SATHER CLASSICAL LECTURES

Volume Fifty-Seven

Shame and Necessity

Shame
and Necessity

Bernard Williams

University of California Press
Berkeley · Los Angeles · London

University of California Press
Berkeley and Los Angeles, California

University of California Press, Ltd.
London, England

© 1993 by
The Regents of the University of California

First Paperback Printing 1994

Library of Congress Cataloging-in-Publication Data

Williams, Bernard Arthur Owen.
    Shame and necessity / Bernard Williams.
      p.   cm.—(Sather classical lectures ; v. 57)
    Includes bibliographical references (p.   ) and index.
    ISBN 0-520-08830-1
    1. Greek poetry—History and criticism.   2. Necessity
(Philosophy) in literature.   3. Philosophy, Ancient, in literature.
4. Ethics in literature.   5. Shame in literature.   I. Title.
II. Series.
PA3095.W5   1993
881'.0109384—dc20   92-2212
                                              CIP

Printed in the United States of America
9 8 7 6 5 4 3

To Patricia

ἐπάμεροι· τί δέ τις; τί δ' οὔ τις; σκιᾶς ὄναρ
ἄνθρωπος. ἀλλ' ὅταν αἴγλα διόσδοτος ἔλθῃ,
λαμπρὸν φέγγος ἔπεστιν ἀνδρῶν καὶ μείλιχος αἰών.

Pindar *Pythian* 8. 95–97

Contents

Preface

This book is based on Sather Lectures that I gave at the University of California at Berkeley in spring 1989. The practice is that lectures in this series are given by extremely distinguished classical scholars, and I owe it to the reader, and also to the Sather Committee who did me the honour of inviting me, an honour that I particularly appreciate, to make it clear that I am not primarily a classical scholar. I am someone who received what used to be called a classical education, became a philosopher, and has kept in touch with Greek studies primarily through work in ancient philosophy.

I must mention this, all the more, because this study does not stay within the limits that this experience might advise. I do discuss some ancient philosophy (most extensively, in chapter 5, some views of Aristotle's), but for much of the book the writers I discuss are not philosophers but poets, and I try to discuss them as poets, not as providing rhythmic examples for philosophy. I say something about my reasons for this in the first chapter. It is true that I am particularly concerned with Greek ideas from periods in which there were no philosophical writers, or from which few and fragmentary philosophical writings survive; but that is not my main reason for turning to poetry.

Philosophers who are guilty of bad scholarship should rightly

be reproached for it. It must be said at the same time that there
are some literary scholars who seem closed to the idea that their
reflections might involve some bad philosophy. They should
perhaps at least be conscious of the risk. That is not to say that
they do wrong to run the risk—while there are standards of
scholarly orthodoxy, philosophy (in the words of an old joke) is
anybody's doxy. But it does mean that scholarship, at least when
it tries to say anything interesting,[1] cannot travel entirely on its
own credentials. The truth is that we all have to do more things
than we can rightly do, if we are to do anything at all. As T. S.
Eliot put it, "of course one can 'go too far' and except in directions in which we can go too far there is no interest in going at
all; and only those who will risk going too far can possibly find
out how far one can go."[2]

Eliot's admirable remark, however, carries not just an encouragement, but, to someone in my situation, a warning as
well. If those who are unused to working with literary texts may
sometimes be too rash to satisfy the demands of scholarship,
they also run the risk of not going far enough, of seeming feeble
or superficial, by the standards of imaginative criticism. An insight that is robustly unaffected by contemporary writing about
literature may turn out merely to represent some unforgotten
prejudice. One can only accept that there is no reliable way of
converting the disadvantages of amateurism into the rewards of
heroism.

In admitting that the instrument for much of my recital is the
violon d'Ingres, I am cheered by the fact that at least I was
introduced to it by some excellent teachers. When I was an un-
dergraduate at Oxford I had the good fortune to be taught by
two of the most remarkable classical scholars of this century,
Eduard Fraenkel and Eric Dodds. They set quite different, but
equally demanding, standards for understanding the ancient
world. Neither, incidentally, was unqualifiedly admired in Oxford. Fraenkel was represented by the malice of the common

rooms as a monster of Teutonic arrogance. He could certainly be alarming when presented with rash or pretentious error, but the quality he conveyed in his teaching and taught one to respect was humility in the face of dense and complex philological fact; and while he possessed classical learning on a scale that I suppose is not matched by anyone now living, he saw himself as poorly informed when compared, for instance, with the master whom he called "the great Leo".

If Fraenkel was sometimes derided by amateurs, Dodds was undervalued by pedants (the pedants and the amateurs were in some cases, needless to say, the same people). Extremely liberal in his political sentiments, interested in the social sciences, a poet and a friend of poets, he was also a deeply imaginative scholar. The Sather Lectures that he gave in 1949–50 yielded one of the most helpful and enduring books in the series,[3] and it is one of the closest in subject matter to the concerns of this study. Since he was also extremely kind to me when I was a student, I should like to feel that my undertaking, even though it is imperfectly related to the kind of scholarship he practised, might count as a homage to him.

I have many people and institutions to thank. I am grateful to la Maison des Sciences de l'Homme in Paris, and its administrator, Clemens Heller, for a productive period of time spent there in 1981. In the same year, I presented an early version of some of the material in this book in the Eliot Lectures that I gave at the University of Kent; I appreciated this invitation, and I am sorry that by turning into their present and very different form the lectures I gave disqualified themselves from appearing among the books that bear the name of that series. An invitation from the Classics Faculty at Cambridge to give the J. H. Gray Lectures in 1986 moved some of my ideas nearer to their present form. More recently, I have had the opportunity to present versions of some of the chapters in lectures or papers given at Yale, UCLA, Haverford College, the University of Michigan,

Warwick University, and New York University. I have benefited from discussions and comments on all these occasions.

Between the time when I was invited to give the Sather Lectures and my giving them, I had become a member of the Berkeley faculty. The members of the classics department, undiscouraged by this unprecedented and strictly irregular situation, extended the same hospitable and warm welcome to a visitor from the philosophy department as they customarily do to Sather lecturers from other institutions. Tony Long, in particular, not only did everything that could be asked of a chairman, but also showed himself a good friend and a generous colleague in giving me the benefit of his own work on subjects related to the lectures, especially to chapter 2. Other members of the classics department to whom I have special reasons for gratitude are Giovanni Ferrari, Mark Griffith, Don Mastronarde, and Tom Rosenmeyer. I thank David Engel and Chris Siciliani for their work as research assistants. Two helpful seminars on the lectures were held in the Doreen B. Townsend Center for the Humanities, for which I am specially grateful to Paul Alpers, Samuel Scheffler, and Hans Sluga.

Other friends and colleagues have been generous with their comments and scholarly help; some have read all or some of the book at various stages of its preparation. I should like to thank Julia Annas, Glen Bowersock, Myles Burnyeat, Ronald Dworkin, Helene Foley, Christopher Gill, Stephen Greenblatt, Stuart Hampshire, Stephen Knapp, Jonathan Lear, Geoffrey Lloyd, Anne Michelini, Amy Mullin, Thomas Nagel, Ruth Padel, Robert Post, Andrew Stewart, Oliver Taplin, and David Wiggins for their various kindnesses. The mistakes are undeniably my own.

CHAPTER ONE

The Liberation of Antiquity

We are now used to thinking of the ancient Greeks as an exotic people. Forty years ago, in the preface to *The Greeks and the Irrational*, Dodds apologised, or rather declined to apologise, for using anthropological material in interpreting an "aspect of the mental world of ancient Greece."[1] Since then, we have become familiar with the activity of applying to the societies of ancient Greece methods similar to those of cultural anthropology. Much has been achieved in these ways, and efforts, in particular, to uncover structures of myth and ritual in such terms have yielded some of the most illuminating work of recent times.[2]

These methods define certain differences between ourselves and the Greeks. Cultural anthropologists, in their well-known role of observers living in a traditional society, may come very close to the people with whom they are living, but they are committed to thinking of that life as different; the point of their visit is to understand and describe another form of human life. The kind of work I have mentioned helps us to understand the Greeks by first making them seem strange—more strange, that is to say, than they seem when their life is too benignly assimilated to modern conceptions. We cannot live with the ancient Greeks or to any substantial degree imagine ourselves doing so.

Much of their life is hidden from us, and just because of that, it is important for us to keep a sense of their otherness, a sense which the methods of cultural anthropology help us to sustain.

This study does not use those methods. Many of the subjects I discuss have been treated in those terms, but I have largely left those discussions to one side.[3] I want to ask a different sort of question about the ancient world, one that places it in a different—and, in just one sense, a closer—relation to our own. But I do not want to deny the otherness of the Greek world. I shall not be saying that Greeks of the fifth century B.C. were after all more modern than we have recently been encouraged to suppose, and that despite gods, daimons, pollutions, blood-guilt, sacrifices, fertility festivals, and slavery, they were really almost as much like Victorian English gentlemen, say, as some Victorian English gentlemen liked to think.[4]

I shall stress some unacknowledged similarities between Greek conceptions and our own. Cultural anthropology of course also invokes similarities, or it could not make the societies it studies intelligible to us. Some of the similarities are very obvious, lying in universal needs: human beings everywhere need a cultural framework to deal with reproduction, eating, death, violence. Some of the similarities may be unobvious, because unconscious; theorists have claimed to make sense of Greek myths and rituals and their reflections in literature by appeal to structures of imagery that at some level we share. Nothing I say will be in conflict with such inquiries, but the similarities I shall stress are at a different level and concern the concepts that we use in interpreting our own and other people's feelings and actions. If these similarities between our own ways of thought and those of the ancient Greeks are, in some cases, unobvious, this is not because they arise from a structure hidden in the unconscious, but because they are, for cultural and historical reasons, unacknowledged. It is an effect of our ethical situation, and of our relations to the ancient Greeks, that we should be blind to some of the ways in which we resemble them.

Cultural anthropologists in the field are not committed to any particular evaluation of the life they are studying, compared with the life back home—what might be called the life of modernity. They have many reasons for not feeling superior to the people they study, but those reasons circle a little warily, perhaps, round the basic asymmetry between the parties, created by the fact that one of them does indeed study the other and brings to their relations a theoretical apparatus that has studied others before. With our relations to the ancient Greeks, the situation is different. They are among our cultural ancestors, and our view of them is intimately connected with our view of ourselves. That has always been the particular point of studying their world. It is not just a matter, as it may be in studying other societies, of our getting to know about human diversity, other social or cultural achievements, or, again, what has been spoiled or set aside by the history of European domination. To learn those things is itself an important aid to self-understanding, but to learn about the Greeks is more immediately part of self-understanding. It will continue to be so even though the modern world stretches round the earth and draws into itself other traditions as well. Those other traditions will give it new and different configurations, but they will not cancel the fact that the Greek past is specially the past of modernity.

The process by which modernity takes in other traditions will not undo the fact that the modern world was a European creation presided over by the Greek past. It might, however, make that fact no longer interesting. Perhaps it might prove more helpful, more productive of a new life, to forget about that fact, at least at any level that claims to be history. It is too late to assume that the Greek past must be interesting just because it is "ours".[5] We need a reason, not so much for saying that the historical study of the Greeks bears a special relation to the ways in which modern societies can understand themselves—so much is obvious enough—but rather that this dimension of self-understanding should be important. I believe that there is such a reason, one that was compactly expressed by Nietzsche: "I cannot imagine what would be the meaning of classical philology in our own age, if it is not to be untimely—that is, to act against the age, and by so doing, to have an effect on the age, and, let us hope, to the benefit of a future age."[6] We, now, should try to understand how our ideas are related to the Greeks' because, if we do so, this can specially help us to see ways in which our ideas may be wrong.

This book is directed to what I call, broadly, ethical ideas of the Greeks: in particular, ideas of responsible action, justice, and the motivations that lead people to do things that are admired and respected. My aim is a philosophical description of an historical reality. What is to be recovered and compared with our kinds of ethical thought is an historical formation, certain ideas of the Greeks; but the comparison is philosophical, because it has to lay bare certain structures of thought and experience and, above all, ask questions about their value to us. In some ways, I shall claim, the basic ethical ideas possessed by the Greeks were different from ours, and also in better condition. In some other respects, it is rather that we rely on much the same conceptions as the Greeks, but we do not acknowledge the extent to which we do so.[7]

Both these claims are opposed to a familiar picture of our ethical relations to the ancient Greeks. No one, certainly, thinks that the Greeks' beliefs about these matters were just the same as ours; no one supposes that there is no real difference between modern morality and outlooks typical of the Greek world. The familiar picture of Greek ethical ideas and their relations to our own is, rather, developmental, evolutionary, and—in an ugly word that I have found no way of avoiding—progressivist. It is directly offered by some modern authors,[8] and taken for granted by many more. According to the progressivist account, the Greeks had primitive ideas of action, responsibility, ethical motivation, and justice, which in the course of history have been replaced by a more complex and refined set of conceptions that define a more mature form of ethical experience. It is agreed, on this account, that the development took a long time; it is also agreed that some of the improvements occurred in the lifetime of Greek antiquity itself, while others were reserved for a later time. Within that framework, however, it is not agreed when various improvements occurred. It is accepted that the world of Homer embodied a shame culture, and that shame was later replaced, in its crucial ethical role, by guilt. Some think that this process had gone a long way by the time of Plato or even the tragedians. Others see all Greek culture as governed by notions that are nearer to shame than to a full notion of moral guilt, with its implications of freedom and autonomy; they believe that moral guilt was attained only by the modern consciousness.[9] Similar disagreements arise about moral agency. Homer's men and women, we are told, were not moral agents; according to one influential theory, which I discuss in the next chapter, they were not even agents. Plato's and Aristotle's people are allowed to have been agents, but they perhaps still fell short of *moral* agency, because—on some of these accounts at least— they lacked a proper conception of the will.

These stories are deeply misleading, both historically and ethically. Many of the questions they generate, of when this, that, or the other element of a developed moral consciousness is supposed to have arisen, are unanswerable, because the notion of a developed moral consciousness that gives rise to these questions is basically a myth. These theories measure the ideas and the experience of the ancient Greeks against modern conceptions of freedom, autonomy, inner responsibility, moral obligation, and so forth, and it is assumed that we have an entirely adequate control of these conceptions themselves. But if we ask ourselves honestly, I believe that we shall find that we have no clear idea of the substance of these conceptions, and hence no clear idea of what it is that, according to the progressivist accounts, the Greeks did not have.

There is indeed a word for what it is that they supposedly did not have, the word "morality", and it is a sure sign that we are in the world of the progressivists when we are told that the Greeks, all or some of them, lacked a *moral* notion of responsibility, approval, or whatever it may be. This word is supposed, it seems, to deliver in itself the crucial assumptions that we enjoy and the Greeks lacked. It is perhaps an indication of some justified anxiety on the part of these writers, whether this word could deliver this (or indeed, by itself, deliver anything), that they find it necessary so often to fortify its saving power by putting it in italics.

The way in which we often think about these matters—about morality, in particular, but also about modernity, liberalism, and progress—is structured in such a simple way that it is very hard to say the kind of thing I have just said without being seen as a classicising reactionary. Moreover, since the recent anthropological studies I mentioned earlier, and the work of distinguished scholars who came before them, have rightly shadowed the Hellenic world with darker images, the kind of classicising reactionary one will be taken to be may well be very black indeed. I must therefore state as soon and as firmly as I can that I do not propose that the modern state should be run on the principles of Theognis, or wish to ally myself with those who suspect that the closing scenes of the *Eumenides* already display a dangerous weakening toward liberalism. I am not suggesting that we should revive the attitudes that the Greeks shared towards slavery, or continue their attitudes—the attitudes of men, that is to say, and no doubt of many women—towards women.

In criticising what I call progressivism, I am not saying that there has been no progress. Indeed, there was progress in the Greek world itself, notably to the extent that the idea of *aretē*, human excellence, was freed to some extent from determination by social position. Still more there are differences, differences we must approve, between ourselves and the Greeks. The question is how these differences are to be understood. My claim is that they cannot best be understood in terms of a shift in basic ethical conceptions of agency, responsibility, shame, or freedom. Rather, by better grasping these conceptions themselves and the extent to which we share them with antiquity, we may be helped to recognize some of our illusions about the modern world, and through this gain a firmer hold on the differences that we value between ourselves and the Greeks. It is not a question of *reviving* anything. What is dead is dead, and in many important respects we would not want to revive it even if we knew what that could mean. What is alive from the Greek world is already alive and is helping (often in hidden ways) to keep us alive.[10]

When I say that our differences from the Greeks cannot best be understood in terms of a shift in basic ethical conceptions, I mean two separate things. First, where our underlying conceptions are different from those of the Greeks, what we most value in our differences does not, typically, come from those conceptions. Moreover—and this is the second point—it is not true that there has been as big a shift in underlying conceptions as the progressivists suppose. How much of a shift there has been, how much we do rely on changed ideas of such things as freedom, responsibility, and the individual agent, is an elusive question that in the end cannot be fully answered; to answer it would involve drawing a firm line between what we think and what we merely think that we think. For the same reason, in saying that the notion of the "developed moral consciousness", contrasted with the supposedly more primitive notions of the Greeks, was a myth, I introduced two different ideas, which inevitably run into one another. To some extent there is such a consciousness, but its distinctive content consists of a myth; to some extent it is a myth that such a consciousness even exists. What is certainly true is that, to a greater extent than the progressivist story claims, we rely on ideas that we share with the Greeks. In my view, that must be so, since the supposedly more developed conceptions do not offer much to rely on. So far as such basic conceptions are concerned, the Greeks were on firm ground—often on firmer ground than ourselves. How that is so, and how some Greeks were in certain respects on firmer ground than others, is the subject of the second, third, and fourth chapters of this study, in which I discuss agency, responsibility, and shame.

If it is true that the basic ethical conceptions of the Greeks were in many ways more secure than our own, then this should lead us not to deny the substantive differences between them and us, on questions of justice, for instance, but to understand them in new ways. Our distance from Greek attitudes to slaves and to women (attitudes that I discuss in chapter 5) is properly measured not by the standards of some new structural conception called "morality", but by considerations that can themselves be traced to the Greek world—considerations of power, fortune, and very elementary forms of justice.

It is tempting to suppose that there can logically be only three basic positions to be taken in comparing our ethical conceptions to those of the Greeks—better, worse, much the same. But besides being a comical oversimplification, the schema puts together two different kinds of question, which are indeed taken together in the attitude of progressivism, but which it is important to separate. It is one question whether we are to understand the history of ethical conceptions from the ancient world to modernity as a story of development, evolution, and so forth, the outcome of which is that our conceptions are more sophisticated and complex replacements for those of the Greeks. It is another matter to distribute admiration between them. This is illustrated in one way by those, such as orthodox Marxists, who have held an evolutionary view but for that very reason have thought that evaluations of ancient ideas and practices were beside the point: Engels would have treated the progressivists' views with the same contempt that he applied to modern moralising about ancient slavery, for instance.[11]

However, the point that there is more than one question here is more interestingly illustrated by people for whom (unlike the Marxists) the sophistication of the modern consciousness is itself part of the problem. One is Nietzsche, a writer with whom my inquiry has relations that are very close and necessarily ambiguous. It is not to the point here to pursue what a recent critic has well called "Nietzsche's painful, polemical, detachment from some aspects of Greece and . . . his agonizing involvement with others,"[12] but two things, at any rate, are obvious about him, one his passion for the Greek world, the other his intense contempt and dislike for most aspects of modernity. The complexity of his attitude comes, in part, from his everpresent sense that his own consciousness would not be possible without the developments that he disliked. In particular his view of things—of the Greeks as much as of anything else—depended on a heightened reflectiveness, self-consciousness, and inwardness that, he thought, it was precisely one of the charms, and indeed the power, of the Greeks to have done without. "The Greeks were superficial out of profundity," he famously said,[13] a remark that will show its strength in more than one area of this inquiry.

Nietzsche was committed to thinking that to fall back into a yearning for this lost world would be absurd. If the progressivist outlook is ridiculous, so is a mere inversion of it. We shall need more than nostalgia if we are to make sense of our ethical relations to the Greeks. One thought that impressed Nietzsche was that in lacking some kinds of reflection and self-consciousness the Greeks—whom he was willing to compare to children[14]—

also lacked the capacity for some forms of self-deceit. In his role of unmasker, ultimately self-destructive pursuer of truthfulness, he uses the idea that the Greeks, or at least the Greeks before Socrates, openly lived manifestations of the will to power that later outlooks, above all Christianity and its offspring liberalism, in their increased self-consciousness, have had to conceal.

These ideas of Nietzsche's, taken by themselves, define the relation of our concepts to those of the Greeks in terms of the reflective to the unreflective, and the oblique to the straightforward. In the light of this, the resemblance or unity between the outlooks, the Greeks' and our own, emerges principally at the level of basic human motives, which are supposed to be more deeply hidden in the modern consciousness than in the archaic. But this picture does not offer enough to support or explain our understanding of the Greeks. I shall claim that if we can come to understand the ethical concepts of the Greeks, we shall recognise them in ourselves. What we recognise is an identity of content, and that recognition goes beyond simply the acknowledgement of a hidden motive that we share with the ancients, the thrill of the nerve touched by the deconstructionist's probe.

In fact, Nietzsche offered more than this line of thought to help us understand our relation to the Greeks. Nietzschean ideas will recur in this inquiry, and, above all, he set its problem, by joining in a radical way the questions of how we understand the Greeks and of how we understand ourselves. He himself did not solve either question. Although he moved beyond the conception of the world as aesthetic phenomenon that is prominent in his major, early, work devoted to the Greeks, *The Birth of Tragedy,*[15] he did not move to any view that offered a coherent politics. He himself provides no way of relating his ethical and psychological insights to an intelligible account of modern society—a failing only thinly concealed by the impression he gives of having thoughts about modern politics that are determinate but terrible.[16] But we need a politics, in the sense of a coherent set of opinions about the ways in which power should be exercised in modern societies, with what limitations and to what ends. If it is true that our ethical ideas have more in common with those of the Greeks than is usually believed, we have to recognise that this is not just an historical but a political truth, which affects the ways in which we should think about our actual condition.

Rejecting the progressivist view, then, had better not leave us with the idea that modernity is just a catastrophic mistake and that outlooks characteristic of the modern world, such as liberalism, for one, are mere illusion. As more than one philosopher has remarked, illusion is itself part of reality, and if many of the values of the Enlightenment are not what their advocates have taken them to be, they are certainly something.[17] It is a demand on an inquiry such as this that it should help to explain how they can be something, despite their failures of self-understanding. In the terms I used earlier, what is it that we rely on? If our modern ethical understanding does involve illusions, it keeps going at all only because it is supported by models of human behaviour that are more realistic than it acknowledges. It is these models that were expressed differently, and in certain respects more directly, in the ancient world. In these relations there is, as the title of this chapter implies, a two-way street between past and present; if we can liberate the Greeks from patronising misunderstandings of them, then that same process may help to free us of misunderstandings of ourselves.

Besides an historical account of the Greeks that is structured by a philosophical interest in their relations to us, there could of course be another and vaster inquiry that would be relevant to these interests, one into the history that links us to the Greeks. But that is not my topic: to pursue it would involve either knowing or ignoring most of the intellectual history of the Western world. It is admittedly tempting to speculate about a different course of history in which the ideas of antiquity might have come in a less disguised and altered form to a modern world. It is beguiling to dream about a history in which it was not true that Christianity, in Nietzsche's words, "robbed us of the harvest of the culture of the ancient world." [18] These dreams should not detain us, but the fact that such speculations are a waste of time does not mean that there could not have been such a world. Most of us do not have Hegelian reasons, or more traditional religious reasons, for thinking that the route from the fifth century B.C. to the present day had to take the course that it did take and, in particular, run through Christianity. As things turned out, the world we actually have is so significantly shaped by Christianity that we cannot endorse Oscar Wilde's engaging remark, "Whatever, in fact, is modern in our life we owe to the Greeks. Whatever is an anachronism is due to medievalism." [19] It will never be correct to see Christianity (to adapt a remark current in Eastern Europe about communism and capitalism) as merely the longest and most painful route from paganism to paganism. But the formative influence of Christianity is something we owe to the way things turned out, and although we can do little with the thought, it may well be true that not only something else, but something else very different, might have been in the place of Christianity. It was, for instance, a special development that, as Peter Brown has shown, "the new way of thinking that emerged in Christian circles in the course of the second century shifted the center of gravity of thought on the nature of human frailty from death to sexuality." [20] The overwhelming role of Christianity in the transition from antiquity to the modern world is necessary, in the sense that if we try to subtract it, we cannot think determinately of an alternative history, and we cannot think of people who would be *ourselves* at all; but while the role of Christianity is in this way necessary, it might not have been.

In trying to recover Greek ideas, I shall turn to sources other than philosophy. There is nothing unusual about this, but the fact that the practice is standard makes it more, rather than less, necessary for me to say something about the ways in which I see works of literature, particularly tragedy, as contributing to my undertaking. It is not of course peculiar to this sort of inquiry, which aims at historical understanding, that philosophy should be concerned with literature. Even when philosophy is not involved in history, it has to make demands on literature. In seeking a reflective understanding of ethical life, for instance, it quite often takes examples from literature. Why not take examples from life? It is a perfectly good question,[21] and it has a short answer: what philosophers will lay before themselves and their readers as an alternative to literature will not be life, but bad literature.

In contrasting philosophy and literature, we should remember that some philosophy is itself literature. Philosophers often suppose that the kinds of difficulties raised for them by a literary text are not presented by texts that they classify as philosophical, but this idea is produced largely by the selective way in which they use them. We should bear in mind how drastically some of these texts are being treated when they are read in this way. The kind of treatment that is needed in order to extract from the text what philosophers mostly look for, argumentative structures, obviously demands more restructuring of some texts than others, and the texts that need the most drastic regimentation may sometimes yield the most interesting results. But this does not mean that those texts do not present literary problems of how they should be read; indeed, they present such problems to people trying to decide how to regiment them. It is merely that historians of philosophy can, for their own purposes, reduce them to texts that are designed not to present those problems.

One philosopher with whom the cost of these processes is especially high is one who will be relevant to this inquiry, Plato. With him, moreover, we meet the special problem that he was the first to offer the categories in which we discuss these questions, the categories of "literature" and "philosophy". It is hardly likely that the works in which he developed these categories should themselves respect them. We should not expect this even if we could suppose him to be straightforward: if we could assume, for instance, that he did not seek to qualify or undermine the doctrines professed by authoritative speakers in the dialogue, above all by Socrates. Moreover, we do not always have reason to assume it.[22]

Even in the difficult case of Plato, it is not that there is anything necessarily wrong in treating texts as the historian of philosophy typically treats them. It is wrong only if it turns out to be unrewarding, or if there is too dominating an idea that we are uncovering the argument that is "really there". If it is freed from obsession, the activity can be creative and illuminating. Some recent critics, in poststructuralist spirit, have attacked historians of philosophy for treating "philosophical" and "literary" texts as quite different from one another, and have at the same time scorned the idea that a determinate or privileged meaning can be extracted from any text. But, taken far enough, the second of these ideas undermines the first. If all that we can do with any text of the past is to play with it, then one satisfying style of play may be to force it into the regimentation demanded by the history of philosophy.

Most of the texts that I consider in this book do not even look like philosophy, and my aim is not to make them do so. Tragedy, in particular, is important to many of the questions I want to ask, but its importance is not going to be discovered by treating it as philosophy, or even, rather more subtly, as a medium for discussion that was replaced by philosophy.[23] By the same token, to point out the obvious fact that these plays are not works of philosophy tells us nothing at all about what their interest for philosophy might be. It may have been some confusion on this point (but not only on this point) that moved the late Sir Denys Page to issue his remarkable end-of-term report on the author of the *Oresteia:* "Aeschylus is first and foremost a great poet and most powerful dramatist. The faculty of acute or profound thought is not among his gifts." And a revealingly bookish phrase: "Religion advances hardly a step in these pages, philosophy has no place in them."[24]

If you think about tragedy in these terms, you not only misunderstand its relation to philosophy, you also disable yourself from understanding it historically. Tragedy is formed round ideas it does not expound, and to understand its history is in some part to understand those ideas and their place in the society that produced it. All the Greek tragedies we possess were written within one century, in one city; they were performed at a religious festival of great civic importance; their material was drawn very largely from a stock of legends.[25] Recent work has brought out ways in which the action of tragedy helped to articulate and express conflicts and tensions within the city's stock of concepts and guiding images.[26] It was a very particular historical situation in which all this was possible, and to understand it must involve asking what pictures of human action and experience tragedy offered or implied, and how such pictures were related to the life of those who took part in its presentation.

It follows that if we are to understand Greek tragedy even from an historical perspective, we have to understand it as tragedy. The tragedy is not just a document that happens to be a drama, or a drama that happens to be in a conventional form styled tragic: to understand it in its historical situation involves grasping, among other things, its tragic effect. That connection, again, read in the opposite direction, may tell us something about this tragic effect itself: that its possibility was related to that same historical situation. As Walter Benjamin said in his admirable discussion of these problems, "the perspectives of the philosophy of history [are] . . . an essential part of the theory of tragedy."[27]

But this leads to an important question about the inquiry that

I am undertaking. Scholars who have given accounts of that historical moment, the moment in which ancient tragedy arose, have mostly agreed that it involved a particular conception of human action in its relations to a divine or supernatural order. Benjamin himself believed this and made the highly suggestive remark, "The tragic is to the daimonic what the paradox is to ambiguity."[28] In his well-known work on Greek tragedy Jean-Pierre Vernant has said, under the title "the historic moment of tragedy":

> You get a tragic consciousness of responsibility when the human and the divine planes are distinct enough from one another to be opposed but nevertheless appear as inseparable. The tragic sense of responsibility arises when human action becomes the subject of a reflection, a debate, but has not yet acquired a status autonomous enough to be self-sufficient. The proper domain of tragedy is situated in a frontier zone where human actions come to be articulated with divine power, and it is in that zone that they reveal their true sense, a sense not known to the agents themselves, who, in taking on their responsibility, insert themselves into an order between man and gods which surpasses the understanding of man.[29]

There is a great deal of truth in this statement, as a claim about the consciousness that is expressed in much of Greek tragedy. For Vernant himself, it is part of an evolutionary story: the tragic outlook is for him "a step in the development of the notion of action."[30] But I do not accept this evolutionary account, and this presents a difficulty. I want to say all of the following: our ideas of action and responsibility and other of our ethical concepts are closer to those of the ancient Greeks than we usually suppose; the significance of those Greek ideas is expressed in ancient tragedy and indeed is central to its effect; tragedy must be understood as a particular historical development, coming about at a particular time; and this historical development involved beliefs about the supernatural, the human, and the daimonic, which we could not possibly accept, which are no part of our world. Can all these things be true together?

The problem will seem even sharper when we reflect that among the tragedians the one who embodies in the most powerful and challenging form the ideas of action and responsibility that are in question is Sophocles. Sophocles' verse can compact into a few words a great range of conflicting, alarming, and carefully controlled associations;[31] his stylistic resources yield a density of reference that can in itself help to alert us to underlying connections of ideas. They also contribute markedly to the sense of a shaping necessity that is such a feature of Sophoclean tragedy (I shall try to say something more about the relation between dramatic and metaphysical necessities in Sophocles in chapter 6, where I consider fatalism and supernatural modes of determination of human action). Generally, the work of this poet is central to many of the ideas I discuss. This sheds an uncompromising light on the difficulty, since Sophocles' images of life, and the relations of human beings to necessity that are expressed in his plays, seem inextricably tied to themes of ancient religion. Charles Segal has called Sophocles "the great master of commingling these two ways of accounting for the violence and suffering in human life, internal and external, psychological and religious."[32] "It was above all Sophocles," Dodds wrote,

> the last great exponent of the archaic world-view, who expressed the full significance of the old religious themes in their unsoftened, unmoralized forms—the overwhelming sense of human helplessness in the face of divine mystery, and of the *ate* that waits on all human achievement—and who made these thoughts part of the cultural inheritance of Western Man.[33]

But these remarks raise the problem in a very obvious way: for how, and in what form, can these thoughts be "part of the inheritance of Western Man" when the archaic worldview certainly is not—in the sense, at least, of our actually possessing it, which is what one hopes of an inheritance?

The most important thing about the problem is that although I have presented it as mine, it is in fact no less a problem for Vernant or other critics who see these works as representing a past stage in the development of ideas of autonomous human action—if, at any rate, those critics can respond, and expect us to respond, to the tragedies. How can we respond to them if their effect is grounded essentially in supernatural conceptions that lie over two thousand years behind us? Admittedly, a response to them may not be immediate and may call for some knowledge; they can appear dull in translation or, only too often, comical in production. But the fact that it takes some knowledge and imagination to see their point does not mean that when we see their point, the experience is just the product of imaginative time-travel—that they mean something to us only to the extent that we pretend to be fifth-century Greeks. If we get to the position of their meaning something to us, then they mean something to *us*. It is important that a modern response to them can be determinately shaped by their dramatic content: it is not adequately described just in terms of the unconscious power of a series of images. Nor is it just a large and unlikely misunderstanding, as though someone became intoxicated with Gregorian chant because he took it for a kind of raga. The fact that we can honestly and not just as tourists respond to the tragedies is almost enough in itself to show that ethically we have more in common with the audience of the tragedies than the progressivist story allows.

Some may say that the contradiction disappears because it is just not true that tragedy and its world of ideas are as closely tied to the historical circumstances in which they arose as Vernant claims. In one sense, that is true, and it is the direction in which we must look. But it is so obvious that the tragedies do involve supernatural conceptions, in particular of necessity,[34] that we cannot merely sidestep that feature of them and feebly fall back on a well-worn notion that was rightly dismissed by Benjamin, of a timeless tragic experience of which these works happened to be, in their time, the expression or trigger. What the tragedies demand is that we should look for analogies in our experience and our sense of the world to the necessities they express.

In some dimensions, we can make a start just with a subtraction. Vernant also said:

> In the tragic perspective, acting, being an agent, has a double character. On the one side, it consists in taking council with oneself, weighing the for and against and doing the best one can to foresee the order of means and ends. On the other hand, it is to make a bet on the unknown and the incomprehensible and to take a risk on a terrain that remains impenetrable to you. It involves entering the play of supernatural forces . . . where one does not know whether they are preparing success or disaster.[35]

In this passage, one might be left with a fairly lively sense of the tragic if one merely deleted the word "supernatural". But that would be only the first step. If the remaining description is to be more than formulaic, we shall need a better understanding of necessity and chance and of what they mean when the daimonic has gone. In other respects as well, the movement from the Greek world and from what is expressed in tragedy to our own consciousness will involve larger and more elaborate structural substitutions. To understand these substitutions properly would be a large task, both historical and philosophical. In this book I hope to situate that task, and to help us, perhaps, to reach an understanding of our relations to the Greeks that will make clearer what the task means.

In a lecture given at Oxford, Wilamowitz said: "To make the ancients speak, we must feed them with our own blood."[36] When the ancients speak, they do not merely tell us about themselves. They tell us about us. They do that in every case in which they can be made to speak, because they tell us who we are. That is, of course, the most general point of our attempts to make them speak. They can tell us not just who we are, but who we are not: they can denounce the falsity or the partiality or the limitations of our images of ourselves. I believe that they can do this for our ideas of human agency, responsibility, regret, and necessity, among others.

CHAPTER TWO

Centres of Agency

Since one can go no farther back in Greek literature than Homer, it is not surprising that the outlook I have labelled "progressivist" should find in him the clearest expression, as it supposes, of an ethical experience that is primitive, unreflective, defective in morality, and, at the limit, incoherent. By an analogy to individual moral development, Homer's characters are seen, in effect, as childish.

One scarcely needs an argument, least of all a philosophical argument, to see that there must be something wrong with these interpretations: they crumble in face of the authority of the poems themselves. Yet that authority, even if it should make the charge of childishness fall silent, will not show exactly what is wrong with it or how systematically mistaken it is. I shall try to show in this chapter and in the two that follow that many of the most basic materials of our ethical outlook are present in Homer and that what the critics find lacking are not so much the benefits of moral maturity as the accretions of misleading philosophy.

First, the Homeric poems contain people who make decisions and act on them. It may seem extraordinary that this should need to be said, but there is a theory, proposed by Bruno Snell and others and still very influential, to the effect that even this fundamental capacity to understand people as being agents was beyond the Homeric reach. "Homer's man does not yet regard himself as the source of his own decisions," Snell wrote.[1] He was not alone in this view; Christian Voigt said that in Homer "man still possesses no concept of . . . deciding for himself." To anyone who has read Homer and not the scholars these remarks must seem surprising. Homer's characters are constantly wondering what to do, coming to some conclusion, and acting. To take just one everyday example from the battlefield:

> and Deiphobos wondered two ways,
> whether to draw back and find some other high-hearted
> Trojan to be his companion, or whether to attempt him singly.
> And as he thought, this way seemed best to him,
> to go for Aineias.[2]

Moreover, they seem able to regret what they have done, wish they had done something else, and much else of the same kind. So what is it that Snell thought was lacking?

I said "Homer's characters"; Snell and Voigt said "Homer's man". The idea lying behind their words is that the language of the poems can act as a guide to the conceptual scheme of the people who originally read or listened to them: the poems were expressed in terms that were natural to their audience. This assumption is not so much wrong as quite indeterminate. On the one hand, no one denies that there are lines in Homer that describe such things as a man throwing a spear or a woman talking to her husband. One could deny such things only by proposing a radically new translation. If the poems describe those things, then those things were intelligible to their audience. On the other hand, no one supposes that early Greek-speakers addressed each other in epic verse or—and here a real question begins to grow—in formulae adapted to epic verse. We can make inferences from the text to its audience only if we are clear about the assumptions we need to make in order to understand its words. For this reason, it makes a difference whether we are reaching conclusions from what can be found or, as Snell did, from what supposedly cannot be found: inferences from presence are one thing, inferences from absence quite another. At the end of this chapter, when absence is once more the issue, I shall come back to this question of how we may move in and out of the poem.

Snell's view about decisions was part of a much wider thesis. One of the reasons for thinking that Homeric man could not decide for himself was that he supposedly had no self to decide for: he was, in his own conception, not what we would regard as a whole person at all. We must consider this wide claim first. There is certainly one thing that Homer's descriptions of people did without, and that was a dualistic distinction between soul and body. It has often been remarked that the word that came to mean something like "soul" by the time of Plato, *psuchē,* stands in Homer for something that is mentioned only when someone is fainting, dying, or dead; when the person is dead, it is pictured as existing in a very flimsy, deprived, and unenviable condition, in the world from which Odysseus summons some of the dead in the eleventh book of the *Odyssey*.[3]

The other half of the dualism is also missing. The later Greek word for the body as opposed to the soul, *sōma,* means a corpse in Homer, as was pointed out already by the Alexandrian scholar Aristarchus;[4] and as Snell remarks,[5] no other word does the job of meaning the soul's dualistic companion. *Demas* comes closest to it, but it refers (I follow Snell in this) to the visible body; it belongs to the same category as the English word "waist".[6] This leads Snell to speak of "a mentality that makes no provision for the body as such," and to say that "early Greeks did not, it seems, either in their language or in the visual arts, grasp the body as a unit." I do not want to discuss the elusive claim about the visual arts; but so far as language goes, it is clear that something has already begun to go wrong.

Snell was impressed by the fact that the Homeric vocabulary does include various words for the limbs, and when he says that the early Greeks "did not grasp the body as a unit," he means that they grasped it only as an assemblage of parts. But every reader of the *Iliad* knows that this cannot be true. When, at the very end of the poem, in one of its most moving scenes, Priam sets out to recover his son's body from Achilles, he asks his companion (who is in fact the god Hermes):

> whether my son still lies
> beside the ships, or whether by now he has been hewn
> limb from limb and thrown before the dogs by Achilles.

Hermes is able to tell him that although Achilles has abused it, dragging it around Patroclus' tomb, the body is miraculously neither damaged nor corrupted:

> So it is that the blessed immortals care for your son,
> though he is nothing but a corpse; because in their hearts they
> loved him.[7]

In wanting Hector's body to be whole, Priam wanted Hector to be as he was when he was alive. The wholeness of the corpse, the wholeness that Priam wanted, was not something acquired only in death: it was the wholeness of Hector.[8]

Not finding in the Homeric picture of things a certain kind of whole, a unity, where he, on his own assumptions, expects to find one, Snell inferred that what the early Greeks did recognise were merely parts of that whole. In doing this, he overlooked the whole that they, and we, and all human beings have recognised, the living person himself. He overlooked what is in front of everyone's eyes; and in the case of Homer and others of the Greeks, this oversight is quite specially destructive of their sensibility, which was basically formed by the thought that this thing that will die, which unless it is properly buried will be eaten by dogs and birds, is exactly the thing that one is.

Snell's formulations have been, and even in their original form continue to be, very influential. Moreover, they rest on assumptions that continue to have a distorting effect even when Snell's own, more extreme, expressions of them have been disowned.[9] Snell does admittedly have some peculiar formulations of his own, which help him not to see where he is going. He is fond of saying, for instance, that if the Homeric Greeks did not recognise a certain item, then that item "did not exist for them," a form of expression that is almost certain to produce some error or other. "Of course the Homeric man had a body exactly like the later Greeks," he writes, "but he did not know it *qua* body, but merely as the sum total of his limbs. This is another way of saying that the Homeric Greeks did not yet have a body in the modern sense of the word";[10] and one can only ask in what sense of the word Homeric man did "of course" have a body. These unhappy formulations do play some role in the argument: they encourage the idea that since the body did not exist for Homeric man, a space is left where it should have been, and unless Homeric man was the Invisible Man, this space must have been filled by something, and that what it was filled by was the set of its parts. But none of this would have enough power to distort the Homeric image so drastically if it were not backed up by something more important—the assumption that, not only in later Greek thought, but truly, a distinction between soul and body describes what we are.[11]

This is very clear when Snell applies to the soul the same pattern of argument that he used for the body. "To express myself accurately," he writes, "I should have to say: what we interpret as the soul, Homeric man splits up into . . . components each of which he defines by the analogy of physical organs."[12] The components include *thumos* and *noos* (translated roughly as "spirit" and "mind"; we shall come back to them). Once again, when he does not find in the Homeric picture the item that his assumptions would lead him to expect—the soul—he finds parts to take its place.[13] Once again, he does not acknowledge the obvious unity, the one that is in front of his eyes. He does not deny that when Odysseus takes thought or Nausikaa regrets his leaving or Hector reflects on death, these characters indeed do these things. On the contrary, he explicitly admits it.[14] But he does not see that, in virtue of this, he has already found what he was looking for. The unities needed to have thoughts and experiences are there. They are just the unities that Homer's characters recognised as thinking and feeling: themselves.

This case, however, is more complicated than that of the body, and it also brings out a deeper point about Snell's underlying reasons. We do indeed have a concept of the body, and we agree that each of us has a body. We do not, *pace* Plato, Descartes, Christianity, and Snell, all agree that we each have a soul. Soul is, in a sense, a more speculative or theoretical conception than body.[15] Similarly, there is nothing theoretical, or very theoretical, about the division of the body into its manifest parts, but *thumos, noos,* and the rest, according to Snell, contribute to a prototheory of the mind. Homeric man, for Snell, had an elementary theory of the mind that invoked merely parts and did not recognise the whole soul: the whole soul figures only in a more elaborate theory of the mind, which on Snell's view is the true theory. I said earlier that Snell assumed the truth of a distinction between soul and body. His assumption now turns out to be rather more complex: that everyone needs a theory of the mind, and the theory of the soul is the true one.[16]

Because of this appeal to theory, the situation is more complicated than it is in the case of the body, but basically the same mistake is being made. The terms *thumos* and *noos* and other terms that Homer uses in relation to psychological functions, such as *phrēn,* belong to a vocabulary in which the person himself plays an essential and irreplaceable role. People think and feel with or in their *thumos;* they standardly reflect or deliberate with or in (*kata*) their *phrēn* and their *thumos.* If people need a *thumos* to think or feel with, it is equally true that a *thumos* needs a person if any thinking or feeling is to go on. This means that if *thumos* and *noos* and the rest are parts of a theory of the mind, so is the person himself: the theory does contain a unity after all. Alternatively, we might say that these terms are too disorganised, informal, and unexplanatory to be part of any theory. In that case, they are not part of a theory later replaced by a more unified theory in terms of the soul: an absence of theory is not a theory of absence. In neither case, then, whether they are seen as theoretical terms or not, do they represent fragments later replaced by a whole. They seem to be fragments only if one supposes that the true unity is the unity of the soul, and so concludes that in overlooking the soul the early Greeks overlooked the only thing that could stop them breaking into mental parts.

A major reason for doubting that the Homeric terms are best seen as part of a theory is that they do not seem intended to have any explanatory force. How far they are intended to be explanatory is an issue closely connected with the question whether *thumos* or *noos,* in particular, do pick out psychological functions in a consistent way. This has been very extensively discussed,[17] and I do not want to contribute to the debate, beyond making one general remark. The search for consistent and illuminating distinctions between these terms has not been very successful, and one reason for this may be that the directions in which people look for the structures underlying the use of these terms are too strongly governed by their own inherited philosophical and psychological assumptions about the division of the mind. An attention to later Greek use of these terms must be appropriate—they are words with a history in one language—but a lot of that later usage is itself philosophical, or shaped by philosophical preoccupations, and one needs a good deal of self-criticism to filter out later associations.

A clear example of this is provided by the uses of certain

words that have encouraged scholars to think that the Greeks had from the beginning a tendency to see character and emotional dispositions in intellectual terms,[18] a habit that supposedly provided natural ground for the equation, which was later made by Socrates, of virtue and knowledge. Thus Patroclus tells Achilles that he has a pitiless *noos: nous* later has the sense of an intellectual faculty, mind or reason, and the association is read back to passages such as this. More striking is the example of the word *eidenai*. This word certainly does mean, in Homeric as in later Greek, "to know" (though even in later Greek it does not necessarily mean "to know that something is the case": it can refer to a skill). In Homeric Greek, however, but not later, it is also applied to states of character and dispositions. It is used to describe friendly relations between Nestor and Agamemnon, for example, and to express the thought "if he were kindly disposed to me."[19] But to argue to an intellectualist understanding of these examples from the later sense of *eidenai* is surely to go in the wrong direction. A better interpretation is that *eidenai* in Homer has a less specific sense, roughly, "to have something in mind", "to have thoughts of a certain kind", a sense that later contracted into the notion of knowledge. This sheds some light on the Greek notion of knowledge, rather than the notion of knowledge shedding light on the early Greek notion of character. An argument for this way of seeing the matter is that if there were a general intellectualist disposition running from Homer to Socrates and expressed in the Homeric use of this word, it is unclear why the Homeric use of the word should ever have changed. A more particular point is that some uses of the expression in Homer are conspicuously unfavourable to an intellectualist interpretation, as when Achilles is compared in these terms to a lion.[20]

If, then, Homeric man does not "decide for himself", it is not because he has no self to decide for, or from. The very general arguments advanced by Snell, to the effect that Homeric man

dissolves into parts, whether mental or physical, are a systematic failure. But there might still be something peculiar about
the Homeric notions of deliberation and action, which more
specifically supported the idea that something is missing from
the Homeric picture: something, for instance, called "the will".
One reason for thinking this that is advanced by Snell and by
others is the role of the gods: "It should be noted especially that
Homer does not know genuine personal decisions: even when a
hero is shown pondering two alternatives the intervention of the
gods plays the key role."[21] If this means that in every case a god
intervenes, it is simply not true. A very frequent verb for someone wondering what to do is *mermērizein,* "to be anxious or
thoughtful", sometimes in constructions introducing the idea
of division, as when Deiphobus was described in the passage
quoted near the beginning of this chapter as "wondering two
ways".[22] Sometimes when someone is in this state the gods do
intervene: so Athene turns Odysseus's *thumos* to the Lycians,
when he has been wondering whether to go against them or to
pursue Sarpedon. But very often they do not intervene. Very
often, the state of uncertainty is ended simply by one course
coming to seem to the agent better than another.[23]

But even if the gods did intervene quite regularly, it would be
wrong to infer that Homer had no conception of deciding, as
the skeptics put it, for oneself. There are two quite different
reasons for this, and each of them, as it seems to me, is decisive.
One is that even when the gods do intervene, they do not standardly do so by simply making people do things—winding them
up, so to speak, and pointing them in a certain direction. (In the
next chapter we shall be concerned with some examples that are
more like this, and they are, precisely, cases in which the normal conditions of deliberated action are to some extent under-
mined.) In some cases, the god's intervention is described merely
in terms of having affected the agent's mind—his *thumos,* for
instance, as in the case above—without our being told exactly

how it was affected. But in other cases, we are given a more detailed picture, in which the god intervenes by giving the agent reasons. So in the famous passage in the first book of the *Iliad* (187 seq.), in which Athene seizes Achilles by the hair, when he is wondering whether to kill Agamemnon on the spot. She speaks to him and tells him that Hera has sent her, and asks for obedience, and he yields:

> Goddess, it is necessary that I obey the word of you two,
> angry though I am in my heart. So it will be better.
> If any man obeys the gods, they listen to him also.

Achilles decides, and he does what seems to him better. The goddess has done more than help him to see that one course of action is better than the other in terms he was already considering; in this case, she has given him an extra and decisive reason, which he did not have before, for thinking that it is better. Of course, if there are no intervening gods, one cannot have that kind of reason for deciding; but this does not mean that it is not a case of deciding what to do, for reasons.

This also brings out the important point that there have to be some considerations in terms of which the agent is addressing the courses of action between which he is hesitating. He is asking which would be the better course. A god may help him answer that question. In Achilles' case, as we have seen, she did so by giving him a new, divine, reason. A god may equally help someone answer the question in its original terms. Yet again, a god may change the terms of the question and add another reason, but it may be a purely human reason. So Diomedes is considering, in the heat of battle, an unusual question, what would be the most *awful* thing to do,[24] and Athene comes and persuades him not to do any of those things, but to head back prudently to the ships. But whatever kind of reason the god gives an agent, the question that the god helps to answer is a question asked by an agent deciding for reasons—and when the agent decides for those reasons and acts on them, he acts on his own reasons.[25] His question was not, and could not have been, "Which course of action is it that some god is going to make me take?" That is a different kind of question altogether, and when divine determination, in some such way, gets too closely involved in the thoughts that are appropriate to deliberation, we meet a special class of problems, involving fatalism. These problems do indeed lurk in the thought world of the Greeks, and they will concern us later, in chapter 6.

These considerations about the ways in which the gods intervene, when they do, provide one of the two reasons I mentioned why we cannot conclude from the role of the gods that Homer had no concept of deciding for oneself. The second reason is embarrassingly simple: that the Homeric gods themselves deliberate and come to conclusions. Their conclusions are certainly their own, not the product of an intervention of another god. No one is going to deny that Homer's gods are thoroughly anthropomorphic,[26] and their decisions are just like those of mortals when no god intervenes: the language of doubt and the formulae of decision are the same. Even if the gods always intervened in human decisions, then, it would still not show that Homer lacked the concept of deciding for oneself. He could not apply to the gods a concept of decision he did not have.

There is indeed a question, of what point is particularly made when Homer does speak of divine intervention in a decision. In many places, a reference to divine intervention simply coexists with an everyday psychological explanation: the way in which the divine agency operates is in the agent's thoughts.[27] Something more needs to be said, however, when (as happens more frequently in the *Odyssey*)[28] Homer contrasts divine intervention with its absence. Here there is still no inconsistency between a divine intervention and the ordinary materials of psychological explanation: it is rather a question of how much the ordinary materials, on these particular occasions, succeed in explaining.

In *Odyssey* 5, a god intervenes to persuade Calypso to let the unhappy Odysseus go. The reader knows that Calypso already had reasons to incline her to do that—she had noticed, for instance, how unhappy he was. It is not clear, though, that those reasons were enough. When Odysseus later tells his host about her and says that she had let him go "whether by a message from Zeus or whether her own mind turned within her," the difference that underlies the alternatives is best understood as that between a decision for which Calypso could have given a complete and determining set of reasons and one for which there are reasons but for which it remains mysterious in the end why those reasons should have prevailed. Similarly, when Medon has to try to explain to the distraught Penelope why Telemachus should have gone off on an expedition to Pylos, and says, "I do not know whether some god moved him, or whether his own mind had the impulse to go to Pylos," it is in reply to a question she is asking because, in particular, there was no reason for Telemachus to go; and Medon is saying that he does not know whether there was enough of what they would call a reason or whether he just went.[29] When the gods give someone a reason, as in the cases I discussed before (and Calypso's case, to her great resentment, is such a case), the space for their intervention is left by the fact that there is no explanation of why that reason should have occurred to the agent or should have prevailed if it occurred. Such spaces still exist in our world. People act for reasons, and those reasons often explain what they do; but why one reason should prevail rather than another, or take over someone's attention, can remain hidden. Homer's gods, in cases such as these, operate in the place of those hidden causes. It is entirely appropriate that Homer should say that the goddess Hera moves as fast as thought—and not just any thought, but the thought of a man who has many desires and is thinking where he might go.[30]

The interventions of the gods, then, operate within a system that ascribes action to human beings; and deliberation, as a result of which they act; and, therefore, reasons on which they act. In ascribing reasons to people, it also ascribes to them desires, beliefs, and purposes. If we are looking for a theory of action in Homer, this system is itself the best candidate for that theory. It is far more pervasive, and, most importantly, it is far more explanatory, than the references to *thumos, noos,* and so on. And if it is a theory of action at all, then it is the same as ours. If it is a theory, then we can see a further reason why Snell and others were looking in the wrong direction. Beliefs and desires are not agents, but properties of agents, and a theory in which they play a role is one that includes the person who is the agent: as I said that the theory of *thumos* and *noos* would have to do if that was indeed to be seen as a theory. But Snell's assumption that the theory of the soul is the correct theory of mind disposes him in addition to try to look for theories that posit an inner agent; so it is not surprising that, seeing Homer's vocabulary not just as a theory, but as a theory of that sort, he sees it as a fragmentary theory of that sort, one that posits several inner agents.

There is one concept that appears in our everyday theory of action (if that is what it is) and for which there is no noun or directly equivalent verb in Homer, and that is *intention;* but, I shall claim in the next chapter, the idea is there. When someone acts in the Homeric world, as in ours, he or she brings about various states of affairs, and only some of them does he or she mean to bring about. That, in itself, is enough to ground the idea of an intention. Indeed, it is hard to see how we could understand the Homeric poems as speaking of human action at all unless we could find in their words the presence of such a notion, and of beliefs, desires, and purposes. These ideas, or ideas very like them, seem constitutive of the notion of human action. If they are constitutive of that notion, this fact itself might be thought a reason for denying that they form a *theory* of action. Perhaps they do not. But the question whether they form a theory or not, though it is important philosophically,[31] does not affect the basic point: beneath the terms that mark differences between Homer and ourselves lies a complex net of concepts in terms of which particular actions are explained, and this net was the same for Homer as it is for us. Indeed, if it were not, could we understand Homer as presenting us with human actions at all? How could the progressivist critics understand him? Only if we can understand him as presenting us with actions, can we go on to discover either the similarities or the differences that exist between Homeric ways of relating actions to people, society, and the nonhuman world, and our own ways of doing those things.

In the middle of all these arguments, we should remind ourselves of the ways in which this set of notions is all the time taken for granted in Homer, and of how rich, explanatory, and totally familiar it is. At the end of the fifth book of the *Odyssey* (464–93), Odysseus crawls ashore on the island of the Phaiakians, exhausted, naked, caked with salt:

Then deeply troubled he spoke to his own great-hearted spirit:
"What will happen now, and what in the long outcome will befall me?
For if I wait out the uncomfortable night by the river,
I fear that the female dew and the evil frost together
will be too much for my damaged strength, I am so exhausted,
and in the morning a chilly wind will blow from the river;
but if I go up the slope and into the shadowy forest, and lie down
to sleep among the dense bushes, even if the chill
and weariness let me be, and a sweet sleep comes upon me,
I fear I may become spoil and prey to the wild animals."

In the division of his heart this last way seemed best,
and he went to look for the wood and found it close to the water
in a conspicuous place, and stopped underneath two bushes
that grew from the same place, one of shrub, and one of wild
    olive,
and neither the force of wet-blowing winds could penetrate these
nor could the shining sun ever strike through with his rays, nor yet
could the rain pass all the way through them, so close together
were they grown, interlacing each other; and under these now
    Odysseus
entered, and with his own hands heaped him a bed to sleep on,
making it wide, since there was a great store of fallen leaves there,
enough for two men to take cover in or even three men
in the winter season, even in the very worst kind of weather.
Seeing this, long-suffering great Odysseus was happy,
and lay down in the middle, and made a pile of leaves over him.

The straightforward intelligence of these practical thoughts, for a man in such an extremity, is itself very moving, and it is specially appropriate that they should be the thoughts of Odysseus the *polumētis* at this stage of the story; for this is the turning point of the *Odyssey,* the moment at which his wanderings are over and he is about to start on the last journey home. What he has brought from the sea, and by taking thought has saved for the next day and for what is to come, is his own life:

As when a man buries a burning log in a black ash heap
in a remote place in the country, where none live near as
    neighbors,
and saves the seed of fire, having no other place to get a light
from, so Odysseus buried himself in the leaves, and Athene
shed a sleep on his eyes so as most quickly to quit him,
by veiling his eyes, from the exhaustion of his hard labors.

Granted that Homer has so much, what is it that he is supposed not to have? What is this concept of the will that, according to these scholars, the early Greeks lacked, and perhaps no Greeks ever fully developed? It is true, as the scholars remarked, that Homer has no word that means, simply, "decide". But he has the notion.[32] For he has the idea of wondering what to do, coming to a conclusion, and doing a particular thing because one has come to that conclusion; and that is what a decision is.[33] He also has the idea of coming to a conclusion about what to do later, and doing that thing at the later time because of that conclusion. All that Homer seems to have left out is the idea of another mental action that is supposed necessarily to lie between coming to a conclusion and acting on it: and he did well in leaving it out, since there is no such action, and the idea of it is the invention of bad philosophy.

Again, Homer has no word that means simply "practical deliberation". The word *mermērizein,* which I have already mentioned, can mean simply "to be worried or thoughtful", "to be in doubt"; the verb *hormainein,* quite often used for practical deliberation, can also mean a state of wondering whether something is so or not.[34] But this is equally true of modern English, as when we speak of "wondering" or "considering" what to do; even the word "decide" itself is not confined to practical connections. The only word that exclusively means "practical deliberation" is "deliberation", and that is now virtually a philosophical term of art. Language itself, our own and Homer's, can help to remind us that decision is not a special kind of action, and also that wondering what to do has something in common with wondering how things are: they are both fully resolved by one's becoming certain.

Perhaps what we are supposed to find lacking is not mere decision, but something more immediately associated with what is ordinarily called the will: for instance, efforts of will. Snell himself does appeal to what I take to be an effort or act of will, or rather its absence; but, if that is what he means, it must be said that the context is very unpropitious. "We believe," he writes, "that a man advances from an earlier situation by an act of his own will, through his own power. If Homer, on the other hand, wants to explain the source of an increase in strength he has no course but to say that the responsibility lies with a god." [35] He refers to a scene in the *Iliad* where Glaukos is wounded in the arm and incapacitated by great pain. Glaukos prays to Apollo:

> I have this strong wound on me, and my arm on both sides
> is driven with sharp pains about, my blood is not able
> to dry and stop running, my shoulder is aching beneath it.
> I cannot hold my spear up steady, I cannot go forward
> to fight against the enemy. . . .
> My lord, make well this strong wound;
> and put the pains to sleep, give me strength. . . .
> So he spoke in prayer, and Phoibos Apollo heard him.
> At once he made the pains stop, and dried away from the hard wound
> the dark running of blood, and put strength into his spirit.

What Apollo did for Glaukos was ease his pain, heal his wound, and make him able to do what he very much wanted to do. If Snell really thought that those services would be replaced in the modern world by an effort of will, I am glad he was not in charge of a hospital. When, on the other hand, things can be effected by making an effort, Homeric characters can make it. [36]

Efforts can also be made within the mind. Homeric characters can in their thoughts bring themselves up short or recall themselves to some consideration. A curious formula is used more than once to express this: a character "addresses his own *thumos*" and in the course of the following speech says, "Yet still, why does the heart within me debate on these things?" [37] Hermann Fränkel had already noticed that remarks made to the *thumos* are then represented as made by it. But the word translated as "debate on", *dielexato,* refers, unsurprisingly, to a two-way discourse,[38] and the formulae capture the idea that in talking to his *thumos* a man is talking to himself. What happens in both cases is that the character pulls back from a course of action he has been considering in favour of a course of action with which he is more identified. The courses of action in the two examples are by no means the same: in one, Odysseus advances, in another, Menelaus retreats—but that difference indeed represents their different identifications.[39]

There is a passage in the *Odyssey* describing self-restraint, which Plato read as showing the power of reason over the emotions (in particular, anger). Odysseus is tempted to kill the maidservants who are consorting with the suitors, and stops himself from doing so:

> He struck himself on the chest and spoke to his heart and scolded
>   it:
> "Bear up, my heart. You have had worse to endure before this
> on that day when the irresistible Cyclops ate up
> my strong companions, but you endured it until intelligence
> got you out of the cave, though you expected to perish."
> So he spoke, addressing his own dear heart within him; and the
> heart in great obedience endured and stood it
> from then on.[40]

Homeric characters, then, are certainly capable of self-control. Homeric ideas of self-control, however, and related notions of endurance—and to some extent the same goes for later Greeks as well—are interestingly different from ours. The suffering of his heart is the suffering that Odysseus has to undergo when he cannot, for reasons of prudence, do what he would very much like to do and has good reason to do. Suffering is the cost of waiting until he can do what intelligence requires, and his endurance, in this case, is the capacity to sustain suffering that comes from an inner cause, though it is inflicted from outside. The painful character of what is going on indeed comes from outside, from what other agents are doing, together with Odysseus's feelings about those things; but the need to wait and the length of the wait are what demand the endurance, and they come from his own *mētis*, his own rational plan. This puts in a new light one of the standard descriptions of Odysseus, *polutlas*, "enduring"; indeed it associates this quality with what he even more famously is, *polumētis*, "resourceful". Odysseus has a will not only to endure what is inflicted on him: he has a will to endure the consequences of his own will to do.

There is a striking illustration of this same connection towards the end of the *Iliad*. In the scene I have already mentioned, when Priam comes to ask for Hector's body, Achilles says to him a strange thing: "You have a heart of iron"— because of what he was prepared to do, not only in coming by himself to the Greek ships, but in being willing to look at a man who had killed many of his sons. Almost that same phrase had been uttered to Achilles himself not long before, in a very different connection, by Hector. When Hector asked him to spare his life, and Achilles gave his dreadful refusal, Hector said that he did not expect anything else from this man: "You have an iron *thumos* in your breast."[41] The "iron" in this second case stands for an unfeeling indifference to a human appeal; with Priam, it stands for a capacity to act against feeling in order to go through with what is necessary in order to satisfy a deep human need. What links the two is not the capacity to endure—Achilles' hardness meant that, faced with Hector's plea, he had no feelings to endure against—but that both are indifferent to the normal objects of feeling to an extent that goes beyond what would be expected.

Odysseus was like Priam in enduring against feeling; and their capacity to endure was in both of them recruited by their

will to do. It was directed, however, against very different kinds
of feelings. More generally, the Greeks tended to regard the capacity to hold out against feeling or desire as the same capacity,
whatever the feeling or desire and however it originated—
whether it was sexual desire or the desire to yield to pain or to
run away or to take revenge. For this reason, they tended to put
together strengths and weaknesses in ways different from those
that have been familiar to what has been, at least until recently,
conventional modern opinion: thus they thought that men were
better at resisting both fear and sexual desire than women were.[42]

The capacity for endurance, for making oneself do things in
the face of desire or disruptive feelings, is regarded by Homer
and many other Greek writers as much the same disposition,
whether it is mere endurance in the face of suffering imposed on
one, or of suffering undergone in the interests of action. Moreover, it is much the same disposition that may be exercised
against different kinds of feelings or desires. And, last of all, it
is much the same disposition, at least in Homer and other writers before Socrates, whatever the motives that impel one to undergo the suffering or resist the desire. Odysseus endures as the
maidservants laugh inside the hall, in the interest of his reclaiming his home; he endured in Polyphemus's cave the screams of
companions who had to be abandoned if any were to be saved.
Priam endured his own hatred and disgust, his fear, and the
prospect of ridicule to perform an act of piety, honour, and love
in reclaiming his son's body.

So what is it, after all this, that is missing? What is the "will"
that the progressivists find absent? At this point, I am tempted
to say that they should tell us. To me, at least, it seems that in
this Homeric world there is surely enough of the basic conceptions of action for human life: the capacities to deliberate, to
conclude, to act, to exert oneself, to make oneself do things, to
endure. Who could ask for anything more?

But more has been asked for, and I shall suggest, not what it would be if it were found (there is no answer to that), but why it is sought. I suggest that the strangeness, to some people, of the Homeric notions of action lies ultimately just in this, that they did *not* revolve round a distinction between moral and nonmoral motivations. What people miss, I suspect, is a "will" that has these two features: it is expressed in action, rather than in endurance, because its operation is supposed itself to be a paradigm of action; and it serves in the interest of only one kind of motive, the motives of morality. In particular, it serves in the interest of duty. Duty in some abstract modern sense is largely unknown to the Greeks, in particular to archaic Greeks, and this is of course one of their characteristics noted by the progressivists.[43] How much is involved in this lack, how great a difference it constitutes between them and us, to what extent we must think our ideas better than theirs in this respect—these are questions that, in various forms, will recur throughout this inquiry. But are they immediately relevant? Whatever the differences with regard to duty, and however much they matter or not, they would not at first sight seem to be differences about the idea of action itself. If the Greeks disagreed with us about duty, this should not—one might suppose—make us think that therefore in the Greek picture of things people did not decide or did not decide for themselves or could not make themselves do things. It would rather be a disagreement about what kinds of reasons people should, or perhaps can, have for their actions, not about whether they act for reasons at all or exercise their will in doing so.

It is not as simple as this. Certain philosophical and religious assumptions can lead people to think that actions done for the agent's advantage, for instance, are determined from without, by desire external to the moral or rational self, and so are not really actions at all.[44] On this view, only purely autonomous moral duty can make what I do—perhaps one should say, the movements I make—more than some kind of reaction. This schema so distorts what we need to say about action that few can want to adopt it if they really consider it. Yet it has no doubt played a part in the confused discussions of what is supposedly lacking in the Homeric Greeks.

There is a less extreme, and historically more important, idea that links notions of action and effort on the one hand to moral or ethical ideas on the other. That is the idea that the basic theory of action itself, the account of what human beings are and how they do anything, is a theory that must be expressed in ethical terms. This is not merely the idea that there must be a psychology of ethics—that is to say, an account of our psychology inasmuch as we have ethical dispositions, beliefs, and feelings: that is obviously correct, but it is not the idea in question. The idea is rather that the functions of the mind, above all with regard to action, are defined in terms of categories that get their significance from ethics. This is an idea that is certainly lacking in Homer and the tragedians. It was left to later Greek thought to invent it, and it has scarcely gone away from us since.

It was invented, it seems, by Plato. The tripartite division of the soul in the *Republic* is the earliest full expression of it, and one of the most extreme. The theory, although it is designed from the beginning with political ends in view, is presented as a psychological model. The model is intended to explain and make intelligible certain kinds of psychic conflict, and it is central to it that only some kinds of psychic conflict demand the explanatory distinctions that it offers. The divisions of the soul are invoked, basically, to describe and explain conflicts between two kinds of motive: rational concerns that aim at the good, and mere desire. Conflicts among the desires themselves are endemic, as Plato is only too eager to remind us, but they do not call for subdivisions within the soul. Conflicting desires have just one location, a department of the soul that will indeed be chronically at war with itself unless order is brought to it by the superior, rational, part. It is only in the light of ethical considerations, and certain ethically significant distinctions of character and motive, that Plato's schema is intelligible. In particular, it is not enough, for the rational part of the soul to be involved, that rational capacities have been exercised in arriving at a course of action, as they may be in finding a way of carrying out some desire—that would merely involve the superior, rational, part in the conflicts of the desiring part.[45] Reason operates as a distinctive part of the soul only to the extent that it controls, dominates, or rises above the desires.

I am not saying that with the ethicised psychology of the *Republic*, Plato introduced the "will" that the critics have been looking for. On the contrary, they, and particularly the more Kantian among them, find the will still absent from Plato.[46] Rather, they can see Plato, because he provided a psychology that gets its significance from ethical categories, as having taken a crucial step in the right direction. By the same token, he seems to those critics not to have gone all the way (though, of course, it remains as unclear as ever where they suppose that you arrive if you do go all the way).[47] From this perspective, Greeks before Plato seem, in a primitive blindness, not even to have glimpsed the road.

In fact, they rightly felt no need for any such journey. They neglected the journey, however, at least in the archaic period, while they were surrounded by other assumptions that eventually came no longer to serve. It seems that once the gods and fate and assumed social expectations were either no longer there or no longer enough to shape the world around human beings, Plato felt it necessary to discover the ethically significant categories inside human nature, and at the most basic level: not just in the form of a capacity for ethical knowledge, as Socrates had already thought, but in the structure of the soul, at the level of the theory of action itself. The tripartite model of the soul, like its companion in the *Republic,* the theory of Ideas, has to do spectacularly diverse things. It provides a theory of motivation, a character typology, and a political analogy, and the soul it describes is, in addition, immortal. Each of these elements provides difficulties, and the combination of them all is perilously unstable. In particular, there are difficulties on the question from which we set out to arrive at this point: what it is to act. Only by weakening the theory in a Homeric direction can one start to get an account of how the soul, or some part of the soul, issues in bodily action; and to weaken it in that direction is already to abandon some of what Plato, in the *Republic,* wanted from it.[48]

The Peripatetics, in their usual patronising way, commended Plato for having discovered that there were nonrational elements in the soul,[49] and they remodelled his divisions in a much less dramatic and more realistic direction. But the basic involvement of ethical categories in the theory of action had come to stay. Aristotle's most famous contribution to these topics is his discussion of *akrasia*—a term usually translated either as "weakness of the will" or "incontinence" (neither, for different reasons, very fortunate). His definition of this condition is entirely shaped by ethical interests: "The *akratēs* knows that what he is doing is bad, but does it through passion; the *enkratēs,* knowing that the desires in question are bad, does not follow them, because of reason."[50] If we now seek to understand *akrasia,* in Donald Davidson's words, as "not essentially a problem in moral philosophy, but a problem in the philosophy of action,"[51] we are trying to detach it from an ancient tradition of defining problems of rational action and decision in a vocabulary that is basically ethical.

We have good reason to move away from that tradition. This particular concept, however, *akrasia,* is very resistant to being detached from its ethical origins: there is something in the very idea that has an ethical significance. It is indeed now recognised that the phenomena appropriately called *akratic* do not necessarily, as Aristotle supposed, represent the temporary victory of the bad over the good, of desire over ethical reason.[52] Nevertheless, *akrasia* is still, in contemporary discussions, identified in terms of the victory of the short-term over the long-term; or the defeat of courses with which one is identified by those with which one is less identified; or, at the very least, one's consciously doing what one has less reason to do instead of what one has more reason to do. A theory of *akrasia* is supposed to offer a structure to explain such happenings. But the search for such a theory still places psychological explanation in an unclear relation to ethical concerns. Why should we assume that happenings identified in these terms form a class of events that have a distinct type of psychological explanation? The relevant descriptions of what happened are available, in many cases, only retrospectively, as part of an interpretation that establishes or reestablishes one's identifications and the importance of one reason rather than another. Consequently, whether an episode was an episode of *akrasia* at all may depend crucially on later understandings. A married man having an affair with another woman and trying to bring it to an end may find himself wavering in that attempt and seeing his lover when they had decided not to meet. If he ends up with his wife, he may well see those episodes as akratic. But if in the end he and his wife separate, and he goes to live with his lover, it may be that those episodes will count not as akratic, but rather as intimations of what were going to prove his truly stronger reasons. It is an illusion to suppose that there had to be at the time of those episodes a particular kind of psychological event that occurred if things turned out in one of those ways, and not if they turned out in the other; yet *akrasia,* to the extent that it offers a psychological explanation, is supposed to explain an event. We have reason to say that *akrasia* is not so much a psychological concept as (in the broad sense) an ethical one, an element that serves to provide an ethically significant narrative.

To the extent that we distinguish between psychological and ethical concepts, and do not demand that the basic operations of the mind should be classified in ineliminably ethical terms, to that extent we return to the Homeric condition. There are of course many valuable categories of psychology that Homer did not have; it goes without saying that we can add much to the basic apparatus that he already possessed. But at the beginning of Western literature, he had the basic items that we need, and he lacked several things that we do not need, in particular the illusion that the basic powers of the mind are inherently constituted in terms of an ethical order.

Several different things, then, might be meant by the "will" that the critics fail to find in Homer; and I have tried to show that of all those things, inasmuch as they can be identified at all, it is true either that Homer had them or that he, and we, are better off without them. And yet, and yet: when we step back from these arguments in the philosophy of mind, there is surely something that needs to be said about the way in which Homer's characters, in particular Homer's heroes, act—something about the nature, or the absence, of their inner life. Hermann Fränkel said that the antithesis of self and not-self did not yet exist in Homer: "In the *Iliad* . . . man is completely part of his world."[53] The Homeric hero has no innerness, no secret motives—he says and does what he is; and though an epic hero is not a tragic hero, we may associate with these thoughts Benjamin's remarks about the "silence" or the "emptiness" of the hero in tragedy.[54] Many critics have noticed something they describe in such terms; they speak to something.

Yes; but at this point we must come back to the question of what the poem itself is doing. Some characteristics of these fig-

ures—the dignity, the distance, the grave acceptance of a fate or
fortune that is given—these, as James Redfield has emphasised,
are features of how they are presented, artefacts of the epic
style.[55] To draw boundaries between the stylistic and the psychological—in the simple sense of psychological concepts that
we could imagine being applied to each other by the people who
heard the poem—can be an exceedingly complex and elusive
pursuit, above all because of the silences that are imposed by
narrative restraint. Between the time that Achilles hears of the
death of Patroclus and that at which he makes his peace with
Agamemnon, are there no changes working in him? Is it just a
sequence of states? At *Iliad* 16.60, when Patroclus was still
alive, he had said to him:

> Still, we will let all this be a thing of the past; and it was not
> in my heart to be angry for ever; and yet I have said
> I would not give over my anger until that time came
> when the fighting . . . came up to my own ships.

At 18.107 he says to his mother, Thetis:

> why, I wish that strife would vanish away from among gods and
>   mortals,
> and gall, which makes a man grow angry for all his great mind,
> that gall of anger that swarms like smoke inside of a man's heart
> and becomes a thing sweeter to him by far than the dripping of
>   honey.
> So it was here that the lord of men Agamemnon angered me.
> Still, we will let all this be a thing of the past, and for all our
> sorrow we must beat down the anger deeply within us.
> Now I shall go.

"We must" here represents a rather vague expression of necessity, which relates to killing Hector.

When at 19.65 Achilles finally confronts Agamemnon, he
says those same last two lines again:

Still, we will let all this be a thing of the past, . . .

and he continues:

Now I cease my anger. It does not become me
unrelentingly to rage on.[56]

The necessity is now to a greater extent internalised, more part
of his view of his relations to others.[57] The formulaic repetitions,
and the fact that we are presented just with expressions, successive stages on the way, naturally serve to reject anecdotal or
biographical speculation about the thoughts that occupy Achilles in the meantime. But they do not strike down the conception
that there could be such thoughts, and the force of the expressions itself comes from a sense, though it remains indeterminate,
that they are expressions of experience, that they do imply a
process.

A harder example, which I shall not try to pursue, is that of
Penelope's behaviour in books 17 to 23 of the *Odyssey*. Questions of whether she recognizes Odysseus, does not recognise
him, "subconsciously" recognizes him, and so on have been
much debated, and judgements have ranged from accusations,
by clumsy analysts, of incoherence and illogicality to the claim
that "any reader who follows with care in Penelope's steps . . .
must come away with the highest admiration for Homer's or-
ganic concept of human thought and deed." [58] However we see
it, clearly there is no route to Penelope's purposes that does not
take very seriously what the narrative itself is doing. The post-
ponements it imposes are necessary for a number of reasons,
and one of them is that the totality of recovery should be expressed in one incident—and that itself is a dimension of psychological representation, because it expresses what this recovery means.[59]

Certainly we cannot reach the psychology implicit in the
Homeric poems merely by methods that neglect the fact that

they are poems. But equally, much of their effect as the poems they are depends on their implied psychology. Above all, it depends precisely on the unity that I have been claiming for their characters: the unity of the person as thinking, acting, and bodily present; the unity of the living and the dead.[60] It is all compressed into the description of the death of the hero Kebriones, for instance, one of many, around whose body the battle raged on,

> but he lay in the whirling dust,
> mightily in his might, having forgotten all his horsemanship.

CHAPTER THREE

Recognising Responsibility

When, towards the end of the *Odyssey,* Odysseus and Telemachus are fighting the suitors, something happens that greatly alarms Odysseus: the suitors are seen putting on armour and handing out spears, which had prudently been put away in a storeroom before the assault. Someone must have opened the storeroom, and Odysseus wonders who it was. "Father, it was my mistake," Telemachus says,

> and no one else is to blame.
> I left the door of the room, which can close tightly,
> open at an angle. One of them was a better observer than I.[1]

This brings out something implicit in the account of action that we found in Homer in the last chapter. Although, as critics have pointed out, Homer has no word equivalent to the abstract noun "intention", there is implicit in this description a notion that we can identify as that of an intention: Telemachus left the door open—that was indeed something he did—but he did not mean to. We cannot, obviously enough, say that Homer has a certain concept simply because he presents us with an incident that we would describe in terms of that concept. It is reasonable, however, to say that there is a certain concept in Homer when he and his characters make distinctions that can be understood

only in terms of that concept. This is certainly true of intention,
with regard to what Telemachus says; and much the same point
is made, if less sharply, by the many passages that describe
people as hitting or missing, and more generally succeeding or
failing in what they are trying to do.[2] Such uses might well be
enough to let us say that Homer had a concept of intention even
if he had no word that was related to the general notion at all.

But in fact he has such a word, *hekōn,* which very often
means "intentionally" or "deliberately" and in the *Iliad* rarely
means anything else. It is used, for instance, to say that when
Diomedes threw a spear at Dolon and missed him, he meant to
miss him, he did so deliberately.[3] It is a very significant fact
about this word that it occurs in the *Iliad* and the *Odyssey* only
in the nominative singular: it works like an adverb, attached to
verbs of action. This in itself focusses its sense on intention. If it
primarily meant, as it sometimes means, "in accordance with
one's desire", there would be no reason for this restriction; one
can have things done to one or happen to one in accordance
with one's desires. Indeed, this is how things stand with *hekōn*'s
negative counterpart, *aekōn*. This word almost always means
"reluctantly", "against one's will", or "contrary to what one
would otherwise want", and it refers very often to what happens
to people (it occurs frequently not in the nominative) as well as
to actions.[4] It is also used, in this same sense, of actions. An
action that a person does in this spirit, reluctantly, must be distinguished from an action that a person does unintentionally.
Indeed the two things exclude one another: an agent in this situation is one who means or intends to do a certain thing but
wishes he did not have to. In their typical uses, then, *hekōn* is
not the opposite or contrary of *aekōn*: they operate in different
spaces. It is this that Homer compactly exploits when he makes
Zeus say that he is conceding what Hera wants *hekōn aekonti
de thumōi*—as Albrecht Dihle accurately expounds it, he "has
deliberately and intentionally delivered Troy to be destroyed by

the anger of Hera, whereas his sympathies told against this measure."⁵

What Telemachus says about his leaving the door open implies the notion of intention. It also deploys some further notions, which are combined in one Greek word. Telemachus says that he and no one else was *aitios,* and this means, first, that he was the cause of what has happened, that the suitors got the weapons; and second, that if anyone is to receive unfavourable comments about what has happened, it is he. He may also, in one way or another, have to make up for his mistake. In just these senses, he is to blame. There is, moreover, a familiar explanation of how he came to do this thing unintentionally, that he did not look what he was doing: one of them was a better observer. There are many everyday mistakes of that sort in Homer (as everywhere else), bad results brought about unintentionally.

Against this background, we can look at a more spectacular and famous example. It has been much discussed by students of the Homeric world, but we should bear in mind that the situation is in several ways untypical. After Achilles has told Agamemnon that his anger is over, Agamemnon explains the state of mind he was in when the quarrel started;⁶ and the words he uses say the opposite of those used by Telemachus: I am not *aitios,* he says,

> but Zeus and Fate and Erinys the mist-walking,
> who in assembly cast fierce *atē* on my wits,
> on that day I myself took Achilles' prize from him.
> But what might I do? It is the god who accomplishes all things.

Then he gives an account of the operations of *atē*—"delusion", "blind madness"—and of how even Zeus can be afflicted by it, about which he tells a very long anecdote.

Telemachus was *aitios* in virtue of something he did unintentionally. Agamemnon is not *aitios,* he says; yet what he did in this matter, he did intentionally. He certainly meant, at the time, to take Briseis from Achilles and keep her for himself; even at the extreme of his elaborate and overstated self-justification he never suggests that what went wrong was an *accident* or that he did not know what he was doing. What he suggests is that when he had that intention, he was in an abnormal state of mind, and that this state of mind had a supernatural explanation. *Atē*, when it means a state of mind, seems always to be divinely caused,[7] and certainly in this case, the fact that the *atē* was caused, indeed purposed, by almost every kind of supernatural agency that he can lay a name to, contributes a lot to Agamemnon's claim that he was not *aitios*.

When Telemachus was to blame, one thing involved in this was that it might be his business to make up for it. But when Agamemnon says, unlike Telemachus, that he was not *aitios*, he does not mean that it is not his business to make up for it. On the contrary:

> But since I was deluded and Zeus took my wits away from me,
> I am willing to make all good and give back gifts in abundance.[8]

However his actions came about, he must compensate Achilles. In that sense, he does accept responsibility.[9] He says, in fact, "*since* I was deluded," but he certainly does not mean by this that if he had not been deluded and had done the same thing in a normal state of mind, he would not have had to make compensation. When he says, "I must pay compensation because Zeus took my wits away," he means "because of what I did when Zeus took my wits away." It is in virtue of what he did that he must pay. So what did he mean when he said that he was not *aitios*? Of course, in saying this he is trying to excuse himself: he needs Achilles back, he cannot possibly offend him again, and yet he must try to save some face. But for these words to help him do that, there must be some sense in what he says, and we may ask what that sense is.

In the case of Telemachus, his being *aitios* contained two

ideas: that he was, through normal action, the cause of what happened and that he might have to make up for it. Agamemnon agrees in his own case that he must make up for it. Moreover, he was immediately the cause of what happened; that is why he must pay. The one sense in which he is not *aitios* is that when he brought those things about, and indeed did so intentionally, he was not in a normal state of mind: he was, if we are prepared to let in that treacherous phrase, not his usual self. He is not dissociating himself from his action; he is, so to speak, dissociating the action from himself.[10]

This reminds us of two further things about Telemachus. One is how normal Telemachus's state of mind was when he made his mistake; he was his usual self. You do not need Zeus and Fate and the mist-treading Erinys and their *atē* to make you do things unintentionally. Everyone does that all the time. The other thing, related and just as familiar, is that the fact that you acted unintentionally does not, in itself, dissociate that action from yourself. Telemachus can be held responsible for things he did unintentionally, and so, of course, can we.

In Agamemnon's case, the gods intervened (or so he says) by making him crazy for a while, but that is not the only way in which divine agency may make action go wrong. The gods also operate at the more everyday level and contribute, often, to things being done contrary to what the agent intended. They may do this at various points in the causal chain. When a warrior aims at one man and hits another, he may aim as well as he ever aims, and the god turn the spear aside on its way. Or the god, by a more intimate intervention, may have made him, on this occasion, aim badly. But that, too, is the kind of thing that can happen to anyone, and the point of mentioning the gods in such cases is, as in the case of deliberations,[11] that it helps to explain things that have no obvious explanation. The dreaded *atē*, on the other hand, involves a large-scale and mysterious subversion of the agent's mental state. In Agamemnon's case, he claimed that his intentions were radically changed, but the psychological subversions of *atē* may take other forms as well. The agent's intentions may remain as they would have been, but his perception of what he is doing be radically altered, so that he is in the most familiar sense deluded. So it was with Sophocles' Ajax, and we shall come to him.

Just from these two Homeric incidents, then, we have four ideas: that in virtue of what he did, someone has brought about a bad state of affairs; that he did or did not intend that state of affairs; that he was or was not in a normal state of mind when he brought it about; and that it is his business, if anyone's, to make up for it. We might label these four elements cause, intention, state, and response. These are the basic elements of any conception of responsibility.

There is not, and there never could be, just one appropriate way of adjusting these elements to one another—as we might put it, just one correct conception of responsibility. Quite apart from the differences between our practices and those of the Greeks, we ourselves, in various circumstances, need different conceptions of it. All the conceptions of it are constructed by interpreting in different ways these four elements and varying the emphasis between them. The four elements are already in Homer, and they would have to be, since the need for them, and for ideas that bring them together in some pattern or other, follows simply from some universal banalities. Everywhere, human beings act, and their actions cause things to happen, and sometimes they intend those things, and sometimes they do not; everywhere, what is brought about is sometimes to be regretted or deplored, by the agent or by others who suffer from it or by both; and when that is so, there may be a demand for some response from that agent, a demand made by himself, by others, or by both. Wherever all this is possible, there must be some interest in the agent's intentions, if only to understand what has happened; manifestly, a Telemachus who had intended to leave the door open would at least have had a very different plan and perhaps would have had very different relations to Odysseus from those of the Telemachus who left it open because he did not think what he was doing. Again, it must be a possible question how the intentions and actions of an agent at a given time fit in with, or fail to fit in with, his intentions and actions at other times. Under any social circumstances at all, that is a question for other people who have to live with him.

These really are universal materials. What we must not suppose is that they are always related to one another in the same way or, indeed, that there is one ideal way in which they should be related to one another. There are many ways of relating them, in particular of relating intention and state to response. There are many ways of interpreting the elements, of deciding what counts as being the cause, for instance, or enough of a cause, of a given state of affairs; what is an adequate response in a given kind of case, and who can demand it; what states of mind might be strange enough to dissociate the act from the agent. Any or all of the four elements, moreover, are liable to attacks by skepticism. Some of the ways that the Greeks had of interpreting and arranging these materials, as we shall see, are different from any that we now have or would want to have. Other ways they had are the same as some of ours, while yet others speak to concerns that we might do better to acknowledge. Above all, what we must not suppose is that we have evolved a definitively just and appropriate way of combining those materials—a way, for instance, called the concept of moral responsibility. We have not.

The first of these elements, cause, is primary: the other issues can arise only in relation to the fact that some agent is the cause of what has come about.[12] Without this, there is no concept of responsibility at all. For this reason, the scapegoat and its relatives, also known in ancient Greece,[13] are on the other side of a conceptual line: the scapegoat is not responsible, in anyone's scheme of things, but is a substitute for someone who is responsible. Analogous distinctions apply in the modern world. There are, admittedly, rules of strict liability in modern law under which people can be held criminally liable not only for outcomes they did not intend—we shall come back to that—but, in some cases, for outcomes they did not even cause. Thus people can be sanctioned for breaches of rules that their employees have committed against their intentions. Where modern ascriptions of strict liability involve neglecting not just intention, but even causality, the idea seems to be that there is a prior and general assumption of responsibility; it is part of what is undertaken, for instance, by one who conducts a certain kind of business that he or she will be liable for certain faults of employees. This introduces, in a sense, responsibility without causality. But in most spheres of our life regulated by ideas of responsibility, the governing rule relates response to cause: the aim is that the response should be applied to a person whose action was the cause of the harm (correspondingly, if the system is corrupted, the pretence has to be that this is how things are).

Of course this truth does not decide whether in some given sphere of our life we should be regulating our affairs by using the structures of responsibility. That is another question. It is a question that we could not possibly decide without knowing what the responses mean and what the point is of making them, and that is something to be borne in mind when we think, in particular, about the responses of the criminal law.

The link between cause and response was for the Greeks built into their language. The verb *aitiaomai* means "to blame" or "censure". "He is a terrible man," Patroclus said about Achilles; "he may blame someone who is *anaitios*," someone who has done nothing wrong.[14] In the case of the blame for quarrels or wars, the causal question is often—naturally enough—the question of who *started* it. The suitors are killed because they were the first to do shameless things,[15] and in the *Iliad* Menelaus, in a startling expression, refers to the many evils that have been suffered "because of my quarrel and the beginning made by Paris."[16] The word *aition* is, from the Hippocratic writings on, a standard word for "cause", and its relative *aitia* kept connections with both kinds of sense: it meant a complaint or an accusation, but already by the time of Herodotus's book it can mean simply "cause" or "explanation".[17]

This primary link to the idea of a cause may help us to understand some Greek views of responsibility that we find more problematical. Creon in the *Oedipus Tyrannus* was sent to the oracle to ask why Thebes was afflicted with a pestilence, and when on his return he tells Oedipus that it is because of the unpunished killing of Laius and that the murderers have to be found, the king, that eager problem solver, instantly starts to search: "Where is it to be found," he asks, "this obscure trace of an ancient crime?" *pou tod'heurethēsetai / ichnos palaias dustekmarton aitias?*[18] But there is a complex message in Sophocles' words. *Aitias* indeed refers to a crime, but in its role as a cause, not as something complained of; there has been no complaint, and that is itself at the root of the city's problems. *Aitia* means "cause", and the word here belongs to the language of diagnosis and of rational inquiry, a language with which the play is filled. Oedipus plans to conquer this problem, as he says,[19] by the same means that he used in overcoming the Sphinx, by *gnōmē*, rational intelligence—the *gnōmē* in terms of which Pericles is represented by Thucydides as speaking of the defeat of the Persians and the conduct of the Peloponnesian war.[20] *Dustekmarton* is equally a term of the rational vocabulary: it is hard, it says, in such a case, to make an inference, *tekmairesthai*.[21] Yet the way in which this vocabulary is applied here is disturbing. *Ichnos* is a term unequivocally associated with living things, and with hunting: it means a human footprint or an animal's spoor, and it speaks of more ancient skills. Moreover, there is a question of what it means for it to be *dus-*

tekmarton. This might mean that it was hard to find or that it was hard to interpret. Oedipus's question implies the first, that it will be hard to find; but he also says *tod'*, "this footprint," which strongly suggests that he has already found it and that he knows what kind of thing it is. Oedipus's very first description of the inquiry already brings the past and the present, the cause and the search, too close for comfort.

What links the ancient cause and the present pestilence is *miasma,* pollution, and what has attracted it, as the oracle has already said, is the murder: that, rather than what later turns out to be incest. The belief was that killing could bring affliction on a family or a whole city and that the supernatural forces underlying this would be appeased only when the person responsible, the person who had done it, was killed or banished. This set of ideas is not fully present in Homer, and so far as this story is concerned, it has often been remarked that in Homer Oedipus's mother, there called Epikaste, hangs herself, but Oedipus continues to reign in Thebes.[22] The belief and the associated purifications may possibly have become a more important feature of life in the course of the seventh century; it is said that some time before 600 B.C. Epimenides of Crete (known to logicians as the person who precipitated the Liar Paradox) in his capacity as a *kathartēs* purified Athens of the Cylonian pollution.[23] Though there were dissident voices, the concept persisted, and it was still a concern for the legislative scheme proposed in Plato's *Laws* in the middle of the fourth century.[24]

Miasma was incurred just as much by unintentional as by intentional killing. It was conceived of, simply, as an effect of killing a human being, and what modern philosophy calls the extensionality of the causal relation implies that if there are any such effects, then an event that is a killing of a human being will have the effect whether it is intended as a killing or not.[25] *Miasma* is a supernatural effect: and the fact that it was seen in these blankly causal terms may make us say that it is a particular kind of supernatural effect, one that belongs with magic rather than merely with religion.

In the special case of Oedipus, however, there is another dimension of the supernatural involved as well. The pollution was the effect of what he did—it was the dreadful curse he called upon himself in ignorance, as he put it[26]—but, of course, the daimonic was involved equally in the cause of what he did, because it was all fated before his birth. When, as we shall see later, Oedipus, about to die at Colonus, reflects on the horrors of many years before and says for the first time that he was not to blame, he mentions and distinguishes those two different things, that he did not intend it and that it was fated anyway.[27] One half of these daimonic involvements—fate, necessity, and divine plans—are not the concern of this chapter: I shall say something about them in chapter 6. But we are concerned here with the meaning of *miasma* and its relation, or lack of relation, to people's intentions.

The point that supernatural effect and supernatural cause can be separated is not merely a poetical, or a philosophical, distinction. The idea of a pollution that could be incurred by even unintentional killing was important in the Athenian law courts when there was no question of divine preordination, let alone of tragic destiny. A striking example of the analysis of everyday problems—and also of the kind of cheery ingenuity that lawyers and philosophers tend to apply to this sort of subject—is offered by the *Tetralogies* ascribed to Antiphon, a work of the fifth century. It consists of three sets of four speeches, each concerned with a case of homicide, each consisting of two speeches by a plaintiff and two by a defendant; it is generally agreed that they were intended for instruction and do not refer to actual cases. Pollution appears in these speeches as an effect of homicide that demands a response. There are even some references to its supernatural operations, especially at the beginning and end of the *Third Tetralogy*. But its main effect on these ingenious and quite sophisticated arguments is structural. The discussions are not about pollution or its expiation, but about causality.[28] However, the problems are set by a condition that comes from the idea of pollution. This condition is that the effect of the action must be met by what may be called a "whole person" response: someone has to be killed or banished. The central issue, therefore, is a particular kind of causal question, Whose action brought about the death? In the *Third Tetralogy*, for instance, one man drunkenly provokes a second, who strikes and injures him; the victim is looked after by an incompetent doctor and later dies.[29] If the question were simply, What brought about his death? it could be said to have been answered in that narration. But what is at issue is a "whole person" social response, so the question has to be, Who brought about his death? That, as the speeches show, is a much more arguable matter.

The case that is the subject of the *Second Tetralogy* is the one that was discussed, we are told, for a whole day by Pericles and the philosopher Protagoras.[30] Here the killing is a misadventure. One young man is practising the javelin in the gymnasium; at the moment he throws it at the target, another boy, on an errand, runs into its path, is hit, and is killed. No one denies that it was an accident; but the question has to be answered, Who caused his death? The speaker for the young man who threw the javelin concedes that he hit the victim, but not that he caused his death:

> He hit him, but he did not kill anyone if you consider the truth of what he did; he incurred, through no fault of his, the *aitia* when someone else harmed himself by his own mistake.[31]

It is agreed that in most other circumstances hitting someone with the javelin *would*, if the victim died, count as causing his death; the speaker points out that if the javelin had fatally hit someone who, for instance, was standing quietly by in the spectators' area, it could not possibly be denied that the action of hitting him with the javelin caused his death (2.4).[32] But, as it was, the victim brought about his own death by his mistake: it is not our doing (*ergon*), the speaker argues, but that of the boy who did not look where he was running (2.5, 8). There is no paradox (the speaker continues) in saying that the victim caused his own death. It does not imply, for instance, as the other side claimed, the absurd consequence that the victim must have thrown the javelin at himself. To claim this is to misunderstand the crucial issue—which is that it was not an action of javelin throwing that killed him.

In support of this the speaker argues that other people also threw javelins in the course of the practice session and did not hit anyone. The explanation of their not hitting anyone was not that they did not throw, but that no one ran in the way. So the explanation of a runner's being hit must lie with the runner, not with the thrower. The plaintiff (who is the victim's father) could have given a ready answer to this: equally, others ran without being hit. In fact he does not put that argument, but he manages to capture some of the middle ground by arguing that at the very least it would have to be granted that thrower and victim jointly brought about the death; but if that is the right account of it, then they both have to pay a penalty, and his son has already paid his, since he is dead.

These arguments take place against a background of a magical belief, but they are not themselves concerned with magic; and they are not stupid, even in the sense of "stupid" in which that is compatible with their being clever. Certainly, we would not discuss these matters in just this way. The *Tetralogies* do assume a quite rigid connection between a certain sort of cause, a killing, and a certain response, the "whole person" response. This connection makes the argument about causality very unyielding, and it demands an inflexible response, which without the magical belief is unjust and unintelligible.[33] The Greeks themselves came to see this connection as unreasonable. Critics have suggested that the whole discussion in the *Tetralogies* rests on a primitive conception of responsibility, essentially connected with magical notions and basically different from our own conception. But while we would not demand a "whole person" response in such a case, it is not true that the conceptions of responsibility being deployed here are all that different from some of our own.

To a considerable extent, the idea that the Greeks thought very differently from ourselves about responsibility, and in particular more primitively, is an illusion generated by thinking only about the criminal law and forgetting the law of torts. We do argue legally about causality, and in not so different a style, in cases where damage follows from what someone unintentionally brings about. Two men run for a departing train. A guard pushes them into it; in the course of this, one of them drops an ordinary-looking package, which, it turns out, contains fireworks. It explodes, throwing down some scales at the other end of the platform. The scales strike and injure a woman, who sues the railroad. This is an actual case. When such things happen, people need compensating, a response is demanded, and under a system of responsibility, that raises the question, not whether the agent intended the outcome—it is clear that he did not—but of what exactly his action may be said to have caused.[34] The connection of an outcome to the agent's causality need not take the drastic form displayed in the *Tetralogies,* but certainly any demand at all on the agent goes beyond what the agent intended. The extent of the disaster must affect the response, and the extent of it is simply, in such cases, a matter of bad luck. For just the kinds of reason rehearsed in the *Second Tetralogy,* the agent may quite legitimately think that he could easily have done just what he did do, and no such disaster have followed. Response in such cases could never be governed merely by inten-

tion. Unless there is some bad result, there is no *aitia,* nothing
to complain about; the mere fact that there is anything to discuss already goes beyond the agent's intentions.

Progressivist writers refer to a concept of moral responsibility
that we supposedly enjoy and the Greeks lacked, but it is unclear what they have in mind. Their thought seems most typically to be that the Greeks, or at least archaic Greeks, blamed
and sanctioned people for things that they did unintentionally,
or again—though this distinction is often neglected—for things
that, like Agamemnon, they did intentionally but in a strange
state of mind. We are thought not to do this, or at least to regard
it as unjust. But if this means that the Greeks paid no attention
to intentions, while we make everything turn on the issue of
intentions, or at least think that we should, this is doubly false.
The case of Telemachus has already reminded us that even archaic Greeks could attend to intentions; equally, we do not, and
could not, adjust our response to harm caused by an action
simply to accord with what was intended.

When we turn to our own criminal proceedings, we find of
course many contrasts with ancient practice, but they are not
simple. We draw distinctions between civil and criminal proceedings that the Greeks did not draw: there was, for instance,
no public prosecutor in ancient Athens. Intentionality plays a
large role in our criminal proceedings, but it by no means determines everything, and there are complex legal discussions of
what it can and should determine, with regard to recklessness,
for instance, and criminal negligence, and in cases in which a
harmful outcome, such as death, can be foreseen but is not intended. At the limit, there are, as I mentioned earlier, offences
of strict liability, which require neither intention nor any other
culpable state of mind; these tend to concern what lawyers call
mala prohibita rather than *mala in se,* and to involve what have
sometimes been called public welfare offences, the courts tend-

ing to resist a complete retreat from intentionality in cases of acts that attract deeper opprobrium.[35]

The fundamental point is that insofar as we do deal differently with criminal responsibility under the law, this is because we have a different view, not of responsibility in general, but of the role of the state in ascribing responsibility, in demanding a response for certain acts and certain harms. The modern world gives to the state powers to do things that were inconceivable in an ancient polity, and at the same time, in liberal societies, hopes to lay down a framework for their exercise. One aim of those arrangements is that a citizen shall not have the punitive power of the state fall upon him unless he puts himself in jeopardy by what he intentionally does (in the matters of strict liability I mentioned earlier this might be said to be done at one remove). It is unclear how far that ideal is realised. It is even less clear, when the state makes its responses to those intentional acts, what those responses are supposed to mean, what the criminal justice system in modern states even thinks it is doing. Progressivist critics of the ancient world sometimes give the impression of thinking that modern penology makes rational sense, but whether they have that strange belief is beside the point. The point is that the question whether this part, or any other, of the legal system is in good shape or not can be discussed only in terms of what we demand of a legal system, and of how we conceive the powers of the state.

We have conceptions of legal responsibility different from any such conception the Greeks had, but that is because we have a different conception of law—not, basically, a different conception of responsibility. It is not that we have managed to substitute for the Greeks' ideas a purified notion of something called moral responsibility, and then do the best we can to embody that in the law of the state. Inasmuch as we are still concerned with responsibility, we use the same elements as the Greeks did.

When we arrange them differently, placing more emphasis on the intentional in some connections—though by no means in all—than they did, this is in part because we have different conceptions of what response is demanded to certain acts. In particular, we have handed many of the responses to a very special formation, the modern state, and we have principles governing what such a state can and should do. An important ideal that helps to shape those principles is that an individual should, so far as possible, have control over his or her life, in relation to the power of the state. This ideal has implications for the law,[36] and for other aspects of life as well. To the extent that our ideas about legal responsibility are shaped by that ideal, they are governed by a certain political theory of freedom in the modern state, not by a moral refinement of the very conception of responsibility.

In the previous chapter, and at the beginning of this, we saw that the Greeks used a notion of the intentional. That they did do so follows from two truths, that they regarded people's actions as among the causes of what happens and that they understood that people's deliberations, their thoughts about what to do, issued in their actions. Both these truths are obvious (though earlier I found it necessary to extricate the second of them from the interpretations of scholars who, looking for things both higher and deeper, lost any view of the earth). The Greeks also, as we have seen, had the conception of things done intentionally in unusual states of mind. Out of these materials it is possible to construct a notion—an inherently vague and limited notion—of the voluntary: a certain thing is done voluntarily if (very roughly) it is an intentional aspect of an action done in a normal state of mind. All conceptions of responsibility make some discriminations, as Telemachus did, between what is voluntary in this sense and what is not; at the same time, no conception of responsibility confines response entirely to the voluntary.

Within the broad space defined by those limits, different cultures lay differing weights on the voluntary. It may be that modern societies make more turn on the voluntary, when it is a matter of important consequences for the individual, than ancient societies did. I am not sure that this is true if we consider the whole range of ascriptions of responsibility, both formal and informal, as opposed to merely some idealised accounts of some aspects of the criminal law. I am not, in any case, concerned to deny it. What I do deny is that such emphasis as we lay on the voluntary is supported at some deeper level by a basic idea of what it is to be "really" responsible, an idea by reference to which we can measure the practices of (in particular) the legal system. Certainly there are purposes that are served by discriminating between actions in terms of the voluntary, and in ways not known to the Greeks. Very importantly, they include some purposes of justice. But these purposes can be identified only by working back to what we require of the law and other agencies that ascribe responsibility, from more general considerations about the relations of the individual to social power. We deceive ourselves if we suppose that public practices of ascribing responsibility can be derived from an antecedent notion of moral responsibility, or that the idea of the voluntary is uniquely important to responsibility.

It is also a mistake to think that the idea of the voluntary can itself be refined beyond a certain point. The idea is useful, and it helps to serve the purposes of justice, but it is essentially superficial. If we push beyond a certain point questions of what outcome, exactly, was intended, whether a state of mind was normal or whether the agent could at a certain moment have controlled himself, we sink into the sands of an everyday, entirely justified, skepticism. This skepticism is indeed everyday, generated by an honest acquaintance with human affairs. It is a mistake to suppose that the notion of the voluntary is a profound conception that is threatened only by some opposing and profound theory about the universe (in particular, to the effect that determinism is true). That supposition underlies the traditional metaphysical problem of the freedom of the will. The problem (I shall have a little more to say about it in chapter 6) exists only for those who have metaphysical expectations. Just as there is a "problem of evil" only for those who expect the world to be good, there is a problem of free will only for those who think that the notion of the voluntary can be metaphysically deepened. In truth, though it may be extended or contracted in various ways, it can hardly be deepened at all. What threatens it is the attempt to make it profound, and the effect of trying to deepen it is to put it beyond all recognition. The Greeks were not involved in those attempts; this is one of the places at which we encounter their gift for being superficial out of profundity.

So far we have been concerned with responses that are demanded by some people, or by a legal system, of other people. But there is another aspect to responsibility, which comes out if we start on the question not from the response that the public or the state or the neighbours or the damaged parties demand of the agent, but from what the agent demands of himself. Here we must turn back again from law and philosophy to tragedy, from the accident in the gymnasium to the mistake at the crossroads.

Oedipus's response, when he made his discovery, was self-imposed: "I have done it with my own hand," he says of his blinding.[37] In the later play, he says that he afterwards came to think that what he had inflicted on himself was excessive.[38] He also, at Colonus, says that he did not really *do* the things for which he blinded himself—and in a notably compacted expression: "I suffered those deeds more than I acted them."[39] "Strained language," a progressivist critic writes, who sees these words as an overtaxed attempt to accommodate language to the kinds of considerations that appear in the *Tetralogies*. I doubt whether Sophocles was struggling to accommodate himself to the growth of the moral consciousness, and I am sure that if he merely wanted to describe what Oedipus did, he had adequate language to do so. What these words express is something much harder: Oedipus's attempt to come to terms with what his *erga,* his deeds, have meant for his life. For what, if one can ask a very ingenuous question, is one supposed to do if one discovers that not just in fantasy but in life one has murdered one's father and married one's mother? Not even Oedipus, as he is represented in his last days, thought that blinding and exile had to be the response. But should there be no response? Is it as though it had never happened? Or rather, to put the right question: Is it as though such things had happened, but not by his agency—that Laius had died, for instance, indeed been killed, but, as Oedipus first believed and then, for a short while, hoped, by someone else? The whole of the *Oedipus Tyrannus,* that dreadful machine, moves to the discovery of just one thing, that *he did it.* Do we understand the terror of that discovery only because we residually share magical beliefs in blood-guilt, or archaic notions of responsibility? Certainly not: we understand it because we know that in the story of one's life there is an authority exercised by what one has done, and not merely by what one has intentionally done.

In the words of Vernant about tragedy that I quoted earlier[40]—though in their significance for tragedy he applied them only to a world in which there were gods—there are two sides to action, that of deliberation and that of result, and there is a necessary gap between them. Regret must be governed, in good part, by results that go beyond intention. Sometimes regret can focus simply on the outside circumstances that made the action go wrong, and the thought is: I acted and deliberated as well as I could, and it is sad that it turned out that way. But regret cannot always be held at that distance, and then it moves back to the moments of deliberation and action, and you regret acting as you did. This still need not imply that you deliberated carelessly; you may have deliberated as well as you could, but you still deeply regret that that was how the deliberation went, and that this was what you did. This is not just a regret about what happened, such as a spectator might have. It is an agent's regret, and it is in the nature of action that such regrets cannot be eliminated, that one's life could not be partitioned into some things that one does intentionally and other things that merely happen to one.

We have already seen that you can be held responsible by others for what you did unintentionally. Those who have been hurt need a response; simply what has happened to them may give them a right to seek it, and where can they look more appropriately than to you, the cause? In the modern world, for some such claims, you may have insurance, but a structure of insurance itself implies that the victims are looking in your direction. Moreover, not every claim, even now, is of a kind that could be met by insurance. Apart from your effects on other people, however, and your attitude to their lives, there is the question of your attitude to your own. Someone may simply have ruined his life, or, if he will not let anything make such an absolute determination of it, at least he may have brought it to a state of dereliction from which large initiatives and a lot of luck would be needed to get it back to anything worth having. If that has happened, then it is something that has happened to him, but at the same time it may be something that he has brought about. *What has happened to him, in fact, is that he has brought it about.* That is the point of Oedipus's words at Colonus. The terrible thing that happened to him, through no fault of his own, was that he did those things.

After his fall, many of his sufferings are merely sufferings, things that happen to him. Some of them happen to him because of other people's reactions to what he did: the horror of the Chorus, for instance, at the beginning of the *Oedipus at Colonus*, when they discover that the person who has come to their sa-

cred grove is this polluted man. Suppose that we lay aside the
idea of pollution; lay aside, too, the conceptions that shape
the end of the play, under which Oedipus, just because of what
he has done and has suffered, becomes in his death a power for
good, a healing force. Lay aside any idea that the difference
made by his actions is that they gave him new causal powers,
for ill or for good. All this laid aside, it is still a truth about him
that he has done these things, and it is a truth in the present
tense: he is the person who did those things.

How far that present truth matters, turns on many things.
How much has been changed by what he did: that he was tri-
umphantly king of Thebes, for instance, and now is not. Or
what he himself now thinks about it; and one of the finest features of the *Oedipus at Colonus* is the way in which this embit-
tered, helpless, and still angry man affects others with his own
picture of his life. When the Chorus moves away from their first
rejection of him, it is not merely that they have been given, as
though by some advocate, a new understanding of his life: they
have been given *his* understanding of it.

It is certainly not an understanding of that life under which it
is as if he had never done those things. That cannot be so even
if *miasma* fades from the scene. Between the time when the
Chorus stops thinking of him exclusively as polluted and before
they come to see him as a chthonic power, they sustain ordinary
human relations with him, relations shaped, in particular, by
pity. Their pity still acknowledges the presence of his past. It is
aroused not just by what he later suffered, but by what he did,
and by his own acknowledgement of what he did: how he sees
what he did and how others see it form, as they must in any
such case, a pair whose parts structure each other.

Pity is the minimal, least vengeful, least magical, human response to someone who has done such things; after that there
is only curiosity or forgetfulness or indifference. To be pitied for
what he did is something that Oedipus now accepts and even

wants. But for some others, this final and least punitive acknowledgement of things done involuntarily is intolerable: in
itself it destroys what their life would have been otherwise. So
it is with Sophocles' Ajax.

Ajax is one whose actions raise these questions not because
of their immediate intentions,[41] but (in the term I used earlier)
because of his state. Slighted by the award of Achilles' arms to
Odysseus, he plans to kill the leaders of the army. To prevent
this, Athene makes him mad. Thinking that he is killing Odysseus and the others, he slaughters the army's flock of sheep and
cattle (and also, though Sophocles makes nothing of it, two
herdsmen). Unlike Agamemnon's condition in the *Iliad,* this
sickness, as it is repeatedly called,[42] affects not his purposes,
but his perceptions: in a vivid phrase, Athene is said to have
"thrown misleading opinions on his eyes." [43] He is first seen unconscious, covered in blood among the mangled beasts, and the
first human reaction he elicits is in fact pity—pity for all of us,
and not simply for him. Athene is boasting:

> Do you see, Odysseus, how great the gods' power is?
> Who was more full of foresight than this man,
> Or abler, do you think, to act with judgment?

And Odysseus replies:

> None that I know of. Yet I pity him . . .
> I think of him, yet also of myself;
> For I see the true state of all of us that live—
> We are dim shapes, no more, and weightless shadow.[44]

Ajax then wakes up and shows that he has recovered his
mind. There is a passionate lyric outburst of despair and, above
all, shame: he has made himself, apart from anything else, utterly absurd.[45] It becomes increasingly clear to him that he can
only kill himself. He knows that he cannot change his *ēthos,* his
character, and he knows that after what he has done, this gro-

tesque humiliation, he cannot live the only kind of life his *ēthos* demands. In the first half of the play, which leads up to his death, he moves from a mere reaction to a deeper understanding of why this should be so, granted what he and the world are like.[46] The unseemly arguments that occupy much of the play's second half indicate that in this, at least, he was right. Being what he is, he could not live as the man who had done these things; it would be merely impossible, in virtue of the relations between what he expects of the world and what the world expects of a man who expects that of it.

Euripides suggested—and Euripides always suggests, he never shows—that there might have been a way out, even for such a man. In *The Madness of Heracles* Heracles for rather similar reasons does a more dreadful thing and in his madness kills his children. When he recovers, he too fixes on suicide, but he is talked out of it. It has been convincingly proposed that the play was intended as a comment on the *Ajax*,[47] and as such, it is very acute, for Theseus uses an argument well directed to such a hero, that to decide on suicide is a very commonplace reaction.[48] When Heracles, having renounced that course, goes off to live in Athens, he is sustained by two things, the friendly support of Theseus and the thought that suicide would have been a form of cowardice.[49] There is not much opportunity for friendship in Ajax's situation; the betrayal of friendship is one of his greatest obsessions and his solitariness is invincible, expressed, for instance, in his killing himself alone on the stage, something unparalleled in extant Greek drama. But the thought of cowardice might have found a place in his mind.

The image of himself that led Ajax to conclude that he could not live as a man who had done these things is indeed founded on values that put a great weight on how you are seen. Such values and the ways in which they can sustain or destroy a proper autonomy will concern us in the next chapter. But what is already clear, I hope, is that it need not be merely some exaggerated sense of looking ridiculous, or any other value that turns simply on appearances, that leads someone to think that he or she cannot live as someone who has done a certain thing, even though it was done unintentionally or with an intention dissociated from that person's usual self. People do not *have* to think that they could not live in that situation; they do not *have* to think any such thing, and this is a type of ethical thought as far removed as may be from the concerns of obligation. But they may sensibly think it if their understanding of their lives and the significance their lives possessed for other people is such that what they did destroyed the only reason they had for going on. Still more, they may recognise that what they unintentionally did, if it did not destroy their lives, changed them radically, and changed them because they did that thing, not just because of what happened to them.

The "silence" of tragic heroes and heroines, to which Benjamin referred, relates in particular to this, that they have a life that is exposed to fortune on that scale, and this is simply manifest: they do not have to explain it to anyone or argue about it. Heracles, when he reasonably listens to Theseus and moves into retirement, is already moving out of tragedy. It is a grave illusion to try to express that silence and grandeur in real life; by what should be a banality, tragedy is a form of art. But one thing it expresses is that the significance of someone's life and its relations to society may be such that someone needs to recognise and express his responsibility for actions when no one else would have the right to make a claim for damages or be in a position to. Moreover, in the earlier part of this chapter I tried to remind us how, when the response is demanded by someone else and there are claims for damages, this itself reaches beyond the intentions of the responsible agent. As the Greeks understood, the responsibilities we have to recognise extend in many ways beyond our normal purposes and what we intentionally do.

CHAPTER FOUR

Shame and Autonomy

Ajax, when he has fixed on suicide, in almost the last words that he addresses to another human being, says:

Now I am going where my way must go.[1]

His word is *poreuteon:* an impersonal expression of necessity, a frequent form of speech with Sophocles' heroes. In similar terms, Oedipus says, "I must rule" and "I must hear it." "What are you doing to me?" says Heracles' son to him in the *Trachiniai*. "What has to be done," he replies.[2] It is just one of the ways in which these characters express insistence, refusal, defiance, and other intransigent attitudes, which often evoke from others, equally, expressions of necessity. The model of these characters is to be found in Homer, above all in Achilles, with his rejection of the embassy, and his terrible refusal of Hector.[3]

What necessity are they expressing? It is an important question, and it is easy to go the wrong way towards answering it. The influence of modern morality and Kantian ideas encourages one to ask first whether this is the "must" of duty, the categorical imperative of morality.[4] The answer to that comes readily: the courses of action that some of these characters are taking, and the reasons they give for them, are enough to show that this is not what is at issue. But if that is so, then all that is left on the

Kantian story is that this should be what Kant called a "hypo-
thetical" imperative: a "must" that is relative merely to what
the agent wants to do, as when one says, "I must go now,"
meaning by it no more than that he must go if he is to do whatever it is he intends to do. Now it is obvious that the Sophoclean
heroes do not straightforwardly mean this. Ajax or Oedipus is
capable of having the thought that some step is necessary merely
in the sense that it is required by some objective he happens to
have; but this is not the thought of either of them in these cases.
They do not happen just to have some objective to which these
actions are necessary: their heroic "must"s are not experienced
as hanging from an "if" at all. The "must" seems, indeed, categorical, and when Ajax says he must go, he means that he must
go: period.

It looks, then, as though this "must" represents neither of
Kant's imperatives. But the Kantian continues past this point
and insists that there is an "if", but it is concealed—concealed
indeed from the agents themselves. The necessity the agents express *is* relative, on this view, but it is relative to some desire
that has merely been taken for granted. This desire—the account continues—provides a psychological pressure that the
agents wrongly take for an absolute demand. What that desire
may be depends on the case. It may be fear of the gods, or an
unreflective disposition to fit in with the demands of public
opinion or, at the Achillean limit, simply the projects of a massive self-assertion. But whatever the desire may be, the Kantian
continues, the hidden structure of the "must" comes out the
same. So long as it has not yet reached the unique categorical
demand of morality itself, "I must do this" can never mean
more than "this course of action is necessary if I am to have
what I want or to avoid what I fear."

Here we see the cunning of the Kantian construction, the
power it has to make its articulation of morality seem inescapable. This can help us to understand its influence in shaping the

progressivist account of the ancient Greek world. Everyone knows that simply to pursue what you want and to avoid what you fear is not the stuff of any morality; if those are your only motives, then you are not within morality, and you do not have—in a broader phrase—any ethical life. If the Kantian diagnosis is correct, then the Greeks do emerge as premoral, with one or two meritorious exceptions in whom some moral illumination filtered through: Antigone, perhaps, on some accounts of her, or Socrates. The Greeks were indeed children, and young children, in a Piagetian tale of moral development, and the Homeric heroes were accurately represented in a verse that was reprinted in the article on Achilles in Bayle's *Dictionnaire:*

Nine years Achilles, fair as Day,
 And valiant as his Sword in battle,
Cry'd for his Mistress, ta'en away,
 Like little Master for his Rattle.[5]

The Kantian account cannot be accepted. It has insoluble problems on its own territory, in particular to give an account of how the unique demand of duty is itself supposed to work; that is not our concern here.[6] What does concern us, and should concern the Kantian, is that in the Greek nursery itself people were able to realise that mere self-indulgence and fear were not all that were expected; they recognised, for instance, virtues of courage and justice. If that is so, there must be options for ethical thought and experience that the Kantian construction conceals. There are; in exploring them it is helpful to bear in mind how Kantian associations constantly work to short-circuit our understanding of them.

This is nowhere more true than with the concept of shame. In the scheme of Kantian oppositions, shame is on the bad side of all the lines. This is well brought out in its notorious association with the notion of losing or saving face. "Face" stands for appearance against reality and the outer versus the inner, so its values are superficial; I lose face or save it only in the eyes of others, so the values are heteronomous; it is simply my face to save or lose, so they are egoistic. These conceptions of what shame has to be, and of how ethical relations that are importantly governed by shame have to work, are all incorrect. Or rather, I am going to argue, if there is anything in them at all, it will be found only at the end of a very long line, at a level where the issues involved are much more interesting and problematic than these handy dismissals would suggest. This is so not merely with developments or sophistications of shame that are found later in Greek antiquity. It is true even where the dismissive view has been most confidently applied, in Homer. There is some truth in the idea that Homeric society was a shame culture,[7] which persisted (if in altered forms) certainly into later antiquity and no doubt longer than that. But if we are to make such a claim, we have to get clearer about what is involved in shame itself.

The basic experience connected with shame is that of being seen, inappropriately, by the wrong people, in the wrong condition.[8] It is straightforwardly connected with nakedness, particularly in sexual connections. The word *aidoia*, a derivative of *aidōs*, "shame",[9] is a standard Greek word for the genitals, and similar terms are found in other languages. The reaction is to cover oneself or to hide, and people naturally take steps to avoid the situations that call for it: Odysseus would be ashamed to walk naked with Nausikaa's companions. From this there is a spread of applications through various kinds of shyness or embarrassment. When the gods went to laugh at the spectacle of Aphrodite and Ares caught inextricably *in flagrante delicto* by Hephaistus's nets, the goddesses stayed at home, *aidōi*, "from shame." In the same vocabulary Homer can describe Nausikaa's embarrassment at the idea of mentioning to her father her desire for marriage, Penelope's refusal to appear by herself before the suitors, and Thetis's hesitation to go and visit the gods. Rather similarly, but farther away from the sexual, Odysseus is embarrassed or ashamed that the Phaiakians should see him crying; and one can place in the same area an isolated occurrence of the noun *aidōs* in the orators, when Isocrates says that in the old days if young men had to cross the *agora,* they did so "with great shame and embarrassment." The avoidance of shame in these cases serves as a motive: you anticipate how you will feel if someone sees you.[10]

A further step is taken when the motive is fear of shame at what people will say about one's actions. In Homer, there are frequent appeals on the battlefield to *aidōs* as a reason for fighting. So Ajax stirs his companions on:

Dear friends, be men; let shame be in your hearts . . .
among men who feel shame, more are saved than die.

Nestor appeals to shame "in the sight of other men," as well as asking the warriors to remember their wives and children, their property and their parents, whether living or dead. Indeed, the one word *aidōs,* "shame", serves as a battle cry.[11]

It is possible to see this kind of prospective shame as a form of fear. The Greeks hesitated in face of Hector "in shame of refusing him, in fear of taking up his challenge," and one can see them as being pushed by fear from two sources, one behind them and one in front. The verbs of shame can take the grammatical constructions of fear. So when Hector repents of the mistakes he made by not listening to Polydamas, and comes to the sense that he has ruined the people by his recklessness, he fears that unless he goes to face Achilles, someone inferior to him will speak badly of him:

I feel shame before the Trojans and the Trojan women with
    trailing
robes, that someone who is less of a man than I will say of me:
"Hector believed in his own strength and ruined his people."[12]

Fear is there, but, as we shall see, fear is not the whole story.

The reaction in Homer to someone who has done something that shame should have prevented is *nemesis,* a reaction that can be understood, according to the context, as ranging from shock, contempt, and malice to righteous rage and indignation.[13] It should not be thought that *nemesis* and its related words are ambiguous. It is defined as a reaction, and what it psychologically consists of properly depends on what particular violation of *aidōs* it is a reaction to. As Redfield has put it, *aidōs* and *nemesis* are "a reflexive pair."[14] When Achilles is described as *aidoios nemesētos,* it means that he is, as we well know, touchy about violations of his honour, violations that other people's sense of *aidōs* should prevent them from making: he has a strong sense of *aidōs* himself, and it should protect him from slights. *Nemessētos* (the standard form) usually means not "prone to indignation", but "worthy of indignation", but it is natural, and indeed basic to the operation of these feelings, that *nemesis,* and *aidōs* itself, can appear on both sides of a social relation. People have at once a sense of their own honour and a respect for other people's honour; they can feel indignation or other forms of anger when honour is violated, in their own case or someone else's. These are shared sentiments with similar objects, and they serve to bind people together in a community of feeling.[15]

It is those connections that Poseidon hopes to mobilise when he urges on the troops by an appeal not just to shame, but to *nemesis* as well (13.122). But the things that are *nemessēta* in Homer, fit objects of these reactions, are not simply running away in battle. In the *Iliad,* they include a common man's speaking in the assembly and a god's being too friendly with a mortal; in the *Odyssey,* sending one's mother away, giving poison for arrows, Odysseus appearing before his wife in rags, and the behaviour of the suitors, who are repeatedly described as *anaideis,* "shameless".[16]

The idea, which is associated particularly with the work of A. H. Adkins, that in the Homeric shame culture individuals were overwhelmingly concerned with their own success at the expense of other people is wrong at the level of principle: the structures of *aidōs* and *nemesis* are essentially interactive between people, and they serve to bond as much as to divide.[17] If the shame system is to be convicted of basic egoism, even in its Homeric embodiment, it will have to be at a deeper level than this. Much the same is true of the idea that the shame system is immaturely heteronomous, in the sense that it supposedly pins the individual's sense of what should be done merely on to expectations of what others will think of him or her. This, too, if it is true at all, is true only at a much deeper level than is usually suggested. Just as it is a mistake to think that Homeric shame has as its object only the competitive successes or failures of the individual, it is another mistake to think that Homeric shame involves merely adjustment to the prejudices of the community. In this case, however, there is not just one mistake involved but two, and they have to be distinguished. One is just a silly mistake, while the other is more interesting.

The silly mistake is to suppose that the reactions of shame depend simply on being found out, that the feeling behind every decision or thought that is governed by shame is literally and immediately the fear of being seen. Suppose someone invites us to believe that the Homeric Achilles, if assured he could get away with it, might have crept out at night and helped himself to the treasure that he had refused when it was offered by the embassy: then he has sadly misunderstood Achilles' character, or what Alexander Pope called his "Manners", of which he wrote, "They are well mark'd; and discover before-hand what Resolutions that Hero will take."[18] If everything depended on the fear of discovery, the motivations of shame would not be internalised at all. No one would have a character, in effect, and, moreover, the very idea of there being a shame *culture*, a coherent system for the regulation of conduct, would be unintelligible.

Even if shame and its motivations always involve in some way or other an idea of the gaze of another, it is important that for many of its operations the imagined gaze of an imagined other will do.[19] It is not so, of course, with the most elementary case, the shame of exposure when naked; someone who was afraid in that case of being exposed to a merely imaginary observer would be afraid of his own nakedness, and his fear would be pathological.[20] But the imaginary observer can enter very early in the progression towards more generalised social shame. Sartre describes a man who is looking through a keyhole and suddenly realises that he is being watched. He might think that it was shameful to do it, not just to be seen doing it, and in that case, an imagined watcher could be enough to trigger the reactions of shame. To overlook the importance of the imagined other is what I just called the silly mistake.

The second and more interesting mistake concerns the identity, and the attitudes, of the other whose gaze is in question. Shame need not be just a matter of being seen, but of being seen by an observer with a certain view. Indeed, the view taken by the observer need not itself be critical: people can be ashamed of being admired by the wrong audience in the wrong way. Equally, they need not be ashamed of being poorly viewed, if the view is that of an observer for whom they feel contempt. Hector was indeed afraid that someone inferior to him would be able to criticise him, but that was because he thought the criticism would be true, and the fact that such a person could make it would only make things worse. The mere fact that such a person had something hostile to say would not in itself necessarily concern him. Similarly on the Greek side of the war, the opinions of Nestor carried weight, and those of Thersites did not.

In some cases, the operations of shame indeed relate just to the attitudes or reactions of a specified social group. What Penelope was weaving, she told the suitors, was a shroud for Odysseus's father,

> lest any
> Achaian woman in this neighborhood hold it against me
> that a man of many conquests lies with no sheet to wind him.[21]

But it is striking even in Homer how someone who is motivated by the idea of shame may not be thinking simply about the reactions of some socially specified reference group. The internalisation of shame does not simply internalise an other who is a representative of the neighbours. Telemachus, complaining to the Ithacan assembly about the behaviour of the suitors, tells them that they must both be outraged themselves and feel shame in the face of other men who live around,[22] and he is not saying the same thing twice. Nausikaa is afraid of what people will say if they see her with the handsome stranger, and that there will be a scandal; but she adds:

And I myself would think badly of a girl who acted so.[23]

I mentioned earlier the bonding, interactive, effects of shame. An agent will be motivated by prospective shame in the face of people who would be angered by conduct that, in turn, they would avoid for those same reasons. Nausikaa is conscious of how she shares with others the reactions that they might have to her. Her case brings out clearly something that was true also on the battlefield, though perhaps it was less obvious there because of the emphasis in the battle on individual feats of arms: there has to be something for these interrelated attitudes to be about. It is not merely a structure by which I know that you will be annoyed with me because you know that I will be annoyed with you. These reciprocal attitudes have a content: some kinds of behaviour are admired, others accepted, others despised, and it is those attitudes that are internalised, not simply the prospect of hostile reactions.[24] If that were not so, there would be, once more, no shame *culture,* no shared ethical attitudes at all.

But this tells us something more about what I have called the internalised other: it explains, in fact, why the other need not be a particular individual or, again, merely the representative of some socially identified group. The other may be identified in ethical terms. He (and I should stress particularly here that the pronoun carries no implications of gender) is conceived as one whose reactions I would respect; equally, he is conceived as someone who would respect those same reactions if they were appropriately directed to him.

But if the other is identified in ethical terms, is he any longer playing any real role in these mental processes? Has he any independent part in my psychology if he is constructed out of my own local materials? If he is imagined to react simply in terms of what I think is the right thing to do, surely he must cancel out: he is not an *other* at all.

It is a mistake to take that reductive step and to suppose that there are only two options: that the other in ethical thought must be an identifiable individual or a representative of the neighbours, on the one hand, or else be nothing at all except an echo chamber for my solitary moral voice. Those alternatives leave out much of the substance of actual ethical life. The internalised other is indeed abstracted and generalised and idealised, but he is potentially somebody rather than nobody, and somebody other than me. He can provide the focus of real social expectations, of how I shall live if I act in one way rather than another, of how my actions and reactions will alter my relations to the world about me.

This is how, in the last chapter, we found it to be with Ajax. He could not go on living, and that was because of just such a reciprocal structure as we have now seen in the workings of shame. It was in virtue of the relations between what he expected of the world and what the world expects of a man who expects that of it. "The world" there is represented in him by an internalised other, and it is not merely any other; he would be as unimpressed by the contempt of some people as he would be by the reassurances of others. But the other in him does represent a real world, in which he would have to live if he went on living. In his particular case, the interlocked expectations between himself and the world are of course peculiarly connected with his status as an heroic warrior, and that is why, in his case, his grotesquely unsuccessful and ridiculous attempt counts for so much.

In Ajax's case, we are shown who the other is, or at least who he must be like. Ajax is considering what to do:

> What countenance can I show my father Telamon?
> How will he bear the sight of me
> If I come before him naked, without any glory,
> When he himself had a great crown of men's praise?
> It is not something to be borne.[25]

Not only is his language full of the most basic images of shame, of sight and nudity, but it expresses directly a reciprocal relation between what he and his father could not bear. But, once again, it is not the mere idea of his father's pain that governs the decision, nor the fact that it is, uniquely, his father. Ajax is identified with the standards of excellence represented by his father's honours. And so he concludes:

> The noble man should either live finely or die finely.[26]

He has no way of living that anyone he respects would respect—which means that he cannot live with any self-respect. That is what he meant when he said *poreuteon,* that he had to go.

It might be thought that the heroic figure in Sophocles who stands in the greatest contrast to Ajax, whose consciousness is most obviously directed to a demand that transcends mere social esteem, and, even more, reaches beyond self-assertion, is Antigone; she has most often been seen so in the course of her

demanding and variegated *Nachleben,* which has been interestingly documented by George Steiner.[27] Indeed she does call, very
famously (454–55), on the "unwritten, solid, laws of the gods"
as opposed to Creon's "instructions"; and her last words appeal
to a value of piety. Though I do not want to say much about
Antigone, I think we should ask, at any rate, how far she transcends self-assertion, and in what ways.

We are not shown her deciding; she is another who arrives
decided, and at the beginning there is a jarring assertion of self
rather than merely an acknowledgement of something required:

> These are the instructions they say the fine Creon has given
> to you and to me—yes, to *me*.[28]

The impression given by these lines is borne out when she con-
temptuously repudiates, later, Ismene's support. At the bottom
of it seems to be not only a project for which she is prepared to
die, but a project of dying. She is in love with her brother's
death.[29]

Because of much that has happened since, particularly because of Hegel, we tend to see this as a play about political
morality. We are led to this by the occasion, the material, of
Antigone's defiance, and then we may be puzzled to find, if we
look closely, less to mirror this in Antigone's representation of
herself than we might have expected. I suspect in fact that Antigone—Sophocles' Antigone, if there is now such a figure—is
even more like Sophocles' Electra, a manifestly obsessed character, than the relations of each to her sister already suggest. It
is of course true that when Antigone gets what she wants, she
does so in nobility, while for Electra the darkness at the end is
thicker than at the beginning, because her hatred has been
turned into blood. But Creon's obstinacy does not simply elicit
a noble response from Antigone. It triggers a ready and massive
self-assertion, and the fact that her end can mean what it does

mean (and, still more, what it has come to mean) is in a sense
Antigone's good luck.

The play of Sophocles that is most remarkably involved in the
workings of shame, the expectation of it and its attempted
avoidance, is the *Philoctetes*. When Odysseus tries to persuade
Neoptolemus to help him in deceiving Philoctetes, he is bril-
liantly shown as seeking to bring about something that is precisely designed to undo the effects of a prospective shame,
namely, to bracket the action from the rest of life. He says:

> I know, my boy, that you are not of a nature
> to say such things or use a low trick;
> but it is pleasant to lay hold of victory,
> so be bold:[30]

—an appeal to courage itself, a well-known persuasive device
against decency, which is still current—*dikaioi d'authis ekpha-
noumetha*. And that means not "another time, we shall appear
to be just," but ". . . we shall be revealed as being just."[31] Then
Odysseus states quite precisely what he wants:

> But now for a short part of a day without shame,
> give me yourself: and then for the rest of time
> you can call yourself the most decent of men.

Neoptolemus refuses at this point, saying rather conventionally:

> My lord,
> I prefer to fail nobly rather than to win shabbily.

When Odysseus eventually persuades him, by appealing to the
reputation he will get for this success, Neoptolemus says:

> All right, I'll do it, and put the shame aside.[32]

The most natural translation of the word I have translated as
"put aside" is "get rid of" or "expel"; but it can also mean

"neglect" or "pass by" something that is still there to be attended to. But I do not think that it can mean, as has been proposed, "I'll put up with the shame."[33] This he cannot do: if it is present to him, he cannot put up with it, and this becomes clear to him later, when he changes his mind. Neoptolemus, although he himself is an heroic warrior, is one for whom the standard by which he measures his own worth quite clearly involves values beyond so-called competitive success, though he is open to the attractions of that, too, which is why he can be temporarily seduced. He learns enough from these experiences to become confident in trying to teach Philoctetes something, in order to reclaim him from savagery and solitude to a shared world. Philoctetes asks him whether, after all this, he is not ashamed to be doing the Atreides' work, and Neoptolemus can say:

How can someone be ashamed, when they are being of help?[34]

when he is helping, now, Philoctetes.

In this discussion, I have been using the English word "shame" in two ways. It has translated certain Greek words, in particular *aidōs*. It has also had its usual modern meaning. I have been able to use it in both these ways without its falling apart, and this shows something significant. What we have discovered about the Greeks' understanding of these reactions, that they can transcend both an assertive egoism and a conventional concern for public opinion, applies equally well to what we recognise in our own world as shame. If it were not so, the translation could not have delivered so much that is familiar to us from our acquaintance with what we call "shame".

Yet we have another word, "guilt", for which the Greeks had no direct equivalent. This determines for us another concept, and perhaps a distinct experience. Some people think that this difference between ourselves and the Greeks is ethically very important. We must ask whether this is so. First we have to consider how shame and guilt are, in our conception of things, related to one another. The mere fact that we have the two words does not, in itself, imply that there is any great psychological difference between shame and guilt. It might merely be that we set up an extra verbal marker within one and the same psychological field, in order to pick out some particular applications of what would otherwise be shame—its application to one's own actions and omissions, perhaps.

This might be so, but I do not think that in fact it is. The distinction between shame and guilt goes deeper than this, and there are some real psychological differences between them. The most primitive experiences of shame are connected with sight and being seen, but it has been interestingly suggested that guilt is rooted in hearing, the sound in oneself of the voice of judgement;[35] it is the moral sentiment of the word. There are further differences in the experience of the two reactions. Gabriele Taylor has well said that "shame is the emotion of self-protection,"[36] and in the experience of shame, one's whole being seems diminished or lessened. In my experience of shame, the other sees all of me and all through me, even if the occasion of the shame is on my surface—for instance, in my appearance; and the expression of shame, in general as well as in the particular form of it that is embarrassment, is not just the desire to hide, or to hide my face, but the desire to disappear, not to be there. It is not even the wish, as people say, to sink through the floor, but rather the wish that the space occupied by me should be instantaneously empty.[37] With guilt, it is not like this; I am more dominated by the thought that even if I disappeared, it would come with me.

These differences in the experience of shame and of guilt can be seen as part of a wider set of contrasts between them.[38] What arouses guilt in an agent is an act or omission of a sort that typically elicits from other people anger, resentment, or indignation. What the agent may offer in order to turn this away is reparation; he may also fear punishment or may inflict it on himself. What arouses shame, on the other hand, is something that typically elicits from others contempt or derision or avoidance. This may equally be an act or omission, but it need not be: it may be some failing or defect. It will lower the agent's self-respect and diminish him in his own eyes. His reaction, as we just saw, is a wish to hide or disappear, and this is one thing that links shame as, minimally, embarrassment with shame as social or personal reduction. More positively, shame may be expressed in attempts to reconstruct or improve oneself.

The discussion in this chapter, as elsewhere in this study, is directed to an historical interpretation from which we can ethically learn something, and I have included psychological materials in it only to the extent that it may help to focus that discussion. A deeper exploration of the relations between shame and guilt is needed if we are going to be able to carry our understanding of these historical and ethical issues farther; as a start on that inquiry, I have added some further speculations on these matters as an appendix (Endnote 1).

The immediate point is that if these distinctions between shame and guilt are even roughly correct, then it looks as though *aidōs* (and the other Greek terms) cannot merely mean "shame", but must cover something like guilt as well. We noticed earlier in this chapter that *nemesis,* the reaction that was appropriate in the Homeric world to breaches of *aidōs,* could include anger, indignation, and resentment as much as contempt or avoidance. The idea of reparation is prominent in Homer, as we saw in the last chapter, and the need for it, for gestures that compensate and heal, must surely be recognised in any society if the notion of holding oneself responsible is to have any content. Along with that recognition, there goes the thought that a victim is owed compensation, or has a right to it, and this was also part of the ideas that we examined in the last chapter. In the Greek world there was room, too, for forgiveness. It is often thought that forgiveness speaks more effectively to guilt than to shame: if the people who have been wronged forgive me, then perhaps the case is withdrawn from the internal judge, but their forgiveness has less power to repair my sense of myself. But forgiveness was as familiar in the Greek world as in ours and was seen as an appropriate and commendable reaction, for several different kinds of reasons.[39]

If all these things—indignation, reparation, forgiveness—are typically associated with what we call "guilt" rather than with what we call "shame", then should we say that even Homeric society was acquainted with guilt as much as with shame? Should we conclude, then, that Homeric society was not, after all, a shame culture and that this contrast between our world and that society has been based simply on a mistake about a word?

I do not think so. It is certainly true that the shame culture has been understood in much too simple a way, and we have seen this much in the course of getting an adequate idea of shame itself. But it has not been simply a mistake to emphasize the importance of shame in Greek societies. Even though some reactions in those societies were structured in the same way as our reactions of guilt, they were not simply guilt if they were not separately recognised as such; just as shame is not the same when it does not have guilt as a contrast. What people's ethical emotions are depends significantly on what they take them to be.[40] The truth about Greek societies, and in particular the Homeric, is not that they failed to recognise any of the reactions that we associate with guilt, but that they did not make of those reactions the special thing that they became when they are separately recognised as guilt.

If we ask exactly how great a difference lies between the Greeks and ourselves in this respect, we run into a problem that I mentioned in the first chapter, of distinguishing what we think from what we think that we think. One thing that a marked contrast between shame and guilt may express is the idea that it is important to distinguish between "moral" and "nonmoral" qualities. Shame itself is neutral on that distinction: we, like the Greeks, can be as mortified or disgraced by a failure in prowess or cunning as by a failure of generosity or loyalty. Guilt, on the other hand, is closely related to the conceptions of morality, and to insist on its particular importance is to insist on those conceptions. It is said that we make a lot of the distinction between the moral and the nonmoral and emphasise the importance of the moral. But how far, and in what ways, is this really true of our life, as opposed to what moralists say about our life? Do we even understand what the distinction is, or how deep it really goes? [41] There is perhaps no single question on which an understanding of the Greeks can join more helpfully with reflection on our own experience. We paralyse both that understanding and that reflection if we simply take it for granted that the distinction is at once deep, important, and self-explanatory.

Once we stop taking this for granted, we may see some advantages in the Greeks' ways of understanding the ethical emotions. One way in which we can be helped by the Greek conception that brings (something like) guilt under a wider conception of (something more than) shame is that it can give us a wiser understanding of the connections between guilt and shame themselves. We can feel both guilt and shame towards the same action. In a moment of cowardice, we let someone down; we feel guilty because we have let them down, ashamed because we have contemptibly fallen short of what we might have hoped of ourselves.[42] As always, the action stands between the inner world of disposition, feeling, and decision and an outer world of harm and wrong. *What I have done* points in one direction towards what has happened to others, in another direction to what I am.

Guilt looks primarily in the first direction, and it need not be guilt about the voluntary. We considered in the last chapter the utterly familiar fact that what has happened to others through our agency can have its own authority over our feelings, even though we brought it about involuntarily. The agent-regret I described there can be psychologically and structurally a manifestation of guilt. It may be said that it is "irrational" guilt, but to say this, unless it is intended as comfort, carries no useful message; it does not mean, for instance (it had better not), that we would be more admirable people if we did not have such feelings. A better candidate for what might be called "irrational" guilt is guilt felt simply at breaking a rule or a resolution, where there is no question of wrong to others or reparation. Robbed of those implications, guilt narrows down suspectly to a desire for punishment. It might then be helpfully replaced by what it should have been in the first place, shame.

Shame looks to what I am. It can be occasioned by many things—actions, as in this kind of case, or thoughts or desires or the reactions of others. Even where it is certainly concerned with an action, it may be a matter of discovery to the agent, and a difficult discovery, what the source of the shame is, whether it is to be found in the intention, the action, or an outcome. Someone might feel shame at the letter he has mailed, because it is (and he knew as he wrote it that it was) a petty and stupid response to a trivial slight; and the shame is lightened, but only to some degree, when it turns out that the letter was never delivered. Just because shame can be obscure in this kind of way, we can fruitfully work to make it more perspicuous, and to understand how a certain action or thought stands to ourselves, to what we are and to what realistically we can want ourselves to be. If we come to understand our shame, we may also better understand our guilt. The structures of shame contain the possibility of controlling and learning from guilt, because they give a conception of one's ethical identity, in relation to which guilt can make sense. Shame can understand guilt, but guilt cannot understand itself.

This is clearly illustrated by a point I have just mentioned, that guilt, insofar as it concerns itself with victims, is not necessarily or obviously restricted to voluntary actions. I may rightly feel that victims have a claim on me and that their anger and suffering looks towards me, even though I have acted involuntarily. The conceptions of modern morality, however, insist at once on the primacy of guilt, its significance in turning us towards victims, and its rational restriction to the voluntary. It is under considerable strain in insisting on all these things at once.[43] In fact, if we want to understand why it might be important for us to distinguish the harms we do voluntarily from those that we do involuntarily, we shall hope to succeed only if we ask what kinds of failing or inadequacy are the source of the harms, and what those failings mean in the context of our own and other people's lives. This is the territory of shame; it is only by moving into it that we may gain some insight into one of the main preoccupations of the morality that centres itself on guilt.

To the modern moral consciousness, guilt seems a more transparent moral emotion than shame. It may seem so, but that is only because, as it presents itself, it is more isolated than shame is from other elements of one's self-image, the rest of one's desires and needs, and because it leaves out a lot even of one's ethical consciousness. It can direct one towards those who have been wronged or damaged, and demand reparation in the name, simply, of what has happened to them. But it cannot by itself help one to understand one's relations to those happenings, or to rebuild the self that has done these things and the world in which that self has to live. Only shame can do that, because it embodies conceptions of what one is and of how one is related to others.

If guilt seems to many people morally self-sufficient, it is probably because they have a distinctive and false picture of the moral life, according to which the truly moral self is characterless. In this picture, I am provided by reason, or perhaps by religious illumination (the picture owes much to Christianity), with a knowledge of the moral law, and I need only the will to obey it. The structures most typical of shame then fall away: what I am, so far as it affects the moral, is already given, and there is only the matter of discerning among temptations and distractions what I ought to do. (This false picture is closely related to illusions that we have examined in earlier chapters, such as the idea of a moralised basic structure of the mind, and the search for an intrinsically just conception of responsibility.) In not isolating a privileged conception of moral guilt, and in placing under a broader conception of shame the social and psychological structures that were near to what we call "guilt", the Greeks, once again, displayed realism, and truthfulness, and a beneficent neglect.

The conception of the moral self as characterless leaves only a limited positive role to other people in one's moral life. Their reactions should not influence one's moral conclusions, except by assisting reason or illumination. If what others will think of me plays an essential role in my moral determinations, then morality is thought to have skidded into the heteronomy that at the beginning of this chapter we recognised as a familiar charge against the mechanisms of shame. There are some important distinctions to be made here, but this conception of the moral does very little to help us make them. On the contrary, the main distinctions that we need are to be found within the workings of shame itself.

By the later fifth century the Greeks had their own distinctions between a shame that merely followed public opinion and a shame that expressed inner personal conviction. In Euripides' *Hippolytus,* such a distinction is not only expressed but does much, in a complex and sophisticated way, to structure the action.[44] Phaedra destroys herself and those around her in her determination to secure for herself an unambiguous and undoubted good reputation. Hippolytus, accused of wrongs he has not committed, becomes so desperate when his purity is not understood and accepted that at the climactic moment of his attempt to justify himself his wish is to be his own audience.[45] He has invoked the buildings of the house as witnesses of his innocence; Theseus grimly replies that he does well to call on testimony that is speechless. Then Hippolytus says:

> Oh! how I wish that I could stand in front of myself,
> and weep at the miseries that I am suffering.

Theseus answers:

> You have always been more inclined to be in awe
> of yourself, then to treat your parents decently.

Hippolytus's wish is not only extraordinary in itself, but it shifts the focus, as Theseus's reply acknowledges, from one kind of inwardness to another. Hippolytus has been struggling with the fact that his father will not believe that he is innocent of an action that he and everyone else would regard as unforgivable. In his wish, he does not call on himself as a witness on his own behalf: as that, he would be as useless as the walls, if for the contrary reason, that he would be all speech and no substance. He wants to be a witness not for, but of, Hippolytus, his only sympathiser, and this shifts attention away from what he knows about himself—the falsity of Phaedra's accusation—and directs it to his virtuous character, his integrity as a man of purity and honour. The starkly narcissistic image that expresses this leads Theseus to the damaging charge that Hippolytus's virtue has always been self-regarding. *Sebein,* "to worship or hold in awe", is the word he uses for Hippolytus's attitude to himself: Hippolytus regards his soul as a holy place, set aside from the necessary business of caring about other people.

This provides a contrast to Phaedra's error, but it is not a simple one. She was obsessed with herself, and so is Hippolytus. In her case, the obsession took the form of conventional shame, an overwhelming concern for her own reputation. That concern is self-directed, but it honours, in a certain way, the existence of others. If, as Phaedra herself puts it, that sort of shame can destroy the house, it is because it is directed only to what others think and say. Hippolytus's self-concern, by contrast, leaves out other people altogether; in regarding himself as an unpolluted place, he has withdrawn entirely from humanity, from both their opinions and their needs.

The *Hippolytus* creates a space in which "inner-directed" and "other-directed" aspects of *aidōs* can be laid against each other in several different contrasts. Hippolytus's view of himself, in his confrontation with Theseus, represents the truth about what he has done as opposed to what others falsely think: at this point, "inner" is to "outer" as reality is to appearance. Theseus's criticism of Hippolytus, however, and of his private virtue of self-protection and purity, identifies the "inner" as a devotion to self that is contrasted with a proper concern for others. With Phaedra, too, the relations between public and private are wrong, but in another direction; she is concerned with others, but overwhelmingly in the form of fear—a fear of the private becoming public and of how her reality will, truly, appear. Charles Segal has rightly said that the play contrasts "inward and outward, private and public realms, 'shame' and 'repute'." [46] Those three oppositions do not all mark the same contrast: indeed, each of them can be used to mark more than one of the contrasts that are at work.

Greek thought itself had the materials, and powerful ones, to bring out the ambivalence and possible betrayals of shame. It is a question not of some moral motivation quite different from shame, but of the articulation of shame itself. Even before we reach the remarkable constructions of the *Hippolytus*, the Greeks' understanding of shame, I have claimed, was strong and complex enough to dispose of the familiar criticism that an ethical life shaped by it is unacceptably heteronomous, crudely dependent on public opinion. But I also said at the beginning of this chapter that if there were anything in those criticisms, it would have to be found at a much deeper level, and the question remains whether there is anything at all to be found at a deeper level. If there is, it will be found in the fact that the internalised other, as I put it, still has some independent identity: that it is not just a screen for one's own ethical ideas but is the locus of some genuine social expectations. If a charge of social heteronomy is to stick at a more interesting level, its claim will have to be that even this abstracted, improved, neighbour lodged in one's inner life represents a compromise of genuine autonomy.

This charge most familiarly comes from distinctively modern, in particular Kantian, conceptions of morality, but a version of it can be found in the Greek world itself. It was made by Plato. The *Republic* pursues by a long and political route a question that Glaukon put in the second book in the form of a thought experiment, one that sets out from the idea of Gyges' Ring of invisibility. We are to suppose the just man and the unjust man in isolation from any corresponding social appearance, abstracted from all the normal conventional forces that respectively encourage and discourage those dispositions:

> The perfectly unjust man, then, must be given the most perfect injustice, and we must not take anything away from him, but rather allow him, although he does the greatest injustice, to fix himself a perfect reputation for justice. . . . Next to him in the argument, let us set up the just man, who will be a simple and noble person, who, as Aeschylus says, wants to be just rather than to seem it. We will have to take away the possibility that he seems just. For if he seems just, there will be the honors and awards that go with that, and it will then be unclear whether he is just for the sake of justice, or for the sake of the honors and awards.[47]

What Plato tries to do in the *Republic* is to show that the isolated and misunderstood man of justice will have a life more worth living than the other. This will be so, according to Plato, because the soul of the just man will be in the best condition, and that will be so because he knows what is just. But more than this is required if this experiment in motivational solipsism is to work. The subject of the experiment will have to know that he knows: he will have to be, in fact, in the condition that Plato requires of his Guardians. The members of the lower classes in the city, we are eventually told, do not have self-supporting motivations of justice; only the Guardians, who have attained the self-revealing state of knowledge, have those. If the other classes could ethically survive at all when not subjected to the actual power of the Guardians—and that is a deeply ambiguous issue in the *Republic*[48]—they *would* need an internalised other: an inner Guardian. The Guardians do not need that, because they have internalised something else, and carry in them a paradigm of justice gained from their intellectual formation (more exactly, revived in them by it).

A great deal is assumed in the formulation of this thought experiment. When we are presented with it, we are simply told that this man *is* just and that he is misunderstood by a perverse or wicked world. This is something we are supposed to understand from outside the imagined situation. We are given the convictions of the just man himself, and those are taken to be both true and unshakable. But suppose we decline to stand outside and to assume the man's justice. Suppose we change the terms of the solipsistic experiment and arrange it from the agent's perspective, rather than from ours or from Plato's; suppose we make it, in effect, an exercise in ethical Cartesianism. Then we should describe the situation in these terms: this is a man who thinks that he is just, but is treated by everyone else as though he were not. If he were given merely that description of himself, it is less clear how steady his motivations would prove. Moreover, it is less clear how steady we think they should prove. For given simply that description, there is nothing to show whether he is a solitary bearer of true justice or a deluded crank.

When we think of people in a situation described as Glaukon describes his thought experiment, we salute them as morally autonomous: as reformers, perhaps, or as people who, in one of Bertrand Russell's favorite phrases, will not follow a multitude to destruction. When we do this, and try to wave to them over time or through the glass of the thought experiment, we are assuming implicitly that they have some essential thing ethically in common with us. Plato, and in quite a different way, Kant, thought that what was in common was the power of reason, and this is why for each of them, in these different ways, the moral self is indeed characterless. But if we now think, plausibly enough, that the power of reason is not enough by itself to distinguish good and bad; if we think, yet more plausibly, that even if it is, it is not very good at making its effects indubitably obvious, then we should hope that there is some limit to these people's autonomy, that there is an internalised other in them that carries some genuine social weight. Without it, the convictions of autonomous self-legislation may become hard to distinguish from an insensate degree of moral egoism.

That word brings out something that has been implicit in this argument from the beginning. When it is complained that the Greek ethical outlook, or at least that of the archaic Greeks, is both egoistic and at the same time heteronomous, because it rests conventionally on the opinion of others, there is a constant and powerful tendency for these two complaints to turn against each other. Which is supposed to be the trouble, that these people thought too much about others' reactions, or too little? The only thing that makes it seem as though the two complaints line up with one another is the simple idea that the ethic of archaic Greece was competitive.[49] A competition is precisely something in which you have the egoistic aim of trying to win, but you also unquestioningly accept rules that have been laid down by someone else. Under the competitive ethic, as it has been conceived, the views of others are invoked, but in favour of conventionally encouraged forms of self-assertion. But as we have already seen, those conceptions are inadequate to describe even the behaviour of men on the Homeric battlefield. As soon as the interpretation of the two complaints changes at all from that given by the simple model of competition, it becomes quite obvious that they cannot be lined up. It is clear in the case of Plato's thought experiment: the thought experiment tries to dispense entirely with heteronomy, but it is designed for a purpose that in progressivist terms is still egoistic (though its egoism is that of self-concern rather than self-assertion). The divergence between these different criticisms helps to explain the notable unease among progressivist writers, about how far Plato may be thought to have reached on the road to true morality: he seems to have got all the way by one measure and hardly to have started by another.

The necessity with which we started, the necessity that Ajax recognised, was grounded in his own identity, his sense of himself as someone who can live in some social circumstances and not others, and what mediated between himself and the world was his sense of shame. He, being a warrior under the heroic code, balanced that identity on a narrow base of personal achievement. So of course did Achilles and Hector in the *Iliad*, but we can catch the note in figures less grand and tragic than these; in the wistful remark of Nestor, for instance, recalling the achievements of his youth: "So I was among men, if I was ever anything."[50] Similar ideas exist in other honour codes. Heroes in Calderón are given to saying *Soy que soy*, "I am what I am," and the same idea is illustrated wonderfully, by subtraction or denial, in the words of Shakespeare's Parolles:

> Yet I am thankful. If my heart were great
> 'Twould burst at this. Captain I'll be no more;
> But I will eat and drink and sleep as soft
> As captain shall. Simply the thing I am
> Shall make me live. . . .

Quiet sword, cool blushes, and Parolles, live
Safest in shame.[51]

But it is not only the particular and perilous demands of the honour code that may involve a sense of one's identity. The structure of shame can be the same without those particular values and expectations. The ethical work that shame did in the ancient world was applied to some values that we do not share, and we also recognise the separate existence of guilt. But shame continues to work for us, as it worked for the Greeks, in essential ways. By giving through the emotions a sense of who one is and of what one hopes to be, it mediates between act, character, and consequence, and also between ethical demands and the rest of life. Whatever it is working on, it requires an internalised other, who is not designated merely as a representative of an independently identified social group, and whose reactions the agent can respect. At the same time, this figure does not merely shrink into a hanger for those same values but embodies intimations of a genuine social reality—in particular, of how it will be for one's life with others if one acts in one way rather than another. This was in substance already the ethical psychology even of the archaic Greeks, and, despite the modern isolation of guilt, it forms a substantial part of our own.

CHAPTER FIVE

Necessary Identities

At this point, we are between two necessities. The Homeric, tragic, in particular Sophoclean, characters are represented to us as experiencing a necessity to act in certain ways, a conviction that they must do certain things, and I suggested in the last chapter that we should understand this in terms of the mechanisms of shame. The source of the necessity is in the agent, an internalised other whose view the agent can respect. Indeed he can identify with this figure, and the respect is to that extent self-respect; but at the same time the figure remains a genuine other, the embodiment of a real social expectation. At the extreme, the sense of this necessity lies in the thought that one could not live and look others in the eye if one did certain things: a thought which may be to varying degrees figurative but can also be in a deadly sense literal, as it was with Ajax. These necessities are internal, grounded in the *ēthos,* the projects, the individual nature of the agent, and in the way he conceives the relation of his life to other people's.

Contrasted with this, at the other end of the universe, as one might say, is a divine necessity. In the Greek world this was not conceived as a unitary world-historical or redemptive enterprise, as it has been by Jews and Christians. When Homer says at the beginning of the *Iliad* that the anger came about, and many were killed, "and the plan of Zeus was fulfilled,"[1] it was not a plan for the world: it was not even a plan for the whole Trojan War, and anyway (as Homer frequently reminds us)[2] the Trojan War was not the whole world. For the Greeks, divine necessity did not even consist of one plan for one individual, except in very special cases. But the world did contain various forces that could make certain outcomes necessary for the individual: they were necessary outcomes because they were, simply, unavoidable. Those divine necessities were purposive, in the sense that events were shaped towards a particular outcome. Sometimes, though not always, they were purposed as well, in the sense that they were designed by a supernatural agency that had a motive. Those external, divine, necessities, and some of the thoughts that go with them, will be the concern of the next chapter.

Agents, typically, are not fully conscious of those supernatural necessities in advance. They may have a sense that there is a necessity involved, but not be sure what it is; for them, the outcome may, at the time, seem like luck. That is the sense in which, in the *Ajax* (803), Tekmessa, trying to prevent Ajax killing himself within the day—the oracle has said that he will live if he survives the day—can ask her friends "to stand in the way of a necessary chance," *anangkaias tuchēs*.

That phrase, in that connection, unnervingly combines most of the thoughts available about supernatural necessity. But Tekmessa had already used that same phrase earlier in the play (485 seq.), indeed in some such sense, but also with a more everyday meaning. She had said to Ajax that there is no greater evil for human beings than "necessary chance", and she cited her own case: she had a free and rich father, but now she is a slave. "So it was decided by the gods, perhaps, and above all, by your hand": and the move from an indeterminate speculation about the gods to a very definite assertion about Ajax brings with it a shift in the idea of an *anangkaia tuchē*. Her bad luck may possibly have been written in the stars, but it was quite certainly imposed on her by force, and it is continued by the threat or presence of force, even if in Tekmessa's own case her attitude to Ajax had put that to one side. This kind of necessity is certainly not hidden from the victim. Indeed, it most usually operates because it is offered clearly to the victim, in the form of a present threat; though if the threat is carried out and the agent is physically coerced, his consciousness may not matter any longer—what happens just happens to him. *Bia,* force, and *kratos,* physical constraint—a pair personified at the beginning of the *Prometheus Vinctus,* as they are in Hesiod—were well known to be the bearers of a certain kind of *anangkē,* necessity. (A shrine of Bia and Anangke on the way up to the Acrocorinth is mentioned by Pausanias.)[3] Thucydides deploys the word in a sinister plural when he says that the Athenians were very exacting to their subjects who failed to pay the tribute, making themselves objectionable by applying *tas anangkas* to unwilling people (1.99).

Coercion may be both the cause and the effect of bad luck, and a paradigm of bad luck throughout the ancient world was being taken into slavery by military conquest, as Hecuba said in the *Iliad* had happened to some of her sons,

> whom at times swift-footed Achilles captured,
> and he would sell them as slaves far across the unresting salt water
> into Samos, and Imbros, and Lemnos in the gloom of the mists.[4]

And this was what, famously, Hector most regretted when he anticipated the fall of Troy: "None of it troubles me," he says to Andromache,

> so much as the thought of you, when some bronze-armoured
> Achaian leads you off, taking away your day of liberty,
> in tears; and in Argos you must work at the loom of another . . .
> all unwilling, but strong will be the necessity upon you.[5]

In this chapter I shall be concerned first with some consequences in the world of ideas of this very basic kind of disaster,
and of slavery more generally; more generally still, with the
Greeks' recognition that in their world one's whole life, all the
ways in which one was treated, one's ethical identity, might depend on a chance.

My concern here is quite particularly with what I called at the
beginning of this study the philosophical understanding of an
historical phenomenon. Much is known about ancient slavery,
and much is not known; unfortunately, much of what is known
is not known to me. What I have to say about it is not meant to
add to our understanding of it as a social institution, but rather
to try to help us understand some things that some Greeks said
about it. I hope that this may also help us to understand better
our own rejection of it, and of certain other Greek practices, as
unjust. In particular, this raises a basic question that we have
met before and shall come to again, of how far our rejection of
that institution, and of other ancient practices that we see as
unjust, depends on modern conceptions that were not available
in the ancient world.

Greek and Roman slavery was, as Moses Finley stressed,[6] a
novel invention, and its pattern has been rare in history. There
was in fact a range of different institutions, which are distinguished by modern theory and to some extent were distinguished in antiquity itself. The helots in Sparta, though they
were regarded by many as slaves, were not chattel slaves but an
entire subject people, perhaps best classified as "state serfs";
they were notorious for being ready to revolt.[7]

Slaves in Athens, however, were chattel slaves in the fullest
sense, pieces of individual property—"living property", in the
phrase of Aristotle, who with his usual capacity to find an interesting point of ordinary language philosophy in an unlikely
place remarks that while a master can of course say that another

man is his slave, equally a slave can say that another man is his master: but only a master can say of another man that he is *his*.[8] In their own person slaves had no legal rights, and in particular none in the area of marriage or family law. Some slaves were allowed to live together as couples, but any such connection and the association of slaves and their children were frequently broken up, a practice that seems not to have been challenged until the fourth century A.D.[9] Slaves were, of course, sexually available to their owners.[10]

It was important for the ideology of this institution that the slaves were mostly barbarians, people who did not speak Greek, usually from the north and the northeast. (In the fifth and early fourth centuries Athens had a police force consisting of Scythian slaves, who lived in tents and were the subject of a great deal of humour.) [11] The supply of slaves had to be renewed, and this was by no means necessarily a matter of regular warfare. The skills involved in capturing people to be slaves are said by Aristotle to be "a kind of hunting"; being a slave trader was regarded as both dangerous and unpopular.[12]

One of the paradoxes of chattel slavery, in the ancient world as in other cases, was the varying social distance between free and slave to be found in different aspects of life. In Greece, the free and the slaves worked side by side. Xenophon says "those who can do so buy slaves so that they can have fellow workers." As Finley has pointed out,[13] there were no slave employments as such, except domestic service and, usually, mining; the only entirely free employments were law, politics, and military service (but not in the navy). We know from the accounts the status of eighty-six workmen who worked on the construction of the Erechtheum at the end of the fifth century: twenty-four citizens, forty-two metics, and twenty slaves, all skilled craftsmen, and those on a daily wage were all paid the same.

Yet at the same time the slave was set apart from the free, in particular by the violence that surrounded his life. The slave was called (as elsewhere) "boy", *pais,* and it was a joke that *pais* came from *paiein,* "to beat".[14] Public slaves, at least, were marked with a brand, which, as Xenophon observed, made them harder to steal than money.[15] The overwhelming difference between free and slave, Demosthenes remarked, was that the slave was answerable with his or her body. Evidence from slaves was acceptable in the courts solely on condition that it had been extracted under torture. In a speech of Lysias, a man's reluctance to allow his slave concubine to be tortured is cited as evidence against him.[16]

Modern experience shows that it is possible for people to work next to each other who have startlingly different sets of rights, and social identities that require them to be treated in quite different ways. What made ancient slavery even more remarkable was the ready way in which a person could change from one of these identities to another. Some were born slaves, but you could become a slave from being free, by being captured, and this, as we have already seen, was a well-known calamity, a piece of ill luck. But equally, you could cease to be a slave, by manumission. In Rome, slaves were manumitted into citizenship, but this was not so among the Greeks: in Athens, a manumitted slave was a metic, a resident alien, a status that carried fewer rights than being a citizen but was already a world away from being a slave. Manumission, which at least from the fourth century B.C. was fairly common, involved an extraordinary transition: as one scholar has put it, the freed slave was transformed from an object to a subject of rights, the most complete metamorphosis one can imagine.[17]

In later antiquity the law of slavery was complex, and its attempts to mitigate some of the arbitrary features seem sometimes only to add another arbitrariness to the system, that of lawyers. Under Roman law, if a woman conceived as a free person but had become a slave by the time that she gave birth, the child was recognised as free: the *Digest* smugly remarks, "The mother's adversity should not prejudice a child in the womb."[18] From the beginning, the arbitrariness of slavery was recognised. Some people, it is clear, went on to conclude from this that it was difficult to defend. Not many of their opinions have been preserved, but there are some famous verses that say:

> If someone is a slave, he has the same flesh, for no one was ever born a slave by nature: it is chance that has enslaved his body.

A similar thought is attributed to the Messenian Oration of Alcidamas (who was a pupil of Gorgias and a contemporary of Isocrates):

> God let everyone set out as free people; nature never made anyone a slave.[19]

As a nineteenth-century commentator on Aristotle remarked,

> it was just the facility of the transition from slavery to freedom and from freedom to slavery, and the dependence of men's status on accident and superior force and the will of men . . . that would give rise to the view that it was based on convention, not nature.[20]

To say that something was conventional was not necessarily to say that it was unjust; it did not necessarily imply this conclusion even in the period in the late fifth century when oppositions between nature and convention played a particularly large part in discussions of questions in politics and ethics. Slavery, however, was not merely conventional but arbitrary in its impact, and granted that it was intensely unpleasant for the slaves (which no one was disposed to deny, at least until the highminded accommodations of later Stoicism), it was not hard to reach the conclusion summarized by Aristotle in his most lapidary manner:

But to some people, holding slaves [*despozein,* "to be their master"] is against nature (for it is by convention that one man is a slave and another is free, and in nature there is no difference); therefore it is not just, either; since it is imposed by force [*biaion gar*].[21]

In the first book of the *Politics,* Aristotle notoriously tried to answer this charge and to show that slavery was in some sense natural. His attempt has not been well received by modern critics, who have been struck by the fact that various things he says in the course of it are not entirely consistent with each other or with things he says elsewhere.[22] Some of these inconsistencies are clearly ideological products, the results of trying to square the ethical circle. Thus he compares the subordination of slave to master with that of body to soul. (The analogy is not even with the relation of emotion to reason; that comparison is reserved for the relations of women to men.) But at the same time he has to allow that slaves have enough reason to understand what they are told. They are in many ways, as he says more than once, like domestic animals, but they are (bizarrely enough) domestic animals who interpret instructions, obey through the understanding, and display better or worse characters. Yet again, the master and the slave should, ideally, be friends; elsewhere Aristotle is less clear about this possibility and says only that one can be friends with a slave "*qua* man but not *qua* slave,"[23] a more than usually evasive deployment of one of his least satisfactory philosophical devices. These inconsistencies and strains are revealing. However, there is also something revealing about the way in which modern commentators have seized upon them. They are obviously embarrassed by the philosopher's conclusions and are relieved to discover in his argument any sign that he may have been embarrassed himself; at the very least, they are glad to find an encouragement from within to detach these positions from the body of his work. As opposed to Plato, who is manifestly and professedly offensive to liberal and democratic opinion, Aristotle can be seen as expressing a more generous and accommodating humanism, and there is a strong motivation to find a centre to that outlook that will push to one side his less congenial opinions. There are motives, too, provided by his methods. No one expects to write, or be, like Plato. Aristotle, though, even when one has dimly recognised the extent of his genius, can seem to provide a comforting assurance to philosophers about the possibility of their subject, in the form of an omnipresent judiciousness, which, in itself, is only too easy to imitate.

In fact, Aristotle's argument about slavery is not an aberration in his work at all. It is, certainly, very unlike other people's treatment of the institution, but the ways in which it is untypical deeply express Aristotle's own view of the world. It is incoherent, but this is so not simply because of what slavery was, but because of Aristotle's own demands on how it was to be understood. I shall consider his argument in some detail, and this is relevant to my purpose in more than one way. It will help us, I hope, to understand the Greek outlook on slavery and, perhaps, our own views of justice. It will also illustrate the truth that if there is something worse than accepting slavery, it consists in defending it.

I have tried in earlier chapters to show that the outlook of the Greeks, particularly of archaic and fifth-century Greeks, is nearer to our own than is often thought. Moreover, we must not assume that the progress of philosophy, the theoretical constructions of Plato and Aristotle, always brought us nearer to what we can understand as an adequate grasp of the matters in question. Here is another example of that point, very different from those that we have encountered before. The Greeks had the institution of chattel slavery, and their way of life, as it actually functioned, presupposed it. (It is a different question whether as an abstract economic necessity they needed it: the point is simply that, granted the actual state of affairs, no way of life was accessible to them that preserved what was worthwhile to them and did without slavery.) Almost all of them took it for granted. But that did not mean that they had no ways of expressing what was wrong with it. A few did so in general and abstract terms, as we have seen. There were also the less theoretical complaints of slaves themselves, frequent in drama and, certainly, in everyday life. It is not hard to say what is bad about the life of a slave, and slaves everywhere have said it. Equally, free people in the Greek world were able to see what an arbitrary calamity it was for someone to become a slave. What they found it much harder to do, once they had the system, was to imagine their world without it. For the same reason, they did not take too seriously the complaints of the slaves. They had nothing to put in the place of the system, and granted the system, it would be surprising if slaves did not complain, and in those terms. What the Greeks were not generally committed to, however, was the idea that if the system were both properly run and properly understood, no one, including the slaves, would have reason to complain. This is the conclusion that Aristotle offered.

A recent writer has said that the debate whether slavery was natural was not about the question "whether there should be slaves, but why there should be."[24] In a way this is right, but it simplifies the issues. Aristotle, and no doubt almost everyone else who discussed the issue, thought that if there was a question whether there should be slaves, it had a quick answer: they were necessary. He thought they were a technological necessity: he explicitly allows, but only at the level of pre-science fiction, that if there were self-propelling tools that could perform the tasks, "either at our bidding or itself perceiving the need," there would be no need of slaves. He is himself not entirely consistent about how necessary slaves are; they are certainly necessary to the household, but with regard to agriculture, while slaves are certainly best, he concedes later in the *Politics* that other arrangements are possible.[25] However, in general he supposes them to be necessary; and this already yields one sense in which he might say that slavery is natural. It is necessary for life in the *polis,* and the *polis* is a natural form of association: it is the natural condition of human beings to live in such a community, with an appropriate division of labour.

If we grant the premisses, Aristotle has already shown why there should be slaves; indeed, he has even shown, in a sense, why it is natural that there should be. But he has not yet even started to argue for that conclusion in his own distinctive sense, and the further step he has to take makes it very clear what he aims to do. What he has shown so far, on his own assumptions, is that some people have to be in the power of other people. This in no way determines who should be in whose power. All we have is that it is necessary and natural that some people should be masters of others; so far, it could be arbitrary which people were which. But if it is arbitrary, then this, as he said, might support the charge of injustice.

Worse—or, at least, worse from Aristotle's general point of view—is the consideration that to leave a blank at this point might generate a conflict within the account of what is natural. Central to Aristotle's thought is a contrast between what is natural and, on the other hand, what is *biaion,* that which is produced by constraint or force applied from outside. In Aristotle's physics this yields the theory of the natural motions of the elements: air and fire move upwards, water and earth downwards, according to their natures, unless they are constrained to move otherwise. For Aristotle's science, the "natural tendencies" of things were basically connected with what sorts of things they were. Human beings also have natural tendencies, and what goes against such a tendency is *biaion* and involves force or constraint.

The same thing is true, to a considerable extent, the other way round: in a healthy, uncorrupted, and adult individual, behaviour that systematically requires constraint in order to elicit it is not natural. But if slavery is arbitrarily imposed, it will require such force: no person who could live a free person's life would want to be a slave. This shows that the life of a slave, for the person who has to lead it, would not be natural. So if we cannot get any farther, the argument from above, as we might call it, that it is natural that there should be slaves, is met by a contrary argument from below, that nobody is naturally a slave. It is vital to the question whether slavery could be seen as a "natural" institution that there are two issues here. If the argument to that conclusion could get only to the point it has reached so far, the theory of slavery as a natural arrangement would turn out to be (roughly) what modern mathematics calls omega-inconsistent: it would be natural and necessary that someone should be a slave, but for each person, it would not be natural that he or she should be one.

Aristotle thus has to take the next step, which yields his distinctive conclusion. He argues not merely that it is natural that someone or other should be a slave, but that there are people for whom it is natural that they, rather than someone else, should be slaves. In fact, all that Aristotle has to show, and he is careful to point this out,[26] is that there are pairs of people naturally related as master to slave. But since the slave's task is identified in terms of being an implement or a workhorse and the condition of being a slave is absolute,[27] sharp distinctions have to be found between slaves and nonslaves. Physical differences are invoked, between the crouching posture natural to a slave and the upright posture of a free man. This is archaic aristocratic material, going back, for instance, to Theognis:

> A slave's head is never upright, but always bent, and he has a
> slanting neck. A rose or a hyacinth never comes from a sea-onion:
> no more does a free child from a slave woman.

But the important point for Aristotle is the supposed mental superiority of masters to slaves. Not surprisingly, he has problems in adjusting this to the required physical differences, as also to any plausible understanding of the observed reality. He admits that there is considerable miscasting as things are:

> Nature aims to make the bodies of free men differ from those of slaves, the latter adapted in strength to necessary employment, the former upright and not suited to such work. . . . But the opposite often happens, and some people have the bodies of free men and others the souls.[28]

The last sentence of this passage is a disaster: it has to accommodate falsehoods he needs to say, and other things he needs not to say (for instance, that there are free men who should be recast as slaves), and it has collapsed under the pressure, generating a great debate among scholars about how, even syntactically, it is to be taken. These ideas, together with a familiar set of Greek prejudices about the slavish nature of barbarians, are the ancestors of the physiognomic and other ideological myths that have been notorious in modern times.[29]

The idea that slavery was natural, so to speak, *all the way down*, and that the argument from above, that slavery was necessary to the type of community in which human life could best develop, was met by an argument from below, that there existed people for whom the role was not contrary to nature and involved no real constraint: these ideas did not have much future in antiquity. They were to be called upon again, much later, in connection with the directly racist ideology of modern slavery, even if there they played a secondary role to Scripture ("learned embroidery" is Finley's phrase for them).[30]

Later antiquity seems rather to have given up the question of slavery as a problem in political philosophy in favour of edifying attempts to show that slavery was not really harmful to the slave; in particular, that real freedom was freedom of the spirit, and that this could be attained as well, perhaps better, by slaves. One of the most explicit, certainly one of the more repulsive, expositions of this attitude is offered by Seneca:

It is a mistake to think that slavery goes all the way down into a man. The better part of him remains outside it. The body belongs to the master and is subject to him, but the soul is autonomous, and is so free that it cannot be held by any prison. . . . It is the body that luck has given over to the master; this he buys and sells; that interior part cannot be handed over as property.

This view and its various Christian relatives are manifestly very different from Aristotle's,[31] because they invoke a dualism, or some similar picture of human beings, by which the most essential characteristics and interests of people transcend the empirical social world and its misfortunes. Aristotle did not have such a picture. But these views, and his, do share an objective: to sustain the belief that life cannot be ultimately or structurally unjust. Seneca and his various associates can let the social world be unjust, because they can, in accordance with one or another of their fantasies, suppose that one can get out of it. Aristotle knew that one could not get out of it, and his fantasy had to be that however imperfect it was likely in practice to be, at least it was not structurally unjust—the world could not be such that the best development of some people necessarily involved the coercion of others against their nature.

The earlier Greeks were not involved in either of those illusions. They were not particularly disposed to think of slavery as unjust, but that was not because they thought of it as a just institution. If they had thought of it as a just institution, they would also have thought that the slaves themselves—free people captured into slavery, for instance—would have been mistaken to complain about it. So it is now with judicial punishment: those who regard it as a just institution think that those who are properly subjected to it have basically no reason to complain. The earlier Greeks thought no such thing about slavery. On the contrary, being captured into slavery was a paradigm of disaster, of which any rational person would complain; and by the same token, they recognised the complaints as indeed com-

plaints, objections made by rational people. Slavery, in most
people's eyes, was not just, but necessary. Because it was necessary, it was not, as an institution, seen as unjust either: to say
that it was unjust would imply that ideally, at least, it should
cease to exist, and few, if any, could see how that might be. If
as an institution it was not seen as either just or unjust, there
was not much to be said about its justice, and indeed it has often
been noticed that in extant Greek literature there are very few
discussions at all of the justice of slavery.

The Greek world recognised the simple truth that slavery
rested on coercion. Aristotle's attempt to justify the institution,
in the literal sense of conferring justice on it rather than accepting that it was necessary, required him to deny this simple truth.
Coercion, the *biaion,* is against nature, and if slavery, properly
conducted, could be natural, then it would not be, in the deepest
sense, coercive. It would be optimistic to have hoped that if slavery were properly conducted it would not involve violence at
all; the point would be, rather, that even if violence had to be
directed to a natural slave, it need not be in the deepest sense
coercive, because slavery, properly allocated, would be a necessary identity. Aristotle's argument, of course, merely sets the
task; it does not provide the intellectual negotiations and eva-
sions that would be needed in real life to see slavery in that light,
and to change it from being what it had always been seen to be,
a contingent and uniquely brutal disaster for its victims. As I
have already said, antiquity did not persist in any attempt to
find those materials, and it is not surprising.

At least in the case of slaves, Aristotle thought that his case
needed some argument. The subordination of women to men,
on the other hand, receives at the crucial point in the *Politics*
only a phrase: "A slave does not have the deliberative faculty at
all, while a woman has it, but it lacks authority." [32] The argument is of basically the same shape as that about slaves: there is
a need for the division of roles, and nature provides the casting.

But the downwards and upwards movements of the argument in this case virtually coincide, since Aristotle seemingly thinks that less needs to be provided and also that the observed facts clearly provide it. This was merely received opinion, and what was in the case of slavery a peculiar and strained conclusion of Aristotle's, that there were people who by nature filled the required role, was the conventional view with regard to women. There was by nature a position to be filled, and there were people who by nature occupied it. In trying to show that being a slave was a necessary identity, Aristotle was, up to a point, suggesting that if slavery were properly conducted, slaves would become what women actually were.

In the role that Aristotle allocated to women, and in what he said about them, he followed prejudices familiar not only among the Greeks, and they hardly need to be catalogued. Not every Athenian, and still less every Greek, accepted the very restrictive description of a woman's role given in the famous passage of Pericles' Funeral Speech, to the effect that the greatest glory of women lay in not being talked about by men for good or ill, and it has been claimed that a woman's life could be more free than has generally been supposed. Some important facts are unclear—for instance, it is still not agreed whether women went to the theatre. Moreover, the effects of segregation, as Kenneth Dover has pointed out, must have varied between social classes. But, whatever the details, it is clear that a respectable woman's life was to a great degree confined to the house.[33]

Athenian women were not citizens, but the "women of Attica". At the same time, there was a relevant difference between being such a woman and not being so, since the Periclean rule required a male citizen to be *ex amphoin aston*—as it cannot quite be translated, "a citizen on both sides".[34] Their duties lay within the house, and contrasts between *oikos* and *polis*, private and public, were deeply involved in the representation of the relations between women and men; the understanding of those contrasts itself varied, with the result, as Sally Humphreys has noted, that *oikos* is itself an ideological word.[35]

As Dover has reminded us, almost every surviving word of classical Greek was written by men.[36] Nevertheless, complaints about the treatment of women, indeed complaints that their treatment was unfair, are by no means unknown. Already in the *Odyssey* Calypso complains about the double standard that is applied to gods and to goddesses with respect to sexual relations with mortals: "You are jealous," she says to the god, "and you resent goddesses sleeping with men, though you do it with mortal women."[37] A woman in a fragment of Sophocles complains of how they are nothing, are sold into marriage and moved around at their husband's will.[38] The most famous—they might almost be called systematic—objections are those of Euripides' Medea. She is something of a special case,[39] but more generally Aristophanes could make Euripides say that in his plays women spoke. It is interesting that Euripides has been thought by some people to be a feminist, and by others a misogynist: we should perhaps entertain the bleak possibility that he was both.[40]

There is a famous remark, which according to the tradition was ascribed by the biographer Hermippus to Thales (that is to say, to some indeterminate sage), though others ascribed it to Socrates: that there were three things for which he gave thanks to luck—that he had been born a human being and not a beast, a man and not a woman, and a Greek and not a barbarian. (It is a partial inversion of this triad that Aeschylus's Agamemnon invokes when he refuses to walk on the carpet, where he distinguishes himself first from a woman, then from a barbarian, finally from a god.)[41]

But what sort of luck is this? What exactly is the object of the gratitude? Thales—let us call him that—doubtless knew what he meant, more or less, when he said that he was thankful that he was not a woman, and it may seem a philosophical absurdity to press heavily on such a familiar kind of thought. But notions of luck, of justice, and of identity are very tightly enmeshed in this area, and a certain amount of pressure is needed to extract them. One thing at any rate is clear: whatever Thales meant, he was not referring to a real possibility avoided. He had no way of supposing, as a risk he had managed to escape, that he, that very Thales, might have been a woman.

Ancient theories of generation gave no support to the idea that someone who was a man might have been a woman. Those theories themselves are ideological, if not quite straightforwardly so. The kind of theory to be found in Aristotle and elaborated later in Galen superficially expresses male-centred ideas. By contrast with the Hippocratic theory over which it prevailed, it ascribes no active or distinctive role to the female. It represents the female parent as a receptacle rather than a contributor, matter rather than form; it also sees the female child as a spoiled or less than perfect male, a fetus to which not enough heat had been applied to dry it off properly or, in particular, to extrude the genital organs. But it is a very striking fact, as Peter Brown has pointed out, that these ideas were not of a kind to reassure a belief in unquestionable male distinctness. Sexual bimorphism came out as a matter of degree and of accidents, rather than an unambiguous signal of incommensurability; indeed, as Thomas Laqueur has shown, the emphasis in traditional studies of anatomy was quite remarkably directed towards supposed homologies between the male and female reproductive systems. (The first detailed female skeleton in an anatomy book appeared only towards the end of the eighteenth century.)[42] So from a purely biological standpoint, Aristotelian or Galenian medicine might be thought to come nearer than modern theory does to the idea that one might have been born to the other gender—if the father's sperm had been a bit cooler, for instance. But it would still not come near enough. Even if it were an accident that a male came from that copulation rather than a female, and that was an accident simply of degree rather than of the identity of a component, as it is now understood, it was still not an accident that befell *that person,* and Aristotle, for one, never for a moment thinks of it in those terms; just as he thinks that if something is a lion, it is necessarily a lion, so if someone is male, he is necessarily male.

An indication that no one was disposed to deny this thought may perhaps be found in quite a different direction. There was in Greek mythology one figure, Teiresias, for whom belonging to one gender had not excluded belonging to the other. There is more than one version of his myth.[43] The one relevant here is that as a young man he saw two serpents copulating. He killed one and turned into a woman. He was told by Apollo that if he saw the same scene and killed the other, he would turn back; after some time, he did encounter the scene again and did revert to being a man. Hera and Zeus quarrelled on the question whether men or women derived more pleasure from sex, and asked the uniquely qualified Teiresias, who said that of ten parts, the woman enjoyed nine and the man one, which agreed with Zeus. Hera, angry, blinded him. But Zeus gave him the gift of divination and a life lasting seven generations.

This is an old myth, going back to the Hesiodic *Melampodia.*[44] Teiresias's prophetic powers are closely connected in the myth to his sexual history; in Euripides' *Bacchae,* moreover, where Teiresias plays a significant if not very dignified part, there is emphasis on bisexual aspects of the god Dionysus and of his worship.[45] Yet at no point here, or in other plays in which he appears, or in any other extant tragedy is Teiresias's mythical history mentioned. One must surely suppose that the tragedians knew the myth, which survived into later antiquity. Perhaps we may conjecture that despite the psychological power of the myth, it lacked any public significance. The idea of having two sexual histories belonged only to the world of personal fantasy; the field of tragedy, which is also a field of social interaction, is so powerfully structured by the distinctions between men and women that this mythical peculiarity of Teiresias remains, so far as we know, quite irrelevant to it.

The triad of things from which a free Greek male distinguished himself more usually took the form not of *animal, woman, barbarian,* but of *barbarian, woman, slave,* and in that form it remained very powerful for centuries.[46] It was also in that form a good deal more socially relevant. If Thales had given thanks to luck that he was not a slave, he would have been thanking the goddess for a very different and more comprehensible intervention than that which saved him (or somebody) from being a woman. In fact, to thank her that he had not been born a slave would be only part of the message. He would have to thank her further for not making him a slave subsequently. In the matter of his not being a slave, it was not merely in some indeterminate sense luck, but very definitely and comprehensibly his luck, that things had turned out better than they might have done. It was not *his* luck that he was not a woman, and no one ever seriously supposed that it was. Being a woman really was a necessary identity; being a slave or a free man, despite Aristotle's desperate efforts to the contrary, was not. That is why, as I put it before, his attempt can be seen as an attempt to assimilate the condition of a slave to that of a woman.

A lot of conventional practice, now and in the past, has made the assimilation the other way round. In expressing aspirations for a better state of affairs, we acknowledge that being a woman is a necessary identity, but distinguish that biological identity from a social one, in terms such as a distinction between sex and gender.[47] Our aim is that no one should be a slave, but it is not anyone's aim, even the most radical, that no one should be a woman: it is a question of the social construction of what it is to be a woman. The double idea that there should be a sharp and unchanging distribution of roles and that females and males were designed to fill those roles has managed to find a remarkable range of political philosophies ready to accommodate it, including some supposedly devoted to ideals of abstract equality. It was no peculiarity of Aristotle, or of his Greek predecessors, to construe a genuinely necessary sexual identity as a naturally given social identity.

There had, indeed, been one famous exception, Plato, who had argued in the *Republic* that women should not be excluded from performing any role in his ideal state, in particular that of a Guardian, simply because they were women. Plato's opinion seems to have been that as a matter of fact women were not talented for mathematics or ruling; but the question, he insisted, did concern their talents and not their sex.[48] For Aristotle, this argument might as well never have been put, but it is not hard to see the reason. Plato's argument is intimately connected in the *Republic* with his proposal that among the Guardians the family should be abolished. For Aristotle the family was a natural institution that one could not conceive of abolishing, and he took it for granted that the traditional role of women was essentially involved in that natural institution.

The role of women could be taken for granted by most Greeks as natural, except for a few utopians such as Plato or intellectual malcontents such as Euripides. Both tragedy and comedy show, in different ways, that it was not at all unimaginable that women should act differently, but those passages only serve to reveal, and perhaps they helped to reinforce, the standard assumption that there was nothing arbitrary or coercive about the traditional arrangements. With slavery it was different, for while it structured to an immense degree the relations between people in the ancient world, they themselves recognised its arbitrariness and violence.

Except for Aristotle (and he spoke less for existing arrangements than for some indeterminate improvement of them) the Greeks saw what slavery involved, and regarded being a slave as a paradigm of bad luck: *anangkaia tuchē,* the bad luck of being in a condition imposed and sustained by force. "Bad luck" was not a notion that they standardly applied to being a woman. In part, this was because it was not a matter of luck, except at the level of a wish that could be represented by such thoughts as Thales' gratitude. It was also not seen, most of the time and in particular by men, as so bad. It was, for instance, less overtly coercive.

Our attitudes to these matters are different from the Greeks' (though I recognise that the "we" embraced by that "our" is less extensive in the case of women than in the case of slavery). But exactly how are they different? In particular, how far do we need, in rejecting those Greek ideas and practices, ethical ideas that were not available to the Greeks themselves? In the case of slavery, it may be that we deploy ethical ideas against it that the Greeks did not have, but we do not need to do so in order to reject it. It was no secret to the Greeks, as I have said, why it was unenviable bad luck to be in the power of another. Moreover, they recognised how arbitrary the impact of that luck was. Those thoughts could provide the materials for the claim that slavery was unjust—*biaion gar,* in the pungent phrase of Aristotle's I quoted earlier, "because it was imposed by force." But slavery was taken to be necessary—necessary, that is to say, to sustaining the kind of political, social, and cultural life that free Greeks enjoyed. Most people did not suppose that because slavery was necessary, it was therefore just; this, as Aristotle very clearly saw, would not be enough, and a further argument would be needed, one that he hopelessly tried to find. The effect of the necessity was, rather, that life proceeded on the basis of slavery and left no space, effectively, for the question of its justice to be raised.

Once the question is raised, it is quite hard not to see slavery as unjust, indeed as a paradigm of injustice, in the light of considerations basically available to the Greeks themselves. (What really needed new materials, of a scriptural and systematically racist kind, were the attempts to *justify* slavery in the modern world, when the question of its justice had for a long time already been raised.) We, now, have no difficulty in seeing slavery as unjust: we have economic arrangements and a conception of a society of citizens with which slavery is straightforwardly incompatible. This may stir a reflex of cultural self-congratulation, or at least satisfaction that in some dimensions there is progress.[49] But the main feature of the Greek attitude to slavery, I have suggested, was not a morally primitive belief in its justice, but the fact that considerations of justice and injustice were immobilised by the demands of what was seen as social and economic necessity. That phenomenon has not so much been eliminated from modern life as shifted to different places.

We have social practices in relation to which we are in a situation much like that of the Greeks with slavery. We recognise arbitrary and brutal ways in which people are handled by society, ways that are conditioned, often, by no more than exposure to luck. We have the intellectual resources to regard the situation of these people, and the systems that allow these things, as unjust, but are uncertain whether to do so, partly because we have seen the corruption and collapse of supposedly alternative systems, partly because we have no settled opinion on the question about which Aristotle tried to contrive a settled opinion, how far the existence of a worthwhile life for some people involves the imposition of suffering on others.

With regard to women, the relations between ancient and modern prejudice are different. For one thing, modern prejudice is to a much vaster extent the same as ancient. Quite apart from the fact that prejudice based on traditional religious conceptions flourishes in the contemporary world, the idea that gender roles are imposed by nature is alive in "modern", scientistic forms. In particular, the more crassly unreflective contributions of sociobiology to this subject represent little more than continuations of Aristotelian anthropology by other means. This is concealed by the fact that it is not Aristotelian *biology* that is being presented. Precisely because it is based on natural selection theory, sociobiology feels confident of being immunised against teleology and against the Aristotelian spirit that reads the universe on an analogy to intelligent construction. But it is not in virtue of its patterns of biological explanation that Aristotelian assumptions have their hold on this style of thinking, but in the more general assumption that there is some relatively simple fit between social gender roles, on the one hand, and, on the other, nature as it is to be biologically understood (however that may be). Changing the picture of nature does not necessarily remove the assumption that nature has something to tell us, in fairly unambiguous terms, about what social roles should be and how they should be distributed.

As we have already seen in several connections, the idea that there was a harmonious fit between social roles, the structure of the human mind, and nature was by no means a belief that all Greeks held, and in its most complete and comforting form it was almost an Aristotelian speciality, one that was to prove immeasurably influential. Other Greeks had more disrupted and disquieting images of the relations of human life to the cosmos, and not simply because they were sophists or skeptics. As we shall see further in the next chapter, a sense of the opacity or inscrutability of things was expressed by earlier writers such as Pindar, and while this could minister to social passivity, the *amēchania* of the archaic world that Dodds memorably captured in the phrase "God's in his Heaven, all's wrong with the world,"[50] it certainly did not speak to any encouraging idea of the harmony of humanity and nature.

In many comparisons between the ancient and the modern world it is assumed that in the ancient world social roles were understood to be rooted in nature. Indeed, it is often thought to be a special mark of modern societies, distinguishing them from all earlier ones, that they have lost this idea. These assumptions are made equally by those who are favourably disposed to modernity and by those who are not. For those critical of the modern world, the loss of the idea leads to alienation and a feeling that human beings have been unrooted and robbed of a harmony between themselves and their world. Those who salute the power of modern enlightenment, on the other hand, find a liberating force in the recognition that any social role can be held up to human criticism and that no such necessities are dictated to us by nature. A central feature of modern liberal conceptions of social justice can indeed be expressed by saying that they altogether deny the existence of necessary social identities.

There are several reasons why it is so readily assumed that a major difference between modern liberal societies and their predecessors can be found in their accepting or rejecting the idea of necessary social identities. Much of the intellectual machinery needed to discuss the question is of course a modern invention, including the idea, consciously expressed, of a social role; discussion is influenced, moreover, by certain general theories about the nature of authority in traditional societies. Above all, a huge shadow is cast, at least onto European and American conceptions, by Aristotelianised Christianity. But if we look to the ancient Greeks, and in particular look behind Aristotle, we can see that it is to a significant extent untrue that the presence or absence of the idea of necessary identities makes the difference between their outlooks on society and our own. It is untrue, above all, with respect to one of the fundamental and most striking social contrasts between them and ourselves, the attitude to slavery. The institution of slavery in the ancient world involved a very conspicuous and important social role. Most people were no doubt disposed to think that it was "natural" just in the sense that the best development of social life required it, but few thought that it was natural in the sense most closely associated with nature and with these interpretations, namely, with regard to the ways in which the role was allocated. Few, that is to say, seriously thought of it as a necessary identity, a role dealt out to an individual by nature speaking a social language.

Modern liberal thought rejects all necessary social identities, but it is not this element in its outlook that distinguishes its attitude to slavery from that of most ancient Greeks. With regard to slavery, as opposed to their attitudes towards women, two concepts particularly governed their thoughts: economic or cultural necessity and individual bad luck. Obviously we do not apply those concepts, as the Greeks did, in such a way that we accept slavery. But we do apply those concepts very extensively to our social experience, and they are still hard at work in the modern world. The real difference in these respects between modern liberal ideas and the outlook of most Greeks lies rather in this, that liberalism demands—more realistically speaking, it hopes—that those concepts, necessity and luck, should not *take the place of* considerations of justice. If an individual's place in society is to be determined by forces of economic and cultural necessity and by that individual's luck, and if, in particular, those elements are going to determine the extent to which he or she is to be (effectively, if not by overt coercion) in the power of others, then the hope is that all this should happen within the framework of institutions that guarantee the justice of these processes and of their outcome. Even if we cannot, and perhaps should not, cancel all effects of mere necessity and luck, at least we hope that they can be placed within a framework that raises the question of justice and can answer it in such a way that the necessities will not be radically coercive and the luck will be no worse than luck.

Modern liberalism already stands at some distance from the ancient world not only in rejecting altogether the idea of a necessary identity, but in setting this problem. It has given itself the task of constructing a framework of social justice to control necessity and chance, in the sense both of mitigating their effects on the individual and of showing that what cannot be mitigated is not unjust. It is a distinctively modern achievement to have set the problem. However, we shall not know how great our distance really is from the ancient world until we are in a position to claim, not merely that there is this task, but that we have some hope of carrying it out.

CHAPTER SIX

Possibility, Freedom, and Power

The last chapter discussed a necessity consisting of the application of power by one person to another, a necessity imposed on some human beings by others. Earlier, I discussed the inner necessity of the practical conclusion, the necessity encountered when an agent concludes that he must act in a certain way. The Greeks in the archaic period, and to some extent into the later fifth century and beyond, believed that over both these things there stood what I have already called supernatural necessity. For much of this chapter I shall be concerned with this kind of necessity, but it will lead us back to the human necessities of power.

The term "supernatural" is admittedly not very satisfactory. It may suggest, wrongly, that the ancient Greeks had our conception of nature and believed that in addition other agencies existed outside nature.[1] Even if we reject that implication and say instead that the Greeks believed in things lying outside our conception of nature (but not, perhaps, outside theirs), we are still left with a severe problem of saying what lies outside our *conception* of nature, as opposed to items that we merely do not believe to exist (such as phlogiston) or explanations that we do not believe to be true. Not everything that fails to be part of nature is supernatural.[2]

Aristotle's theory that the heavenly bodies revolved round the earth, though rejected, might be thought to belong with our conception of nature: its replacement (or rather the replacement of its sophisticated Ptolemaic descendent) by the heliocentric theory is, after all, part of the history of our science. But Aristotle's cosmological theory proceeded without changing step to the conclusion that the sphere of the fixed stars was moved by an unmoved mover who was pure self-directed thought and produced motion through being loved,[3] and this, for us, is no part of a "naturalistic" account at all. Still harder problems arise when the contrast to a "supernatural" explanation is provided by medicine or psychology. How much—how much *more*—is meant when an ancient Greek said that something was brought about by a god, or when modern people, come to that, themselves familiar with medical and psychological explanations, refer some happening to magic?[4] These are questions that belong to anthropology or the philosophy of anthropology, and I do not pretend to answer them. Equally, I do not use the term "supernatural" as a classification that is supposed to be significant in itself. I use it only as a label for a kind of necessity (it is necessity that I shall particularly discuss) that does not belong to our ways of explaining the world. I do not believe that the label itself tells us much about the ways in which this kind of necessity fails to fit our view of the world, but I hope that my description of it may show rather more.

The ideas in question here helped to structure the action of tragedy, and that fact itself shows that they were intelligible at some level to the Greeks—though we shall also have to attend to ways in which the sense of this necessity in tragedy is an artefact of a dramatic style, and not simply a deployment in the theatre of something that everyone believed anyway. We are not cut off from understanding the tragedies in these respects; the ideas in question are intelligible to us, up to a point, though the extent to which we can grasp them is limited, and we have questions that they cannot answer. The fact that we want to press these questions makes the point that this kind of necessity, unlike others that I have discussed, is not part of our world. It also raises a question touched on in chapter 1, of what the tragedies shaped by these necessities can mean to us, and I shall come back to this at the end of the chapter.

To isolate this kind of necessity, it will be helpful to look first at a famous example in which a necessity of this sort intersects in a dramatic and clear way with an inner necessity of the kind we have already explored, the agent's recognition of what he must do. It is an example from tragedy, but not one in which the agent is directly presented as under the necessity; his situation, rather, is described to us. In the great first chorus of Aeschylus's *Agamemnon,* we are told how Agamemnon came, at the beginning of the expedition to Troy, to sacrifice his daughter Iphigeneia. In this story, which was to offer a repeated subject for tragedy, the Greek expedition was held up at Aulis by adverse weather sent by Artemis, and the prophet made it known that only the sacrifice of Agamemnon's daughter would enable the fleet to sail. In some other versions of the story, Artemis had been offended by something Agamemnon himself had done; Aeschylus, as has often been noticed, suppresses this element so that he can insert this episode and Agamemnon's action as directly as possible into the chain of consequences of the earlier crimes in the house of Atreus. Agamemnon is described by the Chorus as having considered, on the one hand, the horror of what he was asked to do, and on the other side, his responsibilities to the expedition and his own position as its commander: "How could I become a deserter?" he asked (212). Neither course was without evils. He decided in favour of sacrifice: "May it be well," he desperately said. When he had decided and, as the Chorus says, "put on the harness of necessity," *anangkas edu lepadnon* (218), a violent frenzy overcame him, and he changed to a state of mind in which he could dare anything (221); in this state of mind he carried out the sacrifice, which is described in vivid detail in what follows.

This passage used to cause great concern to critics caught up in inappropriate conceptions. Albin Lesky started with the unhelpful question, "Was the choice between the possibilities made in full freedom of will?"; did not find an answer to this question, having to say, rather vaguely, that Agamemnon's free will was represented as being overshadowed by the demands of the gods; and concluded, "Here there is no rational consistency."[5] Page, whose unfavourable verdict on Aeschylus's intellectual powers we noticed earlier, produced a good deal of bluster on this issue. Referring, I think, to Kitto and Dodds, he wrote: "The modern critics say that Agamemnon made a voluntary, however painful, decision. Aeschylus says that what he submitted to was necessity. I do not see how these statements can be reconciled."[6] The most striking thing about this judgement is that it simply misrepresents the text. Aeschylus does not say that Agamemnon submitted to necessity. The word *edu*, in the passage I quoted, is a straightforward verb of action, which means (as Page himself elsewhere translates it) "put on", and Agamemnon is said to have put on the harness of necessity as someone puts on armour. This is a very different relation to the yoke of necessity from that experienced by Prometheus, who is "yoked by these necessities" when he is tied by Kratos and Bia to the rock. The force of the verb can be felt from a passage in which Homer uses it to describe Hector's being seized by fury: there, it is the fury that is the subject.[7]

A major difficulty in understanding the passage from the *Agamemnon* has been ethical: the critics could not understand how someone might have to choose between two courses of action both of which involved a grave wrong, so that whatever he does will be bad, and, whatever he does, he will suffer what, in discussing responsibility, I called an agent's regret at what he has done. The ethical question in such a case is not soluble without remainder, and Kierkegaard was wrong, not in saying merely that the tragic hero "stays within the ethical"—that much is true—but in supposing that there is an unambiguous ethical answer. "The tragic hero gives up what is certain for what is still more certain," Kierkegaard said, and this is not right, at least in the case of Aeschylus's Agamemnon. (Kierkegaard had an Agamemnon in mind, but he was Euripides'.)[8]

The matter of ethical conflict and its resolution is now better understood,[9] and I shall not pursue that aspect here. However, it is perhaps a sign of the radical issues raised by this passage that it is defended from one moralistic distortion only to attract another. Martha Nussbaum, having correctly presented the arguments about conflict,[10] goes on to introduce into her reading the suggestion that the Chorus blames Agamemnon, and Aeschylus intends us to blame him, for the murderous fury with which he carried out the killing. Agamemnon wrongly moved, she suggests, from deciding to do it, as perhaps he had to, to wanting to do it, and he should not have done that: he should have shown more regret.

I do not find that this thought is pressed on me by the text. It is true and important that the fury, the murderous state of mind, is represented as being the result of Agamemnon's decision and not its cause. Whatever it is exactly that the Chorus reports Agamemnon as saying as he reaches his decision,[11] they make it entirely clear what then happens: the father slaughters his daughter in a state of bloody rage. One way we might understand this is as a man's being driven mad by extremity. Equally (and indeed in no conflict with that) we might see the rage as something that was necessary to Agamemnon if he was to do this thing at all. This is not a text that invites us very far into psychological interpretation, but still less does it beckon us towards blame. The Chorus is laying before us what happened, and this horror, the father's fury, is part of it. A sense of the work requires a suspension of moral comment at this point, and so does a sense of the event that it describes. Comments on people's decisions, how they reach them and how they carry them out, are particularly relevant when the decision in question is part of a practice, when there is something to be *learned* from the case. That is why reluctances, regrets, a sense of the moral cost of decisions, may be appropriately urged on politicians as part of a practice or a political life.[12] But that does not apply to Agamemnon's situation. It is, probably, hard to apply the sacrificial knife to one's daughter while wringing one's hands, and if we do not think that Agamemnon just made a mistake about what he had to do on that bad day at Aulis, it is better that, rather than telling him what he should have felt, we should be prepared to learn what was involved in getting through it.[13]

When Agamemnon "put on the harness of necessity", he decided that he had to kill Iphigeneia. But there was another necessity lying behind his decision, of the kind with which we are now specially concerned: a necessity arising from supernatural forces that expressed themselves in the situation that called for his decision. About that same situation, Sophocles' Electra, speaking, as she says, on behalf of her dead father, says that Artemis produced the calm (as it is in that version, rather than contrary winds) *so that*[14] he would have to kill Iphigeneia: this puts a straightforward divine purpose in place of the more complex and obscure forces emphasised by Aeschylus, in which Artemis plays one part in a long history. It is not clear how much Agamemnon in Aeschylus is supposed to understand about these forces. But he does, certainly, understand the immediate demand of the goddess: he understands only too well that Artemis has brought it about that if he sacrifices Iphigeneia, the fleet can sail, and if not, not. So far as Artemis's part is concerned, this is not unlike the kinds of divine intervention that we considered earlier in Homer, where a god gives an agent a reason for action he did not have before. But the overall impact of the supernatural order in the *Oresteia* is quite different from that in Homer: it is the long-running necessity that counts.[15] It is because there is this further necessity that the image of the yoke or harness is so exactly right—in putting it on, Agamemnon takes something that is a necessity, and makes it his own. What must happen in virtue of a long-term design becomes, in Agamemnon's decision, something that he must do. *Ēthos anthropōi daimōn*, Heracleitus said, "a man's character is his fate," and more than one writer has observed that an important feature of tragedy can be captured by reading this saying in both directions.[16] The character's motivations are what shape the life he is fated to have: the way his life is shaped by fate is through his motivations. "Each action," Vernant has written, "appears in the line and the logic of a character, of an *ēthos*, at the same time as it reveals the manifestation of a power beyond that, of a *daimōn*." Later in the *Oresteia*, Aeschylus is able to balance these two elements exactly, and in the consciousness of Orestes himself: "She will pay for the dishonour of our father, through the *daimones* and through my hands," he says,[17] and "through" is *hekati*, a word that means "by the will of", and in Homer (it occurs only in the *Odyssey*) is used solely of the gods.

In such a case, Vernant says, "the great art of tragedy lies in making simultaneous what with Aeschylus' Eteocles is still successive."[18] The scene in the earlier play, *Seven against Thebes*, that consists of the speech of Eteocles and his exchange with the Chorus that follows has something important to show us about supernatural necessity and human action. The scene is sometimes called the Decision of Eteocles, but it does not in fact present a decision:[19] Eteocles knows from the beginning that he is going to face his brother at the last of the seven gates and kill him. He recognises, too, that all this is coming about because of the curse that Oedipus laid upon them. What he does is to resist the Chorus's attempt to dissuade him, and in the course of that he comes to a better understanding of the reasons there are for facing his brother: justice, shame, honour. He also recognises a rising passion of destructive anger and understands that this itself is a result of his father's curse.[20] The Chorus tells him that he need not, all the same, press forward, and makes various attempts to persuade him not to go to the battle, their final words being "Do you want to shed the blood of your own brother?" To this Eteocles replies with his last words in the play: "When the gods decree it, you may not escape evil" (718–19).

Eteocles' growing consciousness of the curse, of his situation and his reasons, and his refusal to take what he sees as a cowardly retreat perhaps do earn him the title that he has been given of "der erste 'tragische' Mensch der Weltdichtung."[21] But when Vernant says that in his case *ēthos* and *daimōn* are represented successively, it is a benign understatement. The truth is that there is some obscurity in the relations of Eteocles' *ēthos* to his *daimōn*. The difficulty does not lie between the inner and the outer, between Eteocles' other motivations and the external force of Oedipus's curse: there is no inherent problem in that. It is to be found rather in his recognising this necessity, and the way in which his recognising it affects his motivation.

How are we to read his last line? It seems to express a recognition of that necessity. At the same time, it might be taken to express a reason for his decision to go out and fight. But if that is what it does, there is a puzzle about what exactly his decision can be. Can someone decide to do a certain thing on the basis of recognising that for external reasons he is certainly going to do it? Could Eteocles say, "It has been fixed by the gods that I shall do it, so my decision is that I shall do it?" As a decision, surely, this is incoherent. Agamemnon indeed put on the harness of necessity—he could do it, and there was a reason for him to do it. But he could not have put it on for the following reason: that he had seen that he was already wearing it. It is something like this that Eteocles would be doing if we read his last line as at once recognising an externally imposed necessity and offering it as a reason for his decision.

Of course, we can understand in other ways someone's saying, "I see that I am going to decide to do it, so I will." We can understand these words as expressing a passive reaction rather than a decisive act, as representing not an heroic acceptance of necessity but a collapse, under which deliberation, decision, and purposeful action seem pointless, and one merely does the nearest thing to hand, or nothing. Eteocles' line might even come to make this suggestion to us, because it is easier to read it as a withdrawal from decision than as affirming a decision that is unintelligible.[22]

It is not completely impossible for someone to decide to do a certain thing while recognising that necessarily he will do it anyway: he might know that he will necessarily do it sometime, and decide to do it now. There is room for the choice of a time or a route to an outcome that is itself seen as inevitable. But Eteocles has no such room. This is uniquely the moment of the fated battle, and if he does not march out to meet Polyneices now, he does not meet Polyneices. In this case, if he expresses fatalism, he is expressing what we might call *immediate* fatalism: a fatalistic necessity is applied directly to the action that is being considered. One reason why this is inescapably puzzling is that it simply suppresses the question, "And what if I don't?" If that question were raised, the only answer to it would be, "You will anyway." But when we are dealing with immediate fatalism, the answer "You will anyway" can only mean "Whatever decision you now take, this is the decision you will now take," and that is unintelligible: "Read my lips," he might well reply.

It may seem crass to press Eteocles' line as heavily as these arguments suggest, but there is something to be learned from them, and not just in philosophy but about the line. They locate an apparent unintelligibility that can cloud our understanding of the spirit in which he goes to his death. In fact, this obscurity is not forced on us by what Eteocles says. His words need not be read as involving immediate fatalism, because they need not be taken to present the gods' necessity as itself one of Eteocles' reasons. He has given his reasons; what he last expresses is the necessity of the situation in which these must be his reasons.

The working of supernatural necessity does not in general involve immediate fatalism or anything like it. Sometimes, as in Agamemnon's case (and on the suggested reading, Eteocles' is similar), the necessity presents itself to the agent as having produced the circumstances in which he must act, and he decides in the light of those circumstances. In other cases it shapes events without presenting itself at all. It may not be known to the agent himself or known only after the event, or, most typically, it is known before the event, but in some indeterminate, ambiguous, or riddling form, and it comes to be determinately understood only afterwards. In these cases, the question that might have occurred to Eteocles, "What if I don't?" cannot occur: the working of the necessity makes sure that there is no moment for it. This state of affairs is very characteristic of omens and oracles.

With omens the first ambiguity may well be whether what you have seen is an omen at all: as Eurymachus says in the *Odyssey*, "lots of birds fly around under the rays of the sun, and they don't all mean something." With the oracle, on the other hand, that characteristic device of tragedy,[23] you are supposed to know when you have received one of its predictions. However, oracles do not only issue predictions. Sometimes they give instructions, usually accompanied by predictions of what will happen if the instructions are not obeyed. It may well be possible to disobey the instructions, but the oracle typically offers a reason for carrying them out. Indeed, the fact that they are oracular instructions may itself suggest a reason for carrying them out. These thoughts and others close to them are subtly exploited, to great dramatic effect, in Aeschylus's *Choephoroi*. At 269–70 Orestes reassures the Chorus, who are afraid that Clytemnestra and Aegistheus will be alerted by their conversation; he says that Apollo's oracle, who told him to face this danger, will not let him down. This does not mean, of course, that he will succeed *whatever he does,* but it does mean something to the general effect that he will succeed if he sincerely and sensibly tries to carry out the instruction—that he will not fail through bad luck. At 297 seq., he says that he has reasons for what he is aiming to do, quite apart from trust in the oracle— and it is quite a sensitive question, what "trust in the oracle" here means. At 900, finally, Orestes hesitates at the last instant before killing his mother and turns to Pylades—"Shall I do it?"; and he, in his one intervention, says, "Where will the trusty oracles of Loxias be for the rest of time . . . ?" thus linking obedience to the oracle's commands with saving its predictive credibility. There is complexity here, and an obscurity that comes with the very idea of an oracle, but in the *Choephoroi* Aeschylus revolves the elements of prophecy, supernatural plan, human motive, and divine command with an assurance that prevents them from falling together into immediate fatalism.[24]

Some oracles do just offer a prediction. It is usually an indeterminate prediction, or a determinate prediction that leaves it vitally unclear by what route it will come true. The mere fact that a prediction leaves it unclear how it will come true does not, of course, mean that it is supernatural. You can make many true predictions of that sort without being an oracle: that each of us will die, for instance. That means, moreover, that each of us will die *whatever we do,* but it still does not import any supernatural thought, nor much in the way of fatalism.

A supernatural thought, and with it the possibility of a fatalism that we might call (in contrast to that discussed in Eteocles' case) indeterminate or deferred, comes in only when we get to a more special kind of situation: when we are told that a certain thing will happen whatever we do, although it is just the kind of thing we might hope to avoid by action. Moreover, if efforts to avoid the outcome helped in fact to bring it about, this is a reliable sign, after the event, that the supernatural has been at work. This is what happened with Oedipus; this was the situation with the appointment in Samarra.[25] Fatalism, in this sense of long-term or deferred fatalism, does not require the belief that no action ever has any effect. So far from fatalism ruling out all effective action of any kind, its characteristic quality, on the contrary, demands that some action and decision do have an effect. It is not that people's thoughts and decisions never make a difference, but that, with regard to the vital outcome, they make no difference in the long run, although one might have expected them to do so.

To accept that there is a supernatural necessity is not merely to believe in nonstandard causal connections. Some superstitious beliefs are just that, such as my late grandmother's belief (she was born in the 1860s) that keeping a potato in a pocket of her undergarments helped to prevent rheumatism. But the idea of supernatural necessity involves something else, an idea that the structure of things is purposive: that it is, so to speak, playing against you. Things are arranged in such a way that what you do will make no difference to the eventual outcome, or will even help to bring about what you try to prevent.

Living in a world in which such forces or necessities operate does not, then, mean that you cannot do anything, or that you think that you cannot do anything. You can act; you can deliberate; and so you can think about what different things would have happened if you had acted differently. An element that we saw in chapter 3 to be essential to responsibility, the idea that agents are causes of some things that come about, stays in its place. But at certain crucial points outcomes converge in a pattern that displays the shape of the purposive, and your attempts to avoid the outcome are necessarily ineffective. The usual condition of life is that you do not know exactly what those points are. If you come to recognise one, then you may move to resignation, as Heracles does in the *Trachiniai* (1143 seq.) when he realises that a prophecy has come true. But you may not: in the space of action before the place at which the ways meet, you may still be able to choose to arrive there by one path rather than another.

Philosophy, and not just modern philosophy, will want at this point to press questions that this set of ideas is not well adapted to answering. Action has to be, at least in the short run, effective if these ideas are to have their force. But what does that imply about possibility? In order to see what might be involved in living in a world structured by such necessities, let us take the large step of wrenching the Oedipus story out of myth and tragedy and asking questions about it as though it were an item of *faits divers* (questions that, needless to say, it would be absurd to ask about the play). Faced with the prediction that their infant son would grow up to kill his father, Jocasta and Laius decided, rather than keeping the baby at home, to give him to a servant with the instructions to kill him. What they intended, that the baby die, did not come about, but something they intended, a very short-term thing, did come about—they decided that the servant should take the baby away, and he did so. Seemingly, if they had decided to keep the baby at home, the baby would have stayed at home. Can we say that if he had stayed at home, he would still have grown up to kill his father? Perhaps we can: all that the supernatural necessity required was that in some way or another Oedipus should come to kill his father, and if his parents had kept him at home, then there would have been a route to the killing that started from his being kept at home.

But there could be another picture. On this, we would rather say that if the baby Oedipus had been kept at home, then he would not have grown up to kill his father; but since it was necessary, in this supernatural sense, that he kill his father, it must have been necessary that he not be kept at home. And this implies, in turn, that Jocasta and Laius could not have kept him at home: either any decision they made to keep him there would have been ineffective or they could not have made that decision.

Such patterns of modal bewilderment have a long history, which goes back to Greek philosophy. Aristotle, or others to whom Aristotle was responding, took such problems away from divine or oracular connections and started discussions that have continued to the present day. Those discussions have often fallen into certain confusions, between fatalism, determinism, predictability, and the mere truth of statements about the future.[26] In part, those confusions are produced by the difficulty of the questions, and the obscurity involved, for us as much as for any ancient Greek, in thinking determinately about what might have been. But beyond that, the confusions may be due in part to the origin of these questions, their association with the idea of a supernatural order. That order had a crucially important feature, that the necessity it applied to human actions was purposive or at least had the shape of the purposive. This notion introduces, as we shall see, the idea of being in someone's power.

The supernatural conceptions themselves offered few determinate answers to questions about what might have been. We ourselves often do not have very clear or determinate ideas on such questions, but the peculiarities of supernatural necessity, particularly as expressed by oracles, meant that there were no answers in places where, without the supernatural, there would have been answers. This is finely illustrated by a play to which we have turned several times before, the *Ajax*. The prophet Calchas, the Messenger tells the Chorus, spoke to Teucer

> and urged and pled with him
> to use all shifts to keep his brother safe
> under his tent-roof, and confine him there
> throughout the length of this now present day,
> if ever he wished to see him alive again.
> Only for this one day, the prophet said,
> will the goddess Athena vex him with her anger.[27]

The Messenger bases a hope on that:

> But if he is still alive today, perhaps
> with God's help, we may be his saviors still.

But Ajax has already gone out, and the Chorus fears the worst: "The razor grazes against the skin" (786). Of course, their fears are correct; Tekmessa desperately sends out a search party, but the next thing we see is Ajax killing himself.

Now what Calchas said was true—the anger of Athene indeed pursued Ajax for only this one day: at the end of it he was dead. But what about the Messenger's hope, which after the event might turn into the regretful thought that if they had saved Ajax for that day, they might have saved him altogether? Is that thought true? It was certainly encouraged by Calchas's advice. But how could Ajax have been saved altogether? He could go on living only if he changed his mind, and we have already been given good reason to believe that he could not change his mind, unless he went mad again, since to go on living would have required him to be a different person. Faced with this, the possibility that they might have saved him simply fades away: there is nowhere in the world to accommodate it. On the other hand, it is indeterminate how, exactly, it fades away: how does the necessity of Ajax's decision combine with the prophet's words to make the rescue attempt necessarily useless? There is simply no answer to that question. It is important that here, as in our speculations about the baby Oedipus, we are not dealing simply with the well-known indeterminacies of fiction. The emptiness we encounter is not merely that involved in wondering, for instance, how things would have gone if Shakespeare's Hamlet had killed Claudius when he came upon him praying. There is a special indeterminacy about the operations of the supernatural and the ways in which it can generate necessities and suppress possibilities.

However, the indeterminacies of fiction do play a part in helping us to grasp the idea of these necessities, to the extent that we can grasp it. To some degree, what we encounter here is a difference between our outlook and the Greeks', a difference of belief, but we should not assume too easily that we understand what this difference is or, in particular, that we can grasp the idea of supernatural necessity quite independently of the plays that so powerfully express it. We may think that there was a belief belonging to fifth-century culture, a belief which Sophocles accepted or at any rate exploited, and which he expressed through dramatic incident. At one level this must be true: elements in popular belief enabled Sophocles' audience to recognise what he presented. But once we try to form a more definite picture of what such beliefs involved, we are likely to find that supernatural and dramatic necessity cannot be so simply separated. If we feel that we have some definite sense of what such a necessity might involve, we owe that impression, in good part, to the operations of tragedy. The special feature of supernatural necessity is that there is nothing relevant to be said about ways in which things might have gone differently—either about other routes by which the inevitable outcome might still have come about or about routes which *if* they had been taken (though inevitably they were not), the outcome would have been prevented. This is not at all how it is with human affairs when an outcome is, for familiar and natural reasons, inevitable; we can explain its inevitability, and to explain it involves understanding how, in just these ways, things might have gone otherwise. How can we so much as have the idea of a world, the world of supernatural necessities, in which all this can, on certain occasions, be suspended?

We are helped to have it—or, perhaps we should say, to think that we have it—by a special use of the indeterminacy of fiction. The play represents to us an outcome, together with such things as failed attempts to prevent it, with such power and in such a chain of significance as to kill speculation about alternatives. By compelling our attention and directing our fears to what it presents as actual, tragedy may leave us with no thought, and no need of a thought, about anything else. The general condition with fiction is that, beyond a certain point, there are no interesting or realistic questions about alternatives *to* the action; a special art of Sophoclean tragedy (and the same no doubt applies elsewhere) is to convert this into the sense that there are, at certain points, no alternatives *within* the action. Our earlier speculations about the baby Oedipus, by taking alternatives seriously, started on a path that could lead to the metaphysical collapse of supernatural necessity; it is no accident that at the same time they farcically departed from the tragedy.

Our sense of supernatural necessity in a play such as the *Oedipus* is a product of authorial power, and nothing but authorial power could give us an idea of it that was so strong or so apparently clear. This is not at all to say that this sense of necessity is itself a sense *of* authorial power. A consciousness of Sophocles' powers at this point will leave us only with a feeling of contrivance, while any sense of a higher power, one that might stand to us and the world as Sophocles stands to the play, introduces an altogether different religious conception. Some theologians have indeed thought of the divine in such terms, but their God, the author of our being as the dramatist is of the action, is the author of everything, of the world in which we sometimes prevent things as much as of the things that, for whatever reason, we cannot prevent. Supernatural necessity in the sense of ancient tragedy is, unlike this, a special element in the world, a presence that has to be inserted into it. Sophoclean tragedy has a power to make this insertion compelling, by concealing the fact that there is no particular way in which it comes about.

In the case of the *Oedipus Tyrannus*, the sense of prearranged necessity that holds it so tightly is an artefact of its construction, above all of the dramatic irony that famously surrounds the utterances of Oedipus from the beginning. "I heard about it, I never set eyes on him," he says (105) when Creon first mentions the killing of Laius. Irony can work with such immediate assurance because the audience already knew the story: their knowledge, and hence their advantage over the character, plays an essential part in allowing the text to present an order of things that has the advantage of him.

There are other ways as well in which the relation of the characters to their world is expressed through the engagement of the audience with the text. Although the audience of Greek tragedy knew the story, they did not always all know the same story. "There are various versions of the death of Ajax," says the ancient hypothesis to the play; "some say he committed suicide, among them Sophocles." It may be that in this case the audience did not know what was going to happen. If that is so, then this play will be an inversion of the *Oedipus*. The *Oedipus* and its ironies provide the most straightforward example of what has been called Sophocles' "characteristic technique of making a character speak words that mean more to the audience than to himself."[28] Ajax does that, too, but in the opposite sense: his words, particularly in what used to be called the "deception speech",[29] convey several meanings to the audience, in the sense that they suggest more than one possibility, but for Ajax there is only one possibility. In the same way, the prophecy, the hope, the useless attempts at rescue, arouse ideas of alternatives that in the end are empty: they seem to point to possibilities for which, as I have said, there is really no location. This is not Sophocles merely generating theatrical effects, in the manner in-

sisted upon by Tycho von Wilamowitz;[30] or if they are theatrical
effects, they are not (as Wagner said of Meyerbeer's so-called
"theatre of effect") effects without causes. The *Ajax* does for
possibility what the *Oedipus* does for necessity. The members
of an audience uncertain of the outcome are first disadvantaged
in relation to the character. When they realise in retrospect that
where they had thought that there were several possibilities,
there was all the time only one, this brings home to them the
necessity of his death, by placing them with the characters who
could not grasp it before the event.

It is the relation of the hero to a text that says more than he
does, a hero who nevertheless acts in the fullest consciousness
that he can attain, that more than anything contributes to the
Sophoclean effect; and Euripides' refusal of that effect is marked
above all by his abandoning these expressions of a shaping necessity, and subjecting his audience as much as his characters
to the uncertainties of an unnerving chance. It used to be conventional to contrast Sophocles with Euripides (who was his
younger contemporary) as old-fashioned believer to radical
skeptic. The picture is encouraged by Aristophanes, but Aristophanes was a reactionary or, perhaps, found it a congenial posture for an energetic satirical dramatist to assume.[31] Whether
there was, as a matter of biographical fact, this contrast between
the two poets seems to me open to doubt,[32] but there are certainly some large contrasts between their works. It is the effect
in many cases of Euripides' works to defeat the expectations of
an audience accustomed to Aeschylus or Sophocles—in some
cases, one might say, to defeat any expectation at all.[33] In some
of his plays this seems to have reached extremes worthy of Buñuel: in the *Phaethon,* known to us only in fragments, smoke
from the bridegroom's smouldering corpse disturbs what would
have been his wedding.[34] Euripides was famously called by Aristotle "the most tragic of the poets", but if this is appropriate,

it is in the sense that his plays had a powerful theatrical effect, rather than that he presented tragic agency in its purest form.[35]

Anne Pippin Burnett has suggested that the device of tragic irony is a bad teacher of humility to an audience whom it essentially privileges and that this was one reason why Euripides laid it aside in favour of the operations of mere chance.[36] But I am not sure that because an audience is knowledgeable, it must in that sense be knowing. The *Oedipus* is scarcely a work that ministers to the complacency of its audience, and indeed, it is precisely the more Shavian elements in Euripides that have to guard against a certain knowingness. I also agree with Ann Michelini in doubting whether Euripides was as straightforward an instructor of his audience as Burnett supposes.

It is obvious, at any rate, that the sense of a supernatural necessity is loosened in Euripides. This is very clear in a play that might seem an example in the other direction, the *Hippolytus*. That play starts with a prologue from Aphrodite explaining how she has arranged the whole action: "I have prepared most of the way," she says (22–23); "not much remains to be done." But this divine determination stands outside the action as the prologue stands outside the play. It has been remarked that if the prologue is removed, the play still makes sense, in particular as a representation of the futility of human action; and the appearance of another goddess, Artemis, at the end, with the striking repetitions that Knox has noted of Aphrodite's words and attitudes,[37] does not do much more to bring into the action a sense of guiding necessity. You might say of Aphrodite's declared arrangement of the events of the *Hippolytus* rather what Socrates in Plato's *Phaedo* says about Anaxagoras's claim that Mind guides everything: he claims this, but all it comes to is that whatever happens, happens, and Mind makes it so.[38]

Euripides was not alone in thinking that *tuchē* might not be *anangkaia* at all. In the first speech that Pericles makes in Thucydides' history, just before the beginning of the Peloponnesian war, he says, "It is possible for the circumstances of our affairs to take as blundering a course as men's plans." As Lowell Edmunds, following Syme, has well argued, Pericles (with some irony) means that events run, not "unintelligibly", but "stupidly", as people's plans may do.[39] Adversity is described in terms of human planning, and the implication is that superior *gnōmē* may be able to master it. This view, that we may hope to control the political and practical world by empirical, rational, planning—a view associated with Protagoras—stands revealingly between the archaic outlook, on the one hand, and a Euripidean arbitrariness of chance on the other. We should not suppose that the view he by implication ascribed to Pericles was Thucydides' own. Thucydides certainly believed that the world's course was not governed by supernatural purposes and also that *gnomē* could do something to control it, but he had a powerful sense of the limitations of foresight, and of the uncontrollable impact of chance.

For Solon and other archaic writers, human beings were largely powerless against fate and chance,[40] but this was not simply because there were conditions of life that were unmanageably complex or, as it happened, inaccessible. Fate and chance were forces, and they were deeply, necessarily, significantly, mysterious. Like the Aeschylean and Sophoclean necessities we have been considering, they belong to an order of things that has the shape and the discouraging effect of a hostile plan, a plan that remains incurably hidden from us. When Pindar offers some fairly conventional thoughts about the unexpected reversals of fortune, he does not merely say that "many things have happened to men against what they expected": he says in addition that "no mortal has had a sure token from the gods of how things will turn out; understandings of what is to come are blinded."[41] There is something there, but it is not given to us. For the Euripidean ironist of uncertainty, on the other hand, there is no game, not even a hidden one, and it is simply a banal truth that human affairs are likely to prove unpredictably ruinous. For the Thucydidean Pericles, however, it was possible at one moment to suggest that there is a game against circumstances, but it is one that we might be able to win, because it is stupidly played by the other side.

The relation of human beings to supernatural necessity inevitably invokes the image of being in someone's power. The mere idea that things are shaped, one way or another, in relation to human purposes—in particular, against them—is enough to ground that image. This may help to explain the suppression of possibilities, the way in which, as we saw in the cases of Oedipus and Ajax, counterfactual thought runs into the ground even more readily than it does ordinarily. Supernatural necessity of this sort is like the operation of an effective agent, but this agent, unlike the Homeric gods with their individual schemes, has no characteristics except purpose and power. Since there is nothing more to the supernatural agent than this, he has, so to speak, no style. There are no distinctive ways in which his purposes come about, and so, once such a purpose has been set, there is nothing to be said about alternative circumstances in which it would not be realised or would be realised by a different route. In some cases, the purpose may itself be set by a human action, and that is so with the operations of *miasma:* if Atreus had not committed his crime, no doubt none of the following disasters need have come about. With an unconnected oracular prediction, the idea of the supernatural purpose is even less determinate than this; there is nothing to be said even about how the purpose came to be set.

Living under supernatural necessity was living under a power, a power that typically used no distinctive means. When the world of supernatural necessities went away, this left human beings, to that extent, free; and when we become finally clear that a causal order, the possibility of explaining human desires and actions, is not itself a continuation of the old supernatural necessities, just because it has no purposive or preemptive character, then it will be finally clear that human beings are free. But this news is less exciting that it may sound. What human beings have, and what it will finally be clear they have, is metaphysical freedom—in the sense, that is to say, of freedom from the kinds of constraints that have been discussed, sometimes threatened, by metaphysics. Indeed, human beings are not "free" in the further sense demanded by some metaphysics, of being free from the laws of nature: this freedom they do not need, and, quite literally, there is nothing they could do with it if they had it.[42] Human beings are metaphysically free in the negative sense that there is nothing in the structure of the universe that denies their power to intend, to decide, to act, indeed to take and receive responsibility in the fundamental and intelligible sense that we found, in an earlier chapter, already in Homer. But metaphysical freedom is nothing—at any rate, very little. This is typical of the release from metaphysical terrors: they leave little behind them when they disappear, because we can see, after they have gone, that what they threatened is not only unreal but unintelligible. (A pessimist might say that in offering less when it is present than it promised when it was in doubt, metaphysical freedom resembles not only other things metaphysical, but other kinds of freedom.)

Being metaphysically free, we then have to ask how far we are free. The real obstacles to our freedom, as John Stuart Mill said, are not metaphysical but psychological, social, and political. The obstacles to it are most obvious in the kind of *anangkē* discussed in the previous chapter, constraint exercised by the power of others. We should now go back to that kind of necessity, and, first, press rather harder the question of what it is.

At the limit, it consists of physically moving people, tying them, locking them up: but that is not making people *do* things—it is only putting them into situations in which they can or cannot do certain things. When someone is constrained actually to do something, the typical situation is, rather, that there is an imposed choice: they are given the alternative of doing what is required, or, on the other hand, pain or death or some other outcome less drastic but also undesirable. Being given these alternatives is also, reasonably enough, called "being given no alternative", but there is, literally, another choice, and there are circumstances, some of them heroic, in which it genuinely presents itself as one. This, too, the Greeks called *anangkē*. Their use of the word embodied a truth that was made explicit by Aristotle in his admirable treatment of this subject:[43] that so far as the restriction of the agent's alternatives is concerned, the threatening intentions of another agent are only a special case of something more general. An unpleasant choice may equally be imposed by nature, as in Aristotle's case of the sailors who throw the cargo overboard to save themselves and the ship in a storm. Or it may be imposed on one by the behaviour of others that is not particularly designed as a threat to oneself, but, for all that, promises no good; I take it that this was the situation of the Thessalians faced with the Persian invasion, who, Herodotus says, at first were friendly to the Persians *ex anangkaiēs*, because of their political situation (later, when they were abandoned by their allies, they went over to the Persians "with enthusiasm and no longer in two minds at all").[44]

We have many expressions with this force: one can be "required" or "forced" or indeed "constrained" to do things either by people or by circumstances. But as the word "freedom" is used, not all these constraints are equally said to reduce our freedom. Freedom stands particularly opposed to those constraints that are intentionally imposed by other agents: it is quite reasonable to say that the sailors acted freely in throwing the goods overboard, even though they were forced to do it by the weather, but it would be a great paradox to say that someone acted freely if forced to surrender his goods in a holdup.

Indeed, even the case in which my choices are limited by others' intentional actions is less obviously a limitation of my freedom if the intentions are not directed against me. The reason for this is that being free stands opposed, above all, to being in someone's power; and the mark of that, as we have learned from the supernatural necessities, is that my choices or opportunities are not merely limited, as they are in all these cases, but that they are designedly and systematically limited, by another person who is shaping my actions to his intentions. To lack freedom is paradigmatically not simply to be short of choices, but to be subject to the will of another.

But if that is the centre of the notion, we next have to ask, Why should that be confined to cases where I experience a limitation on my choices? Cannot I be under the will of another without any open reduction of my options at all? The answer to that is "yes", and the Greeks, once again, discovered it, but as a political truth, at least, not until the fifth century. Protarchus in Plato's *Philebus* says, "I often used to hear from Gorgias that the art of persuasion is very different from other arts, since everything is enslaved by it willingly and not by force."[45] The claims of the rhetoricians and sophists that they could bring this about, and the promises they made on this basis to their ambitious pupils, obsessed Plato, and a good deal of his philosophy was shaped by the concern to discredit their arts of persuasion.

Plato was not in the first instance concerned with political freedom. Some would say that he was never concerned with it, and there is some truth in that, except to the extent that he thought that the worst form of government was tyranny, which enslaved everybody. But Plato was more particularly impressed by the idea that among those enslaved was the tyrant himself; the freedom with which Plato was fundamentally concerned was the inner freedom of the soul. In the tripartite soul that he introduced,[46] the requirement was that its highest, reasoning, part should not be tyrannized by its other parts, in particular by its desires. Those desires presented themselves as exigent, as making demands and imposing constraints. He typically speaks of *erōtikai anangkai,* sexual necessities. As a way of referring to needs this was entirely natural; Aristotle discusses such needs in terms of necessity, and a writer of the second century A.D. tells us that the penis was then known as "the Necessity" and represented other kinds of necessity.[47] But Plato feared that these forces were always ready to reach beyond the extent of mere needs and become relentlessly dominant. It was the mark of a healthy and virtuous soul that reason should sustain its domination over them.

A set of oppositions structures much of Plato's philosophy, and they are supposed to parallel one another: soul to body, reason to desire, knowledge to belief, philosophy to politics, and (at least some of the time) argument to persuasion. In each, of course, the first is superior to the second. But there is a deep and persistent ambivalence in Plato on what makes for this superiority (an ambivalence, that is to say, even in the works in which he insists on these contrasts: it is a further point that he does not always do so). Sometimes the contrast is one of reality and appearance, and the inferior item is represented as shadowy, insubstantial, or illusory. Sometimes the contrast is of words and deeds, argument and force, and then the inferior item seems powerful, a dangerous beast like the *dēmos* that, Socrates says in the *Gorgias,* Pericles and the other democrats tried to placate with lumps of meat. The two contrasts appear side by side in the image of the cave in the *Republic,* where the empirical world—the world, in particular, of everyday politics—is an illusion, a shadow show on the wall, but the viewers, until they are liberated by philosophy, are constrained by real force to watch it, because a chain stops them turning their heads.[48]

This ambivalence—which structures, too, his view of art—affects the way in which Plato frames his attacks on the sophistical and rhetorical techniques of persuasion. On the one hand, those arts are based on nothing at all, and they deal in appearances, cosmetics, decoration. On the other, they corrupt, destroy, subvert the soul. Of course any given conflict in such images can be reconciled, and the major text in this vein, the *Gorgias*, gives a lot of attention to unhealthy pastries and, as it were, disfiguring cosmetics, where apparent attractions conceal real dangers. But the central ambivalence remains and pervasively affects Plato's account of politics and the relations of philosophy to it. For within the soul, how is the domination of reason over the desires sustained? It has no force to coerce them; it cannot use persuasion to manipulate them; it certainly cannot stoop to negotiate with them. These may seem literal-minded and pedantic questions to ask about a psychological model, but the tripartite structure of the soul is designed to provide an analogy to the state, and when we move these questions from the soul to the state, silence is replaced by very obvious answers: the dominion of reason over the labouring population is secured certainly by fraud, and at the limit by force. It is a darker version of the reality that is more blandly evaded by Aristotle, when he compares, as we have seen, the relations of master and slave to those of soul and body, and the relations of men to women to those of reason to the emotions.[49]

"How can a grown man leave the city's business and spend his time whispering with two or three youths in a corner, never saying anything that matters?" Plato makes Callicles ask in the *Gorgias* (485D). You do not need to read very deeply to see that it was a question for Plato himself. It was a question about the relation of philosophy to politics, but Plato faced a related question about the activity of philosophy itself, and its involvement with persuasion. Within the soul, reason surveys the world of reality, if it rises that far, and it talks to itself. But philosophy as an activity is supposed to be shared, and one of Plato's repeated demands on that activity, particularly in his more authentically Socratic persona, is that it should consist of dialogue and not monologue, that it is essentially *exchange*. But how could reason exchange anything without persuasion? How could ideas that were being exchanged and tested in a dialogue not take some rhetorical form? There is no way, and nothing insists on that truth more compellingly than the character of Plato's dialogues themselves.[50]

Plato did not always contrast reason and persuasion. Although he writes sometimes as though persuasion and appeals to reason worked by different channels and had different destinations, elsewhere he accepts both verbally and at a deeper level that rational discourse itself is a kind of persuasion.[51] Under this emphasis, the question of how we can be freed from domination by the power of sophistry and irrational politics no longer takes the form of asking how reason can be disembarrassed of persuasion; it is no longer a matter of protecting the channels of rational communication from alien, emotional, interference. The problem becomes, rather, that of distinguishing between acceptable and unacceptable forms of persuasion—in particular, distinguishing between such things as teaching and reasonable political argument on the one hand, and tyrannical control on the other.

When Plato addressed the problem in this form, he was drawn to supposing that everything turned on the issue of whose interests were being served by the persuasion, those of the persuader or those of the persuaded. He felt secure in this answer because he took one's real interests to be those of one's rational self. In the modern world, however, even someone who agreed in some sense with Plato's conception of one's real interests could scarcely accept the enlightened autocracy that, for Plato, was the only political arrangement with any prospect of expressing those interests. Even if some body of rulers could be taken (implausibly) to be unfailingly identified with our real interests, that fact would not in itself legitimate every form of persuasion they might use: it would merely mean that their illegitimate forms of persuasion would be examples of paternalism rather than of exploitation. In any case, someone in the modern world who is seriously concerned with the values of rationality will scarcely accept Plato's account of our real interests: they will think, rather, that our interests include a need not to be treated paternalistically. A modern understanding of political persuasion, and of the limits within which it is acceptable, is more likely to start from the idea that what is wrong with undesirable forms of communication is that they conceal from the listeners what is happening to them and so rob them of control over it.[52] In a modern, and liberal, state, the theory of rational persuasion will be part of the theory of freedom.

Such an approach takes something from the ancient world, but it owes more to modernity, in particular to certain ideals of the Enlightenment. In some of its forms, however, notably in its most Kantian forms, this approach is distorted by the pressure of a delusive ideal, that at the limit rationality and freedom will totally coincide. This ideal involves an idea of ultimate freedom, according to which I am not entirely free so long as there is any ethically significant aspect of myself that belongs to me simply as a result of the process by which I was contingently formed. If my values are mine simply in virtue of social and psychological processes to which I have been exposed, then (the argument goes) it is as though I had been brainwashed: I cannot be a fully free, rational, and responsible agent. Of course, no one can control their upbringing as they receive it, except perhaps marginally and in its later stages. What the ideal demands, rather, is that my whole outlook should in principle be exposed to a critique, as a result of which every value that I hold can become a consideration for me, critically accepted, and should not remain merely something that happens to be part of me.

I have described this ideal in distinctively modern, Kantian, terms. In this form it represents a modern ambition, and it has come into the discussion precisely in contrasting modern conceptions of acceptable or rational speech with those of Plato. Yet at a deep level it shares something with Plato. It presupposes a Platonic idea of the moral self as characterless, an idea which we encountered earlier in discussing shame, guilt, and autonomy.[53] That idea is implicit in the aspiration to a total critique. If the aspiration makes sense, then the criticising self can be separated from everything that a person contingently is—in itself, the criticising self is simply the perspective of reason or morality. The idea of the characterless self is implicit, too, in the original motive for the critique. If I have acquired my values and outlook through mere contingency, from the way I have grown up and, more generally, from what has happened to me, then—the argument went—it is as though I had been brainwashed. But who is the already existing self that is brainwashed by such a process? It can only be, once more, the characterless self. In truth, however, it is not that such a self is misled or blinded by the mere process of being socialised; one's actual self, rather, is constructed by that process.

For some critics, such as Alasdair MacIntyre,[54] the belief in the featureless moral self is a characteristic expression of the Enlightenment and constitutes a major reason why we should abandon its legacy: in the direction, for MacIntyre, of a renovated Aristotelianism. But the Enlightenment, as representing a set of social and political ideals in favour of truthfulness and the criticism of arbitrary and merely traditional power, has no essential need of such images, and if, more generally, we can make better sense of our ethical ideas, we can hope to rethink those ideals in ways that will make it clear that this is so. It has been the argument of this book that we shall make better sense of the ethical ideas that we need if we look back to some ideas of the Greeks. That process need not condemn the ideals of the Enlightenment, inasmuch as they are identified with the pursuit of social and political honesty, rather than with a rationalistic metaphysics of morality.

In these respects, at least, our search will not lead us back to Plato: the idea of the featureless moral self is one that Kantian conceptions share with Plato even if the idea appears in a very modified form in Kant and those who think like him, and is applied to a politics very different from Plato's. However, we should also be wary of the extent to which we allow ourselves to be led back to the ideas of Aristotle. I have already suggested, in chapter 2, that Aristotle also held, if in a less radical form than Plato, an "ethicised" conception of the self: the view that the functions of the mind, especially with regard to action, are defined at the most basic level in terms of categories that get their significance from ethics. In Plato's case, the featureless moral self forms part of such a psychology: it is precisely because the rational powers of the mind are supposed to be distinctively linked to desirable conduct that no other, contingent, features of the agent, such as a character, need come into the account of what the agent must be like in order to lead an ethical life. With Aristotle it is, certainly, not like this: the good person needs a character, one that is formed by contingent circumstances. However, when Aristotle describes the formation of character and tells us how the desires are controlled by reason we are led back to a psychology that is still structured, if more subtly, in ethical terms.

Aristotle indeed says, "Virtue is not natural, but it is not against nature, either,"[55] and at one level, no one could reasonably disagree; but his own view was stronger than this remark at first sight implies. In saying that virtue was "not natural," he was denying only that it expressed itself spontaneously, without training and character formation. This denial leaves room for the belief that in another sense virtue is natural, inasmuch as it represents the correct development of a certain kind of animal, the human being. This was Aristotle's belief, and it comes out clearly in his descriptions of the alternatives to a virtuous character, forms of weakness and wickedness that all represent a malfunction of reason and the domination, in particular, of pleasure. We noticed in the last chapter how Aristotle supposed that the relation of men to women could be modelled on that of reason to the emotions, and how, also, he thought that from a biological point of view a woman was a spoiled or imperfect man. The association of those two ideas expresses a linkage in the structure of Aristotle's ethical thought: more generally, a person whose life fails to be the life of reason is a spoiled, imperfect, or incomplete human being. For Aristotle, ethics is based on psychology, even biology—which means in fact that his psychology is partly ethics.

"What is it that I love in Thucydides?" Nietzsche wrote;[56] "Why do I honour him more highly than Plato?" His answer was in terms of an impartial and comprehensive understanding that he ascribed to Thucydides, a willingness to find good sense in all types of people: "he displays greater practical judgement than Plato; he does not revile or belittle those he does not like or who have harmed him in his life." There is a certain amount that is fanciful or, again, dated in Nietzsche's judgement, but it contains a helpful insight. Thucydides may not be as impartial in a local sense as used to be thought, about Athenian politics, the democracy, or the empire, but he is so in the sense that the psychology he deploys in his explanations is not at the service of his ethical beliefs. At the same time, as Nietzsche's reference to practical judgement significantly brings out, Thucydidean "impartiality" should not be seen as an attempt to produce an entirely "value-free" account of human affairs, one that tries to reduce them to phenomena on the same level as physical transactions. His aim is to *make sense* of social events, and that involves relating them intelligibly to human motivations, and to the ways in which situations appear to agents (the complex role of the speeches is crucial to this process). But Thucydides' conception of an intelligible and typically human motivation is broader and less committed to a distinctive ethical outlook than

Plato's; or rather—the distinction is important—it is broader than the conception acknowledged in Plato's psychological theories. The same is true, if less obviously, in relation to Aristotle.

Aristotle, certainly, was free from the idea of the characterless moral self, and although (I have suggested) there is a strong ethical slant to his account of rational action, in other ways his moral psychology is helpfully realistic. But more generally, I argued in the last chapter, some of Aristotle's favoured models of the world and of society are among the things that modernity has most conspicuously, and justifiably, learned to distrust. If we identify the Enlightenment with ideas of total critique and rationalistic images of society, it is not surprising that we should be tempted to fall back on Aristotle, as on Hegel, to find a philosophy that does not abstract human beings, as pure moral consciousness, from society, but rather sees them as contingently formed by society, as people who owe their ethical identity to the world in which they have grown up. But in that direction there is a different illusion, hidden in the seductively phrased Hegelian claim that human beings are "constituted" by society: the idea that the relations of human beings to society and to each other, if properly understood and properly enacted, can realise a harmonious identity that involves no real loss.

The pursuit of that illusion has formed part of the history of modern political thought. But it is not only from distinctively modern developments that we can learn that there are options involving neither the featureless moral self nor a "constitution" of the self by society in terms that promise the ultimate reconciliation of the two. We can learn it also from reflection on Greek writers before Plato and Aristotle. In the remarks about Thucydides I have already mentioned, praising that special "impartiality", Nietzsche added the name of Sophocles. Just as his judgement on Thucydides should not be taken as a salute to a pure scientist of society, so the reference to Sophocles is not a reversion to the old image of that poet's work as the ultimate expression of disengaged, marmoreal classicism (one of the more surprising literary interpretations, surely, ever to have been widely shared). Free, at any rate, from the discredited conceptions of Thucydides the positivist and Sophocles the Olympian, we need to ask why these two writers might be brought together. Many traditional oppositions work to separate them in our understanding of the later fifth century: the "archaic world-view" (in the phrase of Dodds that I quoted in chapter 1)[57] as against a rationalism influenced by sophists; a sense of human helplessness as against *gnōmē* and intelligent politics; supernatural connections as against psychological and social explicability. These oppositions are not baseless, but we must ask how far they take us if we can no longer rely on the assumptions of progressivism.

If we think of the history of Western ethical experience in Kantian or Hegelian terms, we shall structure it around such contrasts as that between the religious and the secular, or the prerational and the rational; we shall look for the emergence of autonomous human reason, as opposed to conceptions of personal forces lying beyond humanity. These contrasts of course dig a ditch that leaves Sophocles and Thucydides on opposite sides. If we reject the progressivist picture, however, we shall be more open to the thought that the important question—or, at any rate, another important question—is whether or not a given writer or philosophy believes that, beyond some things that human beings have themselves shaped, there is anything at all that is intrinsically shaped to human interests, in particular to human beings' ethical interests. In the light of that question and the distinctions it invites, Plato, Aristotle, Kant, Hegel are all on the same side, all believing in one way or another that the universe or history or the structure of human reason can, when properly understood, yield a pattern that makes sense of human life and human aspirations.[58] Sophocles and Thucydides, by contrast, are alike in leaving us with no such sense. Each of them represents human beings as dealing sensibly, foolishly, sometimes catastrophically, sometimes nobly, with a world that is only partially intelligible to human agency and in itself is not necessarily well adjusted to ethical aspirations. In this perspective the difference between a Sophoclean obscurity of fate and Thucydides' sense of rationality at risk to chance is not so significant.[59] It is less significant than the difference between both of them, on the one hand, together with Homer and others who have been our concern in this study, and, on the other hand, all those who have thought that somehow or other, in this life or the next, morally if not materially, as individuals or as an historical collective, we shall be safe; or, if not safe, at least reassured that at some level of the world's constitution there is something to be discovered that makes ultimate sense of our concerns.

Here we come back to a question that we met at the end of chapter 1. How do we respond to Greek tragedy? What are those "structural substitutions", as I called them, that are needed if it is to relate to our experience? Napoleon remarked to Goethe that what fate was in the ancient world, politics was in the modern, and in the same spirit Benjamin Constant said that the significance of the supernatural in ancient tragedy could be transferred to the modern theatre only in political terms. "If you base a tragedy today on the *fatalité* of the ancients," he wrote, "you will certainly fail. . . . The public will be more moved by the struggle of an individual against the social structure that strips or garrots him, than by Oedipus pursued by destiny, or Orestes by the Furies."[60] Constant was concerned with the question of how to write a modern tragedy, but his remarks have implications for what it is to make ancient tragedy part of modern experience. Greek tragedy precisely refuses to present human beings who are ideally in harmony with their world, and has no room for a world that, if it were understood well enough, could instruct us how to be in harmony with it. There is a gap between what the tragic character is, concretely and contingently, and the ways in which the world acts upon him. In some cases, that gap is comprehensible, in terms of conflicting human purposes. In other cases, it is not fully comprehensible and not under control. That may be as true of social reality as of a world that contains supernatural necessities. The interaction of character or individual project with forces, structures, or circumstances that can destroy them can retain its significance without the presence of gods or oracles.[61]

This is not to suggest that impersonal political reality can take on the strongly purposive aspect, encouraging to fatalism, that the world sometimes displays under the conventions of Sophoclean tragedy. There is indeed a view to the effect that reforming measures, in almost tragic style, inexorably produce an effect opposite to that intended; as Albert Hirschman has pointed out,[62] it is popular with reactionary pessimists. But that is not the point. The significant analogy is with what I called earlier the supernatural power's lack of style, the fact that social reality can act to crush a worthwhile, significant, character or project without displaying either the lively individual purposes of a pagan god or the world-historical significance of a Judaic, a Christian, or a Marxist teleology.

I have said, more than once, that we do well to remember that tragedy is a form of art: there is no suggestion here of anyone behaving as a tragic hero. (That reminder can only be reinforced by bearing in mind the extent to which Sophoclean necessities of fate are themselves the product of art.) I am not suggesting, either, an answer to Constant's question whether a form of art that might be called "tragedy" can be successfully created in the modern world; perhaps, for several kinds of reason, it cannot. The point is only that if we ask what sense the tragedies of antiquity may make to us when we consider our ethical lives and our roles, not as tragic people but simply as people, even their supernatural aspects may find some analogy in our experience. But to pursue that analogy, to spell out in detail the structural substitutions that are needed, remains a further task.

We are in an ethical condition that lies not only beyond Christianity, but beyond its Kantian and its Hegelian legacies. We have an ambivalent sense of what human beings have achieved, and have hopes for how they might live (in particular, in the form of a still powerful ideal that they should live without lies). We know that the world was not made for us, or we for the world, that our history tells no purposive story, and that there is no position outside the world or outside history from which we might hope to authenticate our activities. We have to acknowledge the hideous costs of many human achievements that we value, including this reflective sense itself, and recognise that there is no redemptive Hegelian history or universal Leibnizian cost-benefit analysis to show that it will come out well enough in the end. In important ways, we are, in our ethical situation, more like human beings in antiquity than any Western people have been in the meantime. More particularly, we are like those who, from the fifth century and earlier, have left us traces of a consciousness that had not yet been touched by Plato's and Aristotle's attempts to make our ethical relations to the world fully intelligible.

Perhaps I should say again, as I said at the beginning of this study, that I am not denying that the modern world is through and through different from the ancient world. I am not suggesting either, that we should feel sorry for ourselves because we are not Homeric or tragic or Periclean people. One of the most persistent fantasies, at least of the Western world, is that there was a time when things were both more beautiful and less fragmented; the oldest expression of that fantasy indeed is to be found already in the earliest Greek literature, and it embodies both those grounds of nostalgia.[63] But it is always a fantasy, and no serious study of the ancient world should encourage us to go back to that world to search for a lost unity, in our social relations to one another or, come to that, in our relations to Being. And if we find things of a special beauty and power in what has survived from that world, it is encouraging to think that we might move beyond marvelling at them, to putting them, or bits of them, to modern uses.

An image of Pindar's is right: [64]

Take to heart what may be learned from Oedipus:
If someone with a sharp axe
hacks off the boughs of a great oak tree,
and spoils its handsome shape;
although its fruit has failed, yet it can give an account of itself
if it comes later to a winter fire,
or if it rests on the pillars of some palace
and does a sad task among foreign walls,
when there is nothing left in the place it came from.

Notes

The place and date of publication of books will be found in the Bibliography. In some cases, books or articles that are cited several times are referred to by an abbreviation, which is explained when the works are first cited and also in the Bibliography.

NOTES TO THE PREFACE

1. And when it does not. Relevant to this is the conception of a certain aspect of scholarship, textual criticism, as a purely technical discipline. There are, of course, technical considerations of palaeography and transmission that give power to interpretation, and one ignores them at one's peril, but some editors have exaggerated the extent to which textual criticism can be independent of debatable stylistic and hermeneutical issues. We should be cautious with the medical metaphor that Housman used in his encomium on Bentley: "*Lucida tela diei:* these are the words that come into one's mind when one has halted at some stubborn perplexity of reading or interpretation . . . then turns to Bentley and sees Bentley strike his finger on the place and say *thou ailest here, and here*" (M. Manilii *Astronomicon* Liber I, p. xvi). In the same pages, indeed, Housman issued a significant rebuke: "Though Bentley's faculty for discovering truth has no equal in the history of learning, his wish to discover it was not so strong. Critics like Porson and Lachmann, inferior in εὐστοχία and ἀγχίνοια, put

him to shame by their serious and disinterested purpose and the honesty of their dealings with themselves" (p. xviii). For a striking example of textual criticism out of control, see below, chap. 5, n. 39.

2.   Preface to Harry Crosby, *Transit of Venus,* p. ix. I owe this quotation to Christopher Ricks, *T. S. Eliot and Prejudice,* p. 171.

3.   *The Greeks and the Irrational* [GI].

NOTES TO CHAPTER I

1.   GI p. viii.

2.   A pioneer was Jane Harrison: e.g., *Prolegomena to the Study of Greek Religion.*

3.   I hope that this approach can negotiate a respectable passage for itself within the general terms of the division of labour. The points at which I am conscious of the greatest risks in this neglect are those at which I touch on Greek conceptions of what I call the "supernatural"; on this, see below, chap. 6, esp. pp. 130—32.

4.   On this subject, see Richard Jenkyns, *The Victorians and Ancient Greece;* and for the influence on another culture, E. M. Butler, *The Tyranny of Greece over Germany.*

5.   But not because of the view, which currently has some vogue, that judgements of value associated with the "hegemonic" Western tradition and its works are, all of them, equally and perniciously ideological constructs. This outlook in any case runs into the problem (which gets deeper the more it is understood) that all the critical machinery deployed against the hegemony is itself a product of this tradition. But this book will not deploy arguments against that outlook. Rather, I hope that the works it discusses are themselves an argument against that outlook.

6.   *Vom Nutzen und Nachteil der Historie für das Leben,* in *Unzeitgemäße Betrachtungen,* translated by Gary Brown as "History in the Service and Disservice of Life," in *Unmodern Observations,* ed. William Arrowsmith, p. 88 [UO]. In the quotation, I have replaced "unmodern" with the traditional "untimely" as the translation of *unzeitgemäß;* "unmodern" suggests "postmodern", which at the present moment is too close to "fashionable".

7. More than one friend, reading this book in an earlier version, has asked who this ubiquitous "we" represents. It refers to people in a certain cultural situation, but who is in that situation? Obviously it cannot mean everybody in the world, or everybody in the West. I hope it does not mean only people who already think as I do. The best I can say is that "we" operates not through a previously fixed designation, but through invitation. (The same is true, I believe, of "we" in much philosophy, and particularly in ethics.) It is not a matter of "I" telling "you" what I and others think, but of my asking you to consider to what extent you and I think some things and perhaps need to think others.

8. A well-known and influential example is A. H. Adkins, *Merit and Responsibility: A Study in Greek Values* [MR], and *From the Many to the One: A Study of Personality and Views of Human Nature in the Context of Ancient Greek Society* [MO]. The basic idea is widespread, and not confined to those who directly discuss the Greeks.

9. Dodds held the former view; the latter is dominant in Adkins, MR and MO. Hugh Lloyd-Jones, *The Justice of Zeus* [JZ], very reasonably warns against pressing the distinctions too hard: see in particular p. 25 seq.

10. Nietzsche thought modern culture drastically dilapidated, more in need of redemptive rescue than it will be the aim of this study to claim. One does not have to accept his view in order to agree with his remark: "So if we understand Greek culture, we see that it's gone for good. Hence the classicist is *the great skeptic* in our cultural and educational circumstances" (notes for "Wir Philologen" [III 76], translated as "We Classicists" by William Arrowsmith in UO, p. 345).

11. So Engels, *Anti-Dühring*, Marx-Engels Werke 20, p. 168: "Without slavery, no Greek state, no Greek art and science; without slavery, no Roman Empire. Without Hellenism and the Roman Empire as the base, also no modern Europe. . . . It costs little to inveigh against slavery and the like in general terms, and to pour high moral wrath on such infamies. . . . But that tells us not one word as to how these institutions arose, why they existed, and what role they have played in history" (quoted by M. I. Finley, *Ancient Slavery and Modern Ideology*, p. 12 [AS]).

12.   Heinrich von Staden, "Nietzsche and Marx on Greek Art and Literature: Case Studies in Reception," *Daedalus,* Winter 1976, p. 87.

13.   A remark he used twice, in the preface to the second edition of *The Gay Science* and in the epilogue to *Nietzsche contra Wagner.*

14.   Notably in "We Classicists" [III 49], UO p. 337. However, he also said, "Infancy and childhood have their ends in themselves, they are not *stages*" (ibid. [V 186], UO p. 385). Von Staden points out that the image of the Greeks as children was shared by the young Marx.

15.   For a comprehensive study of this book, see M. S. Silk and J. P. Stern, *Nietzsche on Tragedy.*

16.   Despite its title, Tracy B. Strong's book *Nietzsche and the Politics of Transfiguration* does not really offer a Nietzschean politics. The claim that Nietzsche's politics, such as they were, were not adequate to his own insights, is well argued by Mark Warren, *Nietzsche and Political Thought.*

17.   I do not believe that this point is sufficiently acknowledged by Alasdair MacIntyre, who in his *After Virtue* and, more recently, *Whose Justice? Which Rationality?* indeed rejects what I have been calling the progressivist view, but treats modern outlooks, in particular liberalism, as merely an incoherent assemblage of fragments from past traditions. He thinks that a tradition does run from the Greeks, if I understand him, but the major contributor in antiquity was Aristotle, and it culminated in St. Thomas. For some criticism of his view of modernity, see my review of the later book, *London Review of Books,* January 1989.

18.   *The Anti-Christ,* 60. He was, however, well aware of ways in which Christianity perpetuated classical antiquity: see "We Classicists" [III 13], UO p. 329.

19.   *The Critic as Artist,* in *Intentions* (first published 1891), p. 119.

20.   *The Body and Society,* p. 86. It is one of the merits of this remarkable book that its insight and learning enable one to understand what did happen, while preserving the sense that it might not have happened.

21.   It is raised by Bas van Fraasen, "Peculiar Effects of Love and Desire," in *Perspectives on Self-Deception,* ed. Brian McLaughlin and Amélie Rorty.

22. A central text is the *Phaedrus,* which explores two different contrasts, between rhetoric and philosophy, and between speech and writing; the treatment of the second contrast helps to make the discussion of the first much subtler and more problematic than it is, for instance, in the *Gorgias.* A very helpful examination of the dialogue is G. R. F. Ferrari, *Listening to the Cicadas: A Study of Plato's Phaedrus,* in particular chap. 2, and, for the question whether the attitude to writing expressed by Socrates undermines Plato's own writing, chap. 7.

23. "The concerns of the tragedians are sometimes consigned to the melancholy category of religious philosophy" (Robert Parker, *Miasma,* p. 308). The view that philosophy replaced tragedy is held by Bruno Snell, *Die Entdeckung des Geistes,* translated by T. G. Rosenmeyer, with the addition of an extra chapter, as *The Discovery of the Mind in Greek Philosophy and Literature;* see especially chap. 5. (References to Snell's book will be to the translation.) It must be distinguished from Nietzsche's view that philosophy made tragedy impossible. Martha C. Nussbaum, *The Fragility of Goodness,* p. 12 seq. [FG], argues for the study of tragedy in these connections, but not many of her reasons are specific to tragedy; some of them, such as her emphasis on "complex" and "concrete" characters (p. 13), seem to apply more to the novel than to tragedy.

24. Aeschylus *Agamemnon,* ed. J. D. Denniston and Denys Page, pp. xv–xvi. The introduction, from which these remarks are taken, is by Page (cf. p. vi). Lloyd-Jones, JZ p. 107, offers a good correction on the subject of Aeschylus's intelligence, though he does not take up the relations of tragedy to philosophy.

25. For a useful account, see Simon Goldhill, *Reading Greek Tragedy:* in particular, for the civic aspect, chap. 3.

26. See, among others, Jean-Pierre Vernant and Pierre Vidal-Naquet, *Mythe et tragédie en Grèce ancienne,* vol. 1 [MT], translated by Janet Lloyd as *Tragedy and Myth in Ancient Greece,* and vol. 2; Nicole Loraux, *Façons tragiques de tuer une femme* [FT], translated by Anthony Forster as *Tragic Ways of Killing a Woman;* Charles Segal, *Tragedy and Civilization.* Goldhill gives further references to such work. J. Peter Euben, in his introduction to a collection of essays, *Greek Tragedy and Political Theory,* perhaps moves too easily from the point that the performance of tragedy was a civic event to the idea

that it had a political content; but see now Euben's *The Tragedy of Political Theory: The Road Not Taken.*

27.   *Ursprung des deutschen Trauerspiels,* translated by John Osborne as *The Origin of German Tragic Drama,* p. 101 seq. (References are to this translation.) In the same passage, Benjamin offers a forceful critique of Nietzsche's purely aesthetic view of tragedy.

28.   P. 109. I have changed the translator's "demonic", which may mislead. For an instance of the inherent "ambiguity" of the daimonic, and of the ways in which tragedy can sharpen it into paradox, see the discussion in chap. 6, pp. 139–48 below, of the oracle and its relations to possibility.

29.   MT p. 16. The translation in the text (and below, p. 19) is my own version.

30.   MT p. 63.

31.   For instance, to take one of countless examples, the words of the Paidagogos to Orestes and Pylades as he moves them towards the murder: μέλαινά τ' ἄστρων ἐκλέλοιπεν εὐφρόνη, *Electra* 19. The εὐφρόνη has indeed gone, along with its euphemism, and a dawn has come that can be represented as a new darkness, the moment at which the light of the stars goes out. See further below on the words of Oedipus, chap. 3, p. 58, and chap. 6, p. 147.

32.   *Tragedy and Civilization,* p. 7.

33.   GI p. 49.

34.   As I have already said, the question arises straightforwardly with Sophocles, and the same is largely true for Aeschylus (and for the author of the *Prometheus Vinctus:* for a detailed argument that he was not Aeschylus, see Mark Griffith, *The Authenticity of "Prometheus Bound"*). With Euripides things are different, though it is a complex question, what exactly the differences are. For some remarks on this, see chap. 6, pp. 148–51 below.

35.   MT p. 37.

36.   Hugh Lloyd-Jones, *Blood for the Ghosts,* p. 200, and the epigraph to that book, p. 5. Mr. Mark Migotti has pointed out to me that (ironically, in view of their relations in classical scholarship) Wilamowitz must have got this remark from Nietzsche: "It is only if we give them our soul, that [the works of earlier times] can go on living: it is *our* blood that makes them speak to *us*. A really 'historical' pre-

sentation [*Vortrag*] would speak as a ghost to ghosts" (*Assorted Opinions and Maxims*, 126, in *Human, All Too Human*).

NOTES TO CHAPTER II

1. P. 31. Voigt cited by Dodds, GI p. 20 n. 31.

2. *Il.* 13.455–59. "Wondered two ways" is my, admittedly awkward, translation of διάνδιχα μερμήριξεν, for which see below, n. 23. In quoting Homer, I have generally followed the translations of Richmond Lattimore, modifying them in a more literal direction where it is necessary to the point.

3. There are differences in the ways in which the underworld is represented between the *Iliad* and the *Odyssey*, and to some degree between *Odyssey* 11 and 24. James M. Redfield, *Nature and Culture in the Iliad*, p. 257 n. 52, quotes H. Rahn, who remarked, "Die *psuchai* sind bei Homer soweit dem 'Nichts' genähert, wie er den Menschen überhaupt dem Nichts anschaulich nähern kann," in "Tier und Mensch in der Homerischen Auffassung der Wirklichkeit," *Paideuma* 5 (1953–54), p. 450. The fact that the figures encountered in the underworld bear the names of dead people does not show (despite the point made in n. 8 below) that they are, straightforwardly, those people. They are εἴδωλα (*Od.* 11.476 al.), and, in the Greek world as in ours, names move effortlessly from things to their images.

4. *Il.* 3.23, which relates to the body of an animal, has been claimed as a counterexample, but it is more likely that the item in question is dead—as the Loeb edition translates, a carcass.

5. P. 5 seq.

6. J. L. Austin used to point out the oddness of the sentence *I have a pain in my waist.*

7. *Il.* 24.405–23. The expression of the thought that the corpse is Hector is very strong: ὥς τοι κήδονται μάκαρες θεοὶ υἷος ἑῆος / καὶ νέκυός περ ἐόντος 422: they care for him although he is a corpse. Cf. also Apollo at *Il.* 24.35, speaking to the other gods: τὸν νῦν οὐκ ἔτλητε νέκυν περ ἐόντα σαῶσαι; yet at the end of the same speech (54) he can say that what Achilles is insulting is κωφὴν γαῖαν. For a suggestive account of Achilles' insult, see Vernant, *L'individu, la mort, l'amour*, pp. 68–69 [IMA].

8. "Der einfachste, aller Abstraktion vorausliegende Ausdruck für die durch alle Phasen der Handlung festgehaltene Identität der Person ist der Eigenname" (Albin Lesky, "Göttliche und menschliche Motivation in Homerischen Epos," *SHAW* 1961, p. 11 [GM]).

9. Even Charles Taylor, a philosopher fully alerted to the kind of mistake that distorts Snell's interpretations, cites those interpretations in a discussion of Homer: *Sources of the Self,* pp. 117–18. A position like Snell's, but even more extreme, is advanced by Julian Jaynes in a well-known work of scientific-historical speculation, *The Origin of Consciousness in the Breakdown of the Bicameral Mind:* "There is in general no consciousness in the *Iliad*" (p. 69). Jaynes claims that the gods (who "pushed men about like robots") "are what we now call hallucinations" (pp. 73–74). It is not explained how a creature who lacks consciousness can have a hallucination. Aspects of Snell's treatment have been effectively criticised by A. A. Long, Christopher Gill, and others, in writings referred to elsewhere; cf. also Richard Gaskin, "Do Homeric Heroes Make Real Decisions?" *CQ* n.s. 40 (1990); and R. W. Sharples, "But Why Has My Spirit Spoken with Me Thus?" *Greece and Rome* 30 (1983). See also Lloyd-Jones, JZ p. 9 seq.

10. P. 8.

11. Cf. the passage quoted below, from p. 15. There is a great deal of what seems to be Cartesian material in Snell's text: e.g., the mysterious remarks about sight and "optical impressions" at p. 5.

12. P. 15.

13. I agree in this with the direction of a comment by David Claus: "In a sense this faults the Homeric terminology for failing to achieve a dualistic idea of the self at the same time as it interprets the language in terms of one" (*Toward the Soul,* p. 14 n. 13 [TS]).

14. Introduction, p. ix.

15. But not more theoretical than that of *body as opposed to soul.* It was for this, more theoretical, purpose that Descartes developed, in conscious opposition to ancient tradition, a mechanical conception of the body in terms of which it would be true that the difference between the body of a living person and the body of a dead one would be like that between a functioning watch and a broken one (*The Passions of the Soul,* 1:6). This kind of conception seems now to have become our conception of a body. It is important that it is not merely

Aristotelian ideas that are rejected by this conception. Though Plato's idea of a living person differs from Aristotle's and resembles Descartes's to the extent that it is dualistic, its conception of *life* is not a modern one. Contrast the passage quoted from *The Passions of the Soul* (and also 1 : 5, the soul leaves because the body dies) with the last argument for immortality in the *Phaedo,* 102A seq.

16. We shall see below, p. 33, that the assumption is still more complex than this reveals.

17. For a detailed account of the material, see Claus, TS. See also Redfield, p. 175 seq.; Norman Austin, *Archery at the Dark of the Moon,* p. 106 seq.; and there is much other work on the subject. Some of Claus's contentions are not borne out by his own evidence. He claims that if one lays aside an idiomatic use of θυμῷ (roughly to mean "exceedingly") and the formula κατὰ θυμόν, "it can be seen that 'affection' is the only really important category added by θυμός to the 'life' uses of the other words" (that is to say, the use of "soul" words to signify energy, strength, or being alive). But cf., among other examples, *Od.* 4. 452–53 οὐδέ τι θυμῷ / ὠίσθη δόλον εἶναι; 12.57–58 ἀλλὰ καὶ αὐτὸς / θυμῷ βουλεύειν (how to sail between Scylla and Charybdis); 10.415 δόκησε δ' ἄρα σφίσι θυμός (that they had come home); 1.200, 9.213, *Il.* 7.44 (foreboding, prophecy, understanding a divine decision); *Il.* 9.189 τῇ ὅ γε θυμὸν ἔτερπεν (of Achilles singing to the lyre); cf. *Od.* 1.107 (the suitors enjoying a game of draughts).

Thomas Jahn, *Zum Wortfeld 'Seele-Geist' in der Sprache Homers* (Munich, 1987), concludes that θυμός and six other terms, including φρήν/φρένες, κῆρ, and κραδίη, are semantically interchangeable and are exploited according to their metrical possibilities. See now the review of this book in CR n.s. 42 (1992) by A. A. Long, to whom I owe this reference.

18. For references, see Dodds, GI p. 16 seq. and notes. Dodds himself accepts the phenomenon. He indeed warns us against regarding this "habitual intellectualism" as a conscious expression; rather, he revealingly says, "It is the inevitable result of the absence of the concept of the will."

19. εἴ μοι . . . / ἤπια εἰδείη *Il.* 16.72–3. Similarly αἴσιμα, ἄρτια: *Od.* 14.433, 19.248; and the Cyclops ἀπάνευθεν ἐὼν ἀθεμίστια ᾔδη: 9.189. Patroclus, above: *Il.* 16.35; Nestor and Agamem-

non: *Od.* 3.277. Michael J. O'Brien reaches the same conclusion about this usage and makes further points on the same lines in *The Socratic Paradoxes and the Greek Mind,* p. 39 seq.: see in particular p. 43: "The simplest explanation of this variety [sc. in the use of οἶδα] is not that all other meanings derive from the first but that the word in Homer transcends the distinctions we put upon it." (I owe this reference to a member of the Sather Committee acting anonymously as referee.)

20. λέων δ' ὣς ἄγρια οἶδεν *Il.* 24.41; the comparison with the lion continues after this phrase. Hermann Fränkel, *Early Greek Poetry and Philosophy* [EGP] (references are to this translation), resists the proposal in the text on the strength of *Od.* 19.329, ἀπηνὴς αὐτὸς ἔῃ καὶ ἀπηνέα εἰδῇ, but the view I am defending does not entail that these two clauses are synonymous; even if they were, the καὶ could be by a familiar construction epexegetic.

21. Snell, p. 20.

22. *Il.* 13.455 seq. Δηΐφοβος δὲ διάνδιχα μερμήριξεν, ἢ . . . ἢ . . . ; cf. 1.188; δίχα δὲ φρεσὶ *Od.* 22.333.

23. This is expressed in such formulae as ὧδε δέ οἱ φρονέοντι δοάσσετο κέρδιον εἶναι (e.g., *Il.* 13.458; *Od.* 22.338, 24.239) and ἥδε δέ οἱ κατὰ θυμὸν ἀρίστη φαίνετο βουλή (e.g., *Il.* 2.5, 14.161). Odysseus and the Lycians: *Il.* 5.671–74.

24. *Il.* 10.503 seq. The word is κύντατον, formed from κύων, "dog", which though masculine, is applied as a term of abuse to women, as in Helen's description of herself at *Il.* 6.344, 356. On this, and the determinately masculine form of ἀλεκτρύων that provides a joke at Ar. *Nub.* 659–66, see Nicole Loraux, *Les expériences de Tirèsias,* pp. 8 seq., 239.

25. Cf. Lesky, GM p. 18 seq.

26. At *Il.* 21.455, a mortal, Laomedon, is reported to have threatened to cut off the ears of Apollo and Poseidon: there is nothing to suggest he did not know who they were. Laomedon, Priam's father, was, strictly speaking, 1/32d part divine, being five generations from Zeus (20.213 seq.), but that can hardly make the difference. On this subject, see Nicole Loraux, "Corps des dieux," *Le temps de la réflexion* 7 (1986), pp. 335–54.

27. Lesky, GM p. 23, points out that *Il.* 9.600–601, ἀλλὰ σὺ μή

μοι ταῦτα νόει φρεσί, μηδέ σε δαίμων / ἐνταῦθα τρέψειε, does not present alternatives and also that Lattimore's translation ("let not the spirit within you turn that way") is modernising. Similarly, 702–3, ὁππότε κέν μιν / θυμὸς ἐνὶ στήθεσσιν ἀνώγῃ καὶ θεὸς ὄρσῃ, on which he remarks: "Die Regungen im Inneren des Menschen und die göttliche Einwirkung in ein und denselben Akt münden" (p. 24).

28.   Lesky remarks (GM p. 34) that there is no clear parallel in the *Iliad* to *Od.* 3.26–27, ἄλλα μὲν αὐτὸς ἐνὶ φρεσὶ σῇσι νοήσεις, / ἄλλα δὲ καὶ δαίμων ὑποθήσεται.

29.   Odysseus's description of Calypso: *Od.* 7.262; Medon: 4.712–13; Penelope's question: 4.707. In both these examples, the nondivine alternative is introduced by ἦ καί. καί must be intensive, "or, again": cf. *Il.* 1.62–63, ἀλλ᾽ ἄγε δή τινα μάντιν ἐρείομεν ἢ ἱερῆα / ἦ καὶ ὀνειροπόλον, and other examples in Denniston, *The Greek Particles,* 2d ed., p. 306. An additive καί (such that "P ἦ καὶ Q" meant "P or P & Q") would make no sense on anyone's account of the matter.

30.   *Il.* 15.82; μενοινήῃσί (subjunctive, Aristarchus; μενοινήσειε, optative, codd.) means "desire eagerly", and it refers to desires rather than mere wishes; cf. *Od.* 2.248, 285; Soph. *Ajax* 341. The gods did not always move so lightly; contrast the comical complaints of Hermes—of all gods—about a long and tiresome journey over the sea at *Od.* 5.100 seq. Vernant is disposed to exaggerate the gods' powers in this respect: I see no basis for interpreting *Od.* 1.22–26, as he does (IMA p. 34), as saying that Poseidon is simultaneously at both extremities of the earth.

31.   The basic question is what the data are, that this set of concepts might be supposed to theorise. The obvious answer is "observable behaviour". The difficulty is to find a relevant notion of "behaviour" that does not already incorporate the supposed theory: cf. Jennifer Hornsby, "Bodily Movements, Actions, and Mental Epistemology," *Midwest Studies in Philosophy* 10 (1986). If we do say that explanations in terms of beliefs, desires, and so on constitute a theory, this must be separated from the further notion entertained by "eliminative materialists", that it is a primitive, "folk psychological" theory which, like the idea of witchcraft, will be replaced by scientific explanations; for the most convincing exposition of this utterly unconvinc-

ing view, see Stephen Stich, *From Folk Psychology to Cognitive Science: The Case against Belief.*

32. Is this is a counterexample to Snell's "lexical" principle, that unless Homer had a word for something, he had no idea of it? Only if the principle assumes that if Homer "had a word" for a certain thing, then he had a word that meant that thing in every context in which it occurred, and in no context meant something else. (In saying that a word "means a certain thing in a given context," I mean the following: if we are to understand the point that is being made in the context, we have to understand the word as marking that distinction rather than some other.) But in that form, the principle is obviously unacceptable: see below and n. 34; also chap. 3, p. 51 and nn. 3 and 4, on intention.

33. Strictly speaking, it is what a deliberated decision is. There is, equally, no lack in Homer of decision without extended deliberation. Of course, for this to be an account of decision it is important that what results from the thoughts should be *doing,* and not *finding oneself doing;* but in Homer, as in life, it usually is.

34. In the practical sense, it is often associated, like μερμηρίζειν, with expressions of division: *Il.* 14.20–21, δαϊζόμενος κατὰ θυμὸν / διχθάδι'; *Il.* 16.435, Zeus says διχθὰ δέ μοι κραδίη μέμονε φρεσὶν ὁρμαίνοντι, and at 443 Hera, in reply, sharply says ἔρδ' ("do it"). For the other sense, cf. *Od.* 4.789, where Penelope is wondering whether Telemachus will get killed, and 15.300, where Telemachus is wondering the same thing. Gaskin, p. 9, says, "Homeric decisions are never labelled as such"; what he means by this, I suppose, is given by "they are never signalled by such verbs as hairein or haireisthai." But it is unclear why this word is thought to be special. αἱρεῖσθαι can mean "decide" (e.g., Hdt. 1.11), but it can mean several other things as well, in particular "prefer": at Plato *Ap.* 38E, αἱροῦμαι does not mean "I am deciding."

35. P. 20; *Il.* 16.513 seq.

36. The idea is presupposed by the frequent thought that men as they now are must make great efforts to do what Homeric heroes could do easily: *Il.* 20.285–87 ὁ δὲ χερμάδιον λάβε χειρὶ / Αἰνείας, μέγα ἔργον, ὃ οὐ δύο γ' ἄνδρε φέροιεν, / οἵοι νῦν βροτοί εἰσ'· ὁ δέ μιν ῥέα πάλλε καὶ οἶος. The same formula at 5.304, 12.449; and cf. 12.383.

37.   *Il.* 11.407; 17.97; well discussed by Sharples, who describes it as a formula for "distancing" the agent from the rejected course of action. Fränkel, EGP p. 79.

38.   πρὸς ἀλλήλους Plato *Pol.* 272C et saep.; ἀνὴρ ἀνδρὶ Thuc. 8.93. Lesky, GM p. 10, refers to parallels in other ancient languages.

39.   Noted by Lesky, GM pp. 13–14. The concept of identification is used in this connection by Dodds (GI, chap. 1), but he associates it with the idea, which I would reject for the reason given in the text, that θυμός represents "not-self". He also (p. 25 n. 98) gives as an example of the same kind of phenomenon *Od.* 9.299 seq., τὸν μὲν ἐγὼ βούλευσα . . . 302 ἕτερος δέ με θυμὸς ἔρυκεν; and Sharples says that the second course here is one that the agent adopts "reluctantly." This assimilates it to 20.17 seq., discussed below, and obviously there is some reason to do that; but it is not quite obvious that the "endurance" there refers to this very moment. So far as these lines are concerned, it could as well be that Odysseus thinks of what at first seems a good idea, and then a decisive objection occurs to him.

40.   *Od.* 20.17 seq. "From then on" seems to me closer to νωλεμέως than Lattimore's "without complaint", which in this connection is rather misleading. "In great obedience" translates the obscure phrase ἐν πείσει: the scholiast paraphrased it ἐν δεσμοῖς. Plato's quotation is at *Rep.* 441B, in the passage setting up the tripartite division of the soul, discussed below.

41.   *Il.* 22.357: ἐν φρεσὶ best codd.; ἔνδοθι cett. Achilles' description of Priam occurs at *Il.* 24.518 seq.: ἔτλης 519, of both the things Priam was prepared to do. LSJ s.v. *τλάω offers a helpful commentary on the range of this word. Priam's conduct is thought quite extraordinary: note the startling comparison at 480 seq., where the amazement of Achilles and the others on first seeing him is likened to that of people seeing a man who comes to a rich man's house in another country, when ἄτη πυκινὴ has led him to kill someone.

42.   Cf. K. J. Dover, *Greek Popular Morality in the Time of Plato and Aristotle,* pp. 98–102 [GPM].

43.   Cf. Adkins's remark, "In this respect, at least, we are all Kantians now" (MR p. 2); the respect in question is that of taking duty and responsibility to be the central concepts of ethics and supposing that What is my duty in these circumstances? "is the basic question which

the agent must ask himself in any matter which requires a moral decision." For an account of τὸ δέον in Aristotle and its relations to "duty", and of the sense in which reason or the ὀρθὸς λόγος *commands,* see Gauthier-Jolif, vol. 2, pp. 568–75; the account is helpful and states the irrelevance of Kantian notions, but it remains interestingly caught in some assumptions of such a morality.

44.   There are strong hints of such ideas in Snell, p. 103. It is unfair to Kant to call this schema Kantian, but his philosophy must bear some responsibility for it.

45.   Equally, the role of τὸ θυμοειδές can only be explained through ethical, and ultimately political, distinctions: on this aspect, see my "The Analogy of City and Soul in Plato's *Republic,*" in *Exegesis and Argument: Essays Presented to Gregory Vlastos,* ed. E. N. Lee, A. P. Mourelatos, and R. M. Rorty. There are many disputable questions about the division of the soul and the arguments for it in *Republic* 4, in particular, about the status of the "principle of contraries": at some points psychic conflict is modelled on an opposition of forces, at others on a contrariety (or, possibly, contradiction) of commands. For discussion and references, see in particular T. H. Irwin, *Plato's Moral Theory: The Early and Middle Dialogues;* John Cooper, "Plato's Theory of Human Motivation," *Hist. Phil. Quarterly* 1 (1985); Michael Woods, "Plato's Division of the Soul," *PBA* 73 (1987).

46.   For instance, in addition to writers already mentioned, Albrecht Dihle in *The Theory of Will in Classical Antiquity;* for further comment, see below, chap. 3, n. 5.

47.   One version of the destination is the type of psychology exposed by Nietzsche and diagnosed by him in terms of the operations of *ressentiment,* which posits a gap between doer and deed and fills it with free will: see in particular *The Genealogy of Morals,* I 13. This version is particularly obscure, and no doubt also particularly powerful. However, I think it may be more helpful, both historically and philosophically, to consider how far our illusions can be traced to a more general phenomenon, the desire for a basically ethicised psychology, of which this is only a specially malign case.

48.   Sharples rightly points out that Plato's account of the soul represents it as less unified than Homer's does.

ers. . . . Socrates is a winner. . . . Desiring the kind of happiness he does, he can't lose." Granted this, and still more if one adds an expectation of immortality (which Socrates is prepared to entertain, 40E seq., and which may perhaps be heard in the word ἔνθαδε), the Homeric words take on a very different tone. On Socrates as hero, cf. Nicole Loraux, "Socrate, contrepoison de l'oraison funèbre," *L'antiquité classique* 43 (1974), cited by Vernant, IAM p. 42. Kebriones: *Il.* 16.775–76.

NOTES TO CHAPTER III

1. *Od.* 22.154–56 ὦ πάτερ, αὐτὸς ἐγὼ τόδε γ᾽ ἤμβροτον—οὐδέ τις ἄλλος / αἴτιος, ὃς θαλαμοῖο θύρην πυκινῶς ἀραρυῖαν / κάλλιπον ἀγκλίνας· Τῶν δὲ σκοπὸς ἦεν ἀμείνων.

2. Cf. in particular the use of τυγχάνω with another verb to mean success in doing that very thing: e.g., *Il.* 4.106–8 ὑπὸ στέρνοιο τυχήσας / . . . βεβλήκει; 23.466 οὐκ ἐτύχησεν ἐλίξας.

3. 10.372 Ἦ ῥα, καὶ ἔγχος ἀφῆκεν, ἑκὼν δ᾽ ἡμάρτανε φωτός. Out of nine occurrences, another five clearly have this sense: 4.43, discussed in the text; 23.434–35, 585, of driving the horses to avoid a crash; 6.523, Hector reproving Paris for idleness in battle, ἀλλὰ ἑκὼν μεθιεῖς τε καὶ οὐκ ἐθέλεις, which notably says that he is not only unwilling, but deliberately so; and 3.66, the gifts of the gods are not to be thrown aside, ὅσσα κεν αὐτοὶ δῶσιν, ἑκὼν δ᾽ οὐκ ἄν τις ἕλοιτο, where the point is not that a person would not willingly get them—of course he would—but that he would not get them *by setting out to*. At 7.197 it seems to have only rhetorical force (Aristarchus read ἑλών). At 8.81 and 13.234 it may mean merely that someone does something willingly, the sense in which it is the contrary of ἀέκων (see below in the text, and n. 4). This is the usual sense in the *Odyssey*, clearly expressed at 4.646–47, ἦ σε βίῃ ἀέκοντος ἀπηύρα νῆα μέλαιναν, / ἦε ἑκὼν οἱ δῶκας. At 22.351–53, ὡς ἐγὼ οὔ τι ἑκὼν ἐς σὸν δόμον οὐδὲ χατίζων / πωλεύμην . . . / ἀλλὰ πολὺ πλέονες καὶ κρείσσονες ἦγον ἀνάγκῃ, the suggestion is neither that the minstrel came into the house unwillingly nor that he came into it unintentionally, but rather that he was dragged into it, which was not an action of his at all. Problems on this boundary are endemic to coercion. See

chap. 6 below, pp. 152–54, with n. 43, and the reference there to Aristotle; cf. his careful formulation in *EN* 1110a2–4, βίαιον δὲ οὗ ἡ ἀρχὴ ἔξωθεν, τοιαύτη οὖσα ἐν ᾗ μηδὲν συμβάλλεται ὁ πράττων ἢ ὁ πάσχων, οἷον εἰ πνεῦμα κομίσαι ποι ἢ ἄνθρωποι·κύριοι ὄντες. The phrase ὁ πράττων ἢ ὁ πάσχων does not mean "the doer or the sufferer, as the case may be", but "the doer or, as we may rather call him, the sufferer", as Burnet. (The example of the wind seems to refer to a ship's being blown off course to an undesired destination: see Gauthier-Jolif ad loc.)

4. The usual use of the negative expressions is illustrated, too, by the frequent construction ἀέκητι + gen., to mean "against someone's will". There is just one passage in Homer in which ἀέκων unequivo-cally means "unintentionally": *Il.* 16.263–64, where it is used of the travelling man who disturbs the wasps in a hedge; he is contrasted with naughty boys who stir them up for fun.

5. *Il.* 4.43; Dihle, p. 26. Kirk ad loc. says that this is "a subtle piece of psychology on Homer's part"; rather, it is a brilliant expression of some everyday psychology. It must also be said that Dihle does not always represent so sharply what is in front of him; he is another, despite the learning and subtlety of his book, whose view is distorted by unfocussed philosophical assumptions. Thus he quotes some straightforward words of Hesiod about perjury (*Op.* 280 seq.): εἰ γὰρ τίς κ' ἐθέλῃ τὰ δίκαι' ἀγορεῦσαι / γιγνώσκων . . . / ὅς δέ κε μαρτυρίῃσιν ἑκὼν ἐπίορκον ὀμόσσας / ψεύσεται . . . , and comments that "the connotation of intentionality is introduced only by γιγνώσκων and ἑκών." In fact, γιγνώσκων has little to do with intentionality here, though ἐθέλῃ does: the first clause refers to someone who wants to give true witness and is in a position to do so, and the second to someone who intentionally perjures himself. The idea that anything *else* might be needed to express these thoughts seems to be the product, like much else in his treatment, of an old-fashioned triadic psychology in terms of reason, emotion, and will (the "rational", the "affective", and the "conative"). This is a descendent of Plato's division of the soul: see above, chap. 2, p. 43.

6. *Il.* 19.86 seq., the passage often called Agamemnon's apology. Dodds, who discusses it in chapter 1 of GI, is among those who connect the references to Zeus to the famous words of 1.5 (themselves

already much discussed in antiquity) Διὸς δ᾽ ἐτελείετο βουλή, on which cf. chap. 5 below, pp. 103–4.

7. It is not restricted in this way when it means a state of affairs—ruin or disaster: nor is the verb that is associated with the noun. Poor Elpenor was indeed put into this state of mind by a conjunction of wine and δαίμονος αἶσα κακή (*Od.* 11.61), but the Centaur (21.297) simply put himself into it by wine. At 10.68, ἄασάν μ᾽ ἕταροί τε κακοὶ πρὸς τοῖσί τε ὕπνος, ἄασαν does not refer to a state of mind; it corresponds to the "state of affairs" sense of ἄτη and means that they plunged him into disaster.

8. *Il.* 19.137.

9. As is seen by Lloyd-Jones, JZ p. 23 (the reference to Zeus "helps Agamemnon to save face, but it does not cancel his responsibility"); Redfield, p. 97. Adkins, MR pp. 51–52, says, "To plead *ate* cannot be an attempt to evade responsibility for one's actions," but he goes on, "In this sense, responsibility is not moral, but cannot be avoided . . . such are the implications of the competitive scheme of values. *Moral* [his emphasis] responsibility has no place in them." For decisive criticism of Adkins's use of a distinction between "competitive" and "cooperative" values, see A. A. Long, "Morals and Values in Homer," *JHS* 90 (1970) [MV]; and see below, chap. 4, p. 100 seq. For the assumption that there is a determinate notion of "moral" responsibility, see below, p. 56, pp. 64 seq.

10. One danger in using these expressions for action in an abnormal state of mind is that we may forget the case of agents who are normally in an abnormal state of mind. The many difficulties in interpreting such cases are, needless to say, of great importance for juridical practice, but they lie outside the range of the present inquiry.

11. See above, chap. 2, p. 32.

12. There are, of course, particularly in any complex society, endless problems that arise about this point, such as the allocation of causality between several agents who have between them brought about some effect. There are issues, too, about collective responsibility. But these are difficulties in applying the primitive idea I am discussing.

13. For an account of various such rituals, see Walter Burkert, *Griechische Religion der archaischen und klassischen Epoche,* translated by John Raffan as *Greek Religion,* pp. 82–84 (references are to

the translation); Parker, *Miasma,* p. 258 seq., who makes the point that in practice (unsurprisingly) scapegoats and offenders regarded as causes of pollution were not always distinguished.

14. *Il.* 11.654 δεινὸς ἀνήρ· τάχα κεν καὶ ἀναίτιον αἰτιόῳτο. Cf. also 13.775; *Od.* 20.135.

15. *Od.* 20.394 πρότεροι γὰρ ἀεικέα μηχανόωντο. I owe this point and that about ἀρχή in *Il.* 3.100 (see n. 16) to Oliver Taplin.

16. 3.100 καὶ 'Αλεξάνδρου ἕνεκ' ἀρχῆς. Zenodotus read ἄτης, which, although there are variants, seems to be correct in the similar passages 6.356 and 24.28. See Kirk ad loc. for the issues. Kirk himself, though he does not change the text, is inclined to favor ἄτης, but Monro gives a convincing defence of ἀρχῆς, citing Hdt. 8.142, where all MSS read περὶ τῆς ὑμετέρας ἀρχῆς ὁ ἀγὼν ἐγένετο. Editors have emended that passage, under the impression that ἀρχῆς would have to mean "empire", but cf. 5.97.3, referring to the matter in question (the Athenian support of the Ionian revolt), αὗται αἱ νῆες ἀρχὴ κακῶν ἐγένετο 'Ελλησί τε καὶ βαρβαροῖσι.

17. Hdt. 1.1 δι' ἣν αἰτίην ἐπολέμησαν. In the famous contrast at Thuc. 1.23.5–6 between the αἰτίαι and the ἀληθεστάτη πρόφασις of the war, αἰτία carries both its senses. Joined as it is with τὰς διαφοράς, it relates to the issues of complaint that led to the treaty being revoked; but they are also the immediate cause of the war, ἐξ ὅτου it came about. See A. W. Gomme, *A Historical Commentary on Thucydides,* vol. 1, pp. 153–54; G. E. M. de Ste. Croix, *The Origins of the Peloponnesian War,* p. 51 seq.

18. *OT* 109.

19. 398, where γνώμη is opposed to the reliance on oracular signs.

20. Thuc 1.144; more generally for the role of γνώμη and rational inquiry, see Edmunds, CI. The importance of such language in the *Oedipus Tyrannus* has often been remarked, notably by Bernard Knox in his brilliant article "Why Is Oedipus Called Tyrannos?" *CJ* 50 (1954), reprinted in his *Word and Action* [WA], with its compelling suggestion that what Oedipus resembles is Periclean Athens itself.

21. As Herodotus puts it (2.33), τοῖσι ἐμφανέσι τὰ μὴ γινωσκό-μενα. At *OT* 915–16 Jocasta refers to an inference in the other direction, ἀνὴρ / ἔννους τὰ καινὰ τοῖς πάλαι τεκμαίρεται, and says that

Oedipus is no longer behaving as such a man. In fact, that is just what he is beginning to do.

22. *Od.* 11.271 seq.: Epikaste, in her ignorance, μέγα ἔργον ἔρεξεν, a monstrous thing; cf. Aesch. *Ag.* 1546, of what Clytemnestra did. It is significant that Epikaste left Oedipus with many woes, ὅσσα τε μητρὸς Ἐρινύες ἐκτελέουσιν, 280.

23. Arist. *Ath. Pol.* 1; Plut. *Solon* 12. I owe these points to Burkert, p. 77 seq. The idea that belief in blood pollution grew up in the post-Homeric period was advanced by Dodds in GI, but it is possible that its absence from Homer follows some familiar patterns of Homeric reticence. Parker, p. 16 (and cf. pp. 66 seq., 130), suggests that the impression of a rise in the belief is largely based on comparing two genres, epic and tragedy: what needs explaining is the rise of tragedy, with its typical subject matter of violence in the family. For purification as "a science of division", a drawing of boundaries, see Parker, chap. 1 (and his reference to Mr. Jaggers, pp. 18–19).

24. Plato *Leg.* 831A, 865 seq. There are, as usual, skeptical voices to be heard in Euripides (cf. *IT* 380 seq., *HF* 1234), though Dodds's remark (GI chap. 2, n. 43) that Euripides "protested against it" is surely too strong. For rationalistic comments on the associated matter of purifications for mental disturbance, see Hippoc. *De morb sacr.* 1.42. See G. E. R. Lloyd, *Magic, Reason and Experience,* pp. 44–45 al., who emphasises the continuities between religious purifications and practices closer to a medical science.

25. For the relations of event, action, causality, and intention, the fundamental work is that of Donald Davidson: see his *Essays on Actions and Events.*

26. *OT* 744–45.

27. *OC* 960 seq.

28. Parker, p. 130, writes, "It seems that the author of the *Tetralogies* has taken the doctrine of pollution to a theoretical extreme some way beyond the level of unease that in practice it created." In a sense this is correct, but Parker means, I think, that the concern of the *Tetralogies* involves the unease itself, and there seems to me no reason to believe this. They represent casuistry, not religion. Adkins, MR p. 102 seq., takes the arguments about causality to be entirely motivated by anxiety about pollution.

29.   Modern readers may not be surprised to learn that the physician, at any rate, was not going to pay the penalty: he was indemnified, 3 *Tetral.* 3.5.

30.   Plut. *Per.* 36.

31.   2 *Tetral.* 2.3, ἔβαλε μέν e.q.s. ἔβαλε must mean "hit"; cf. 2.5, οὐδένα γὰρ ἔβαλε, and 3.5, the parallelism of βαλόντα and τρῶσαι. The argument is simply that the defendant's hitting him was not the cause of his death.

32.   In modern law, a spectator can be held to have put himself at risk by attending and be barred from recovering damages when he is struck by a puck hit out of the rink during an ice-hockey match: Murray v. Harringay Arena Ltd. [1951] 2 K.B. 529, cited by H. L. A. Hart and A. M. Honoré, *Causation in the Law,* p. 199.

33.   This does not mean that it is unintelligible in nonmagical terms that the Greeks should have had the practice. Plato *Leg.* 865E refers to the anger of the victim's relatives at seeing the killer in his usual haunts; such anger can lead to vendetta. Cf. Parker, p. 118.

34.   Palsgraf v. Long Island Railroad Co. (1928) 248 N.Y. 339, 162 N.E. 99. The agent must have been in some degree negligent, but round a very small seed of negligence there can grow a large crystal of liability. Cf. *Restatement of the Law of Torts,* par. 430: "In order that a negligent actor shall be liable for another's harm, it is necessary . . . that the negligence of the actor be the legal cause of the other's harm"; and one requirement of the negligent conduct being a "legal cause" of the harm is that it be "a substantial factor in bringing about the harm" (431). The interpretation of "a substantial factor" and related matters (cf. 432 seq.) brings in questions of what is a necessary condition, a contributing cause, and so forth, which would be entirely recognisable to the author of the *Tetralogies.* For a type of case in which different conclusions were reached about causation (and a plaintiff in New Jersey succeeded, while a plaintiff in Pennsylvania failed, on almost identical facts) see Hart and Honoré p. 95.

Hart and Honoré hold it as an aim of jurisprudence that the causal construal of the happening should be made independently of the need for recompense. It is disputed whether this ideal can be met. For a forceful statement of the contrary view, cf. Cardozo ChJ in *Palsgraf:* "A cause, but not the proximate cause. What we . . . mean by the word 'proximate' is that because of convenience, of public policy, of a rough sense of justice, the law arbitrarily declines to trace a series of events beyond a certain point. This is not logic. It is practical politics." In *Palsgraf*, in fact, the courts finally found for the railroad; what happened to the plaintiff was thought to be (very roughly speaking) too remotely connected to the act.

35. For a classic statement in United States law, see Jackson's judgement in Morisette v. U.S., 342 US 246 (1951). On the question of intention and foresight, mentioned above, see H. L. A. Hart, *Punishment and Responsibility*, p. 119 seq.; and on negligence, p. 145 seq.

36. The idea is emphasised by Hart, who most helpfully insists (*Punishment*, p. 38 seq.) that the (broad) restriction of punishment to the voluntary can be based on a general demand of freedom and need not be attached to a notion of "moral culpability". It is important, however, that his argument is concerned with *punishment*. The civil law, as I have said in the text, raises further issues. There, the aim of increasing citizens' control over their lives can take other forms, such as no-fault insurance. These issues raise a very basic question, whether the liberal aim is to be understood as merely restrictive, protecting the citizen against unpredictable incursions specifically by the state, or as positively encouraging policies to advance individual freedom and control more broadly.

37. *OT* 1331 αὐτόχειρ, the same word that he applied at 266 to the murderer of Laius.

38. *OC* 437 seq. According to the *Oedipus at Colonus*, his banishment was not self-inflicted and came a long time after the blinding.

39. *OC* 266–67 τά γ᾽ ἔργα μου / πεπονθότ᾽ ἐστὶ μᾶλλον ἢ δεδρακότα (translation in text by Robert Fitzgerald). Cf. 539 οὐκ ἔρεξα. The quoted comment is by Adkins, MR p. 105 (he connects the passage immediately to his discussion of the *Tetralogies*).

40. Chap. 1, p. 19.

41. It is not suggested that the project of murdering the leaders was in itself a sign of insanity. As the reported words of Calchas show (758 seq.), Ajax has always been περισσός, ὠμός, δεινός; as the Chorus says after his death, he was στερεόφρων (926), ὠμόφρων (930). The significance of what he actually has done lies in its contrast with his normal ἦθος: cf. 182–83 οὔποτε γὰρ φρενόθεν γ᾽ ἐπ᾽ ἀριστερά /

. . . ἔβας. For a different emphasis, stressing a sense in which Ajax's normal ἦθος is itself abnormal, see R. P. Winnington-Ingram, *Sophocles: An Interpretation,* chap. 2; see also Goldhill, pp. 181–98. Inasmuch as the conception of Ajax's general abnormality rests on a contrast with Homeric prototypes, there is a useful corrective in Vernant's characterization (IMA pp. 43–45) of the extremity of Achilles.

42.   59, 66, 207, 215, 452 al.

43.   51–52; and cf. Ajax's own description at 447–48, κεἰ μὴ τόδ᾽ ὄμμα καὶ φρένες διάστροφοι / γνώμης ἀπῇξαν τῆς ἐμῆς, where γνώμη plays a different role, as his normal judgement or plan.

44.   118 seq.; trans. John Moore. This remarkable speech already shows an Odysseus who is not trapped at the level of the later arguments, and the point is underlined when Menelaus dismissively refers to Ajax at 1257 as ἀνδρὸς οὐκέτ᾽ ὄντος, ἀλλ᾽ ἤδη σκιᾶς: Odysseus knows that it is not dying that makes one that.

45.   γέλωτος 367.

46.   I take it that at no point does he go back on his decision. The boring controversy whether the great speech at 647 seq. is sincere or a *Trugrede* has now been overcome, in particular by the work of M. Sicherl, "The Tragic Issue in Sophocles' *Ajax,*" YCS 25 (1977). As Sicherl excellently says, about his death Ajax speaks as Heracleitus says of the oracle at Delphi: οὔτε λέγει οὔτε κρύπτει, ἀλλὰ σημαίνει. He is not speaking to the others—indeed he does not address them, except at the end; and he is not speaking to himself either—as Goldhill points out (p. 192), that in itself would not solve any problems. But he is speaking from himself. Perhaps the most remarkable of the ambiguities, pointed out by many critics, is at 658–59: γαίας is to be understood with ὀρύξας, not with ἔνθα, which refers to his body: this is confirmed by the phrase in Tekmessa's announcement at 899, κρυφαίῳ φασγάνῳ περιπτυχής.

47.   By David Furley, "Euripides on the Sanity of Herakles," *Studies in Honour of T. B. L. Webster,* vol. 1, ed. J. H. Betts, J. T. Hooker, and J. R. Green. He points out that the same case was made independently by Jacqueline de Romilly, "Le refus du suicide dans l'*Heraclès* d'Euripide," *Archaiognosia* 1 (1980). On the general disposition of characters in Euripides, as opposed to other tragedy, to change their

minds, see Bernard Knox, "Second Thoughts in Greek Tragedy," *Greek, Roman and Byzantine Studies* 7 (1966), reprinted in WA.

48.   εἴρηκας ἐπιτυχόντος ἀνθρώπου λόγους *HF* 1248. Later Theseus promises him gifts, fame, and, after his death, sacrifices: but this speech (1311–39) itself ends with the consideration that what Heracles needs is a φίλος.

49.   *HF* 1348. "Friendly support" is a (weak) rendering of φιλία, a term that, as many writers have pointed out, has broader social implications than "friendship": see, for example, Goldhill, chap. 4; and Mary Whitlock-Blundell, *Helping Friends and Harming Enemies: A Study in Sophocles and Greek Ethics.*

NOTES TO CHAPTER IV

1.   *Ajax* 690; trans. John Moore.

2.   ἀρκτέον *OT* 628, ἀκουστέον 1170; ὁποῖα δραστέ᾽ ἐστίν *Trach.* 1204. There are many other examples.

3.   *Il.* 9.379 seq. οὐδ᾽ εἴ μοι δεκάκις τε καὶ εἰκοσάκις τόσα δοίη; 22.349 seq. Bernard Knox has well detailed this characteristic of Sophoclean heroes in *The Heroic Temper.* On the Homeric influence on Sophocles, see in particular Knox, and Pat Easterling, "The Tragic Homer," *BICS* 31 (1984).

4.   Adkins is full of such assumptions. Cf. also, on the Homeric Hector, W. J. Verdenius, quoted by Redfield, p. 119: "[Die] Möglichkeit des Zweifels kommt für Hektor nicht einmal in Frage. Seine Ehre treibt ihn nicht mit einem mahnendem 'Du Sollst' zum Kampfe, sondern sie geht unmittelbar und von selbst in die Tat über." On this speech of Hector's, see below, p. 79 and n. 12.

5.   English translation, 1734–38; the original verse was by Jean-François Sarrasin (1603–54). I owe this quotation to Howard Clarke, *Homer's Readers,* p. 133. The idea that the psychology of Achilles and other Homeric heroes is literally infantile is accepted by W. Thomas MacCary, *Childlike Achilles: Ontogeny and Phylogeny in the Iliad,* who aims to "speak simultaneously of the ontogeny of the ego in Freudian terms and the phylogeny of Western man in Hegelian terms." Not surprisingly, his project is heavily dependent on Snell.

6. Many who use the Kantian categories, for instance in discussing the Greeks, fail to realise how much of Kant's own philosophy they would have to accept if they were to have any basis for the contrasts they take for granted. On this point, see my *Ethics and the Limits of Philosophy*, esp. chap. 4.

7. The description has recently been challenged by J. T. Hooker in an article ("Homeric Society: A Shame-culture?" *Greece and Rome* 34 [1987]) that is unpersuasive because it never makes clear what is being denied. I shall claim later (see p. 91 seq. below) that there is something misleading in the description, but that it nevertheless marks some real contrasts between the archaic world (and later Greek society as well) and our own.

8. For a rather more complex account of the basic experiences of shame and how they come to be elaborated, see Endnote 1.

9. There are two Greek roots bearing the sense of "shame": αἰδ-, as here and in the noun αἰδώς, and αἰσχυν-, as in the noun αἰσχύνη. I have not been generally concerned to separate uses of the two kinds of word. Not much turns on the distinction, for my purposes, and, in particular, many of the variations are diachronic: in most connections, αἰσχυν- terms tend to replace αἰδ- ones. G. P. Shipp (*Studies in the Language of Homer,* 2d ed., p. 191) points out that the middle αἰσχύνομαι occurs only three times in Homer, and only in the *Odyssey:* "This is the beginning of the replacement of αἰδέομαι, completed in Attic prose." Cf. *Il.* 22.105–6, discussed later in the text (p. 79), with *Od.* 21.323–4. Herodotus, Shipp continues, uses both verbs, with a differentiation of sense: αἰδέομαι + acc., to "respect the power etc. of"; αἰσχύνομαι, to "be ashamed". In Attic, αἰσχύνομαι took over both these senses: cf. Eur. *Ion* 934 αἰσχύνομαι μέν σ᾽, ὦ γέρον, λέξω δ᾽ ὅμως with *HF* 1160 αἰσχύνομαι γὰρ τοῖς δεδραμένοις κακοῖς. See also Barrett on Eur. *Hipp.* 244.

10. Odysseus naked: *Od.* 6.221–22 (and see below, n. 24); Aphrodite and Ares: 8.234; Nausikaa's marriage: 6.66; Penelope: 18.184; Thetis: *Il.* 24.90–91; crying: *Od.* 8.86; Isoc. 7.48.

11. Ajax: *Il.* 15.561; Nestor: 661; battle cry: e.g., 5.787. Here and elsewhere for Homeric materials I am indebted to Redfield, p. 115 seq. The Greeks in front of Hector, below, 7.93. Such passages make it mysterious what Hooker can mean when he says that the passage

about Hector's feelings referred to in the next note and the related passage in book 6 are the only places in the *Iliad* where "'shame' before specific persons [is] adduced as a motive for a certain course of conduct" (p. 122).

12.   *Il.* 22.105 seq. On this speech as a whole, see (contra Verdenius at n. 4 above) Redfield's remark that the most significant fact about it is that Hector makes it about himself: "In describing himself he lets us know that he is aware that others are different and that he could have been different" (p. 119). There is a very similar formula at *Od.* 21.323–24. For more on the associations of αἰδώς and fear, see n. 24 below.

13.   The fact that it covers such a range is very important for the character of αἰδώς. In particular, it is central to the question whether the term covers not only what we call "shame" but also some aspects of what we call "guilt". See below, p. 90 and Endnote 1.

14.   P. 115. Achilles: *Il.* 11.649.

15.   Cf. Redfield, p. 158, on αἰδώς as a "socializing emotion".

16.   Poseidon: *Il.* 13.122. The other examples: *Il.* 2.223, 24.463; *Od.* 2.136, 1.263, 22.489, 2.64 al.; Redfield, p. 117. On the suitors, cf. Long, MV p. 139: "Since the only coercion, short of force in Homer, is through *aidos,* the intention of the poet is to paint them as little better than the Cyclopes, the *athemistoi,* men who have put themselves beyond the pale of acceptable human conduct."

17.   This point is related to one made by Long (MV p. 122 seq.) in criticism of Adkins's dichotomy between "competitive" and "cooperative" virtues, that since the competitive virtues aim, according to Adkins, at success, and the archaic Greeks knew well that cooperation was necessary to success, the competitive virtues would have to embrace some of the cooperative ones.

18.   Quoted by Clarke, p. 137. For what it is that makes the gifts odious to Achilles, see Vernant's admirable description, IMA p. 48.

19.   This is compatible, of course, with the recognition by the Greeks that, as Dover puts it (GPM p. 228), "the hope of praise is a major incentive to virtue and the fear of reproach a major deterrent to wrong-doing." Some of the passages he cites directly make this point, such as Dem. 25.93: the majority "through fear of the courts and the pain inflicted by shaming words and reproaches" take care to do no

wrong. But it is significant that several of the passages he cites say various rather different things. Demosthenes at 4.10 and 1.27 merely says that [shame] is a great penalty or compulsion on free or right-thinking men, and the phrases he uses (ἡ τῶν πραγμάτων αἰσχύνη, τὴν ὑπὲρ τῶν πραγμάτων αἰσχύνην) emphasise a reaction to events rather than the force of public opinion. At 8.51 he distinguishes between a free man who dreads adverse opinion and a slave who is motivated only by fear of bodily pain; this says nothing about what the free man's other motives may be. Lycurg. *Leoc.* 46 says that praise is "the only reward that good men expect for the dangers they accept," which does not say or imply that they do everything for reward; while Xen. *Cyr.* 1.5.12 is making the converse, and again very different, point that if you want praise, you must face dangers.

20.   Members of some religious groups have insisted on covering themselves when naked, for instance when bathing: this is presumably in face of supernatural observation. Cf. St. Paul's cryptic remark that women should be veiled διὰ τοὺς ἀγγέλους, "because of the angels" (I Cor. 11.10); many, after Tertullian, have connected this with Genesis 6.1–4. "'Is it true that God is present everywhere?' a little girl asked her mother. 'I think that's indecent'": Nietzsche, *The Gay Science,* preface to the second edition, sec. 4.

21.   *Od.* 19.146 = 24.136; "hold it against me" is νεμεσήσῃ.

22.   νεμεσσήθητε καὶ αὐτοί, / ἄλλους τ' αἰδέσθητε περικτίονας ἀνθρώπους *Od.* 2.64–65.

23.   ὥς ἐρέουσιν, ἐμοὶ δέ κ' ὀνείδεα ταῦτα γένοιτο. / καὶ δ' ἄλλῃ νεμεσῶ, ἥ τις τοιαῦτά γε ῥέζοι *Od.* 6.285–86; Lattimore has "disapprove" for νεμεσῶ, which is entirely appropriate, but in the context of the present discussion begs some questions.

24.   The Greeks found it easy to associate fear and αἰδώς, but this itself has to be understood in the light of the point emphasised in the text, that an agent may fear public opinion or an individual's reactions and at the same time have internalised feelings about the behaviour that is expected of him; his fear may indeed imply such feelings. Not only is there a gradation from simple fear to more complexly social feelings; there are also relevant gradations in what fear may be of— blows, abuse, disapproval, rejection by an admired figure or group. This is illustrated in Homer even with feelings directed to individuals:

Il. 24.435 τὸν μὲν ἐγὼ δείδοικα καὶ αἰδέομαι περὶ κῆρι, about Achilles; *Od.* 17.188, a similar formula for fear of a master's anger. It is interesting to compare a passage already mentioned, *Od.* 6.221–22, where Odysseus says simply αἰδέομαι γὰρ / γυμνοῦσθαι κούρῃσιν ἐυπλοκάμοισι μετελθών, with the account that he gives to Alkinous of the same incident (7.305–6), ἀλλ' ἐγὼ οὐκ ἔθελον δείσας αἰσχυνόμενός τε, / μή πως καὶ σοὶ θυμὸς ἐπισκύσσαιτο ἰδόντι. This is not the motive he was expressing in the earlier passage, but equally it is not a motive of an entirely different sort.

Δέος is sometimes directly associated with αἰδώς or αἰσχύνη in public and political connections, for instance at Soph. *Ajax* 1073–80. This and other similar passages are interestingly discussed by Edmunds, CI p. 59 seq. and Appendix, in arguing for his solution to a much discussed obscurity at Thuc. 2.42.2, where he takes δέους to represent the fallen citizens' courage and public spirit, aptly citing Plut. *Cleom.* 9 τὴν ἀνδρείαν δέ μοι δοκοῦσιν οὐκ ἀφοβίαν ἀλλὰ φόβον ψόγου καὶ δέος ἀδοξίας οἱ παλαιοὶ νομίζειν. The point in the text might be put by saying that one cannot fear ἀδοξία without having some attitudes towards those things that make for δόξα.

25.   *Ajax* 462 seq.

26.   479–80. "should" is χρή, and, as often, it represents the internalisation of these conceptions: cf. chap. 2, n. 57.

27.   *Antigones.*

28.   *Ant.* 31.

29.   The sexual imagery has often been remarked; it is recurrent from 73 φίλη μετ' αὐτοῦ κείσομαι, φίλου μέτα to the later (e.g., 891) images of marriage.

30.   *Phil.* 79 seq. Notice the repetition in φύσει . . . πεφυκότα, which by stressing the matter of character prepares the way to setting it aside; and ἀλλ' ἡδὺ γάρ, which in two words moves from offering an opposing consideration to giving it as a reason. On Neoptolemus as γενναῖος, see Martha Nussbaum, "Consequences and Character in Sophocles' *Philoctetes*," *Philosophy and Literature* 1 (1976–77). The whole play rewards study from the point of view of the operations of shame.

31.   As at *Il.* 13.278 ὅ τε δειλὸς ἀνὴρ ὅς τ' ἄλκιμος ἐξεφαάνθη.

32.   Neoptolemus's lines are at 94–95, and 120: ἴτω ποήσω,

πᾶσαν αἰσχύνην ἀφείς. Notice Neoptolemus's question at 110: "How do you look at someone when you are deceiving them?" For ἀφεῖναι meaning "neglect", cf. *OC* 1537 τὰ θεῖ' ἀφείς.

33. Gregory Vlastos, "Happiness and Virtue in Socrates' Moral Theory," *PCPS* 1984, p. 188.

34. *Phil.* 1383.

35. For this and other differences, see the very brief but very suggestive discussion by Herbert Morris, "Guilt and Shame," in his *On Guilt and Innocence*. For an illuminating discussion from a psychoanalytical perspective, which reaches some conclusions similar to my own and suggests further some ineliminable functions of guilt, see Richard Wollheim, *The Thread of Life,* chap. 7, especially pp. 220–21.

36. *Pride, Shame and Guilt,* p. 81.

37. It is typical of shame that one cannot meet another's eye, as in the case of Ajax and Telamon (see above, p. 85). Cf. Agathon frag. 22 Nauck ἀδικεῖν νομίζων ὄψιν αἰδοῦμαι φίλων; Dover, GPM p. 236.

38. For accounts broadly on the lines that follow, see John Rawls, *A Theory of Justice,* secs. 67, 70–75; and Alan Gibbard, *Wise Choices, Apt Feelings,* chap. 7. These two treatments do differ substantially, but in respects that are not the present concern. Gibbard suggests, though he does not insist on, ways in which the distinction between shame and guilt might be related to the ethology of cooperation.

39. See Dover, GPM p. 195 seq. (and references at p. 195 to earlier discussions in the book), p. 200 seq.

40. Gibbard makes this point in his discussion of self-ascription. He also interestingly refers to some other types of ethical experience, drawn from other societies, which occupy roughly the same area as guilt and shame, but which are considerably more exotic, from our point of view, than those of the Homeric Greeks.

41. On the question of how effectively moral and nonmoral dispositions can be distinguished at all, the admirable appendix IV of Hume's *Enquiry Concerning the Principles of Morals* remains an indispensable text.

42. Rawls gives a good account of such a case, in terms of his own theory of the moral emotions, at p. 445.

43. Another incoherence is added when the ideal of autonomy (discussed later in this chapter) is added to these three. On this, see Endnote 1, p. 219.

44. The direct expression is at 373 seq. The passage presents several difficulties, and commentators have called into question what distinction, if any, it makes between kinds of αἰδώς. I discuss the difficulties and argue for the interpretation mentioned in the text in Endnote 2, p. 225. For a compact description of Phaedra's relations to shame and reputation, cf. the words of the Chorus in their prescient description of her suicide, 772–75: δαίμονα στυγνὸν καται-δεσθεῖσα τάν τ' εὔ/δοξον ἀνθαιρουμένα φήμαν ἀπαλλάσ/σουσά τ' ἀλγεινὸν φρενῶν ἔρωτα. καταιδεῖσθαι + acc. often means "to feel reverence before", "to stand in awe of" (cf. *Or.* 682), and LSJ cites the present passage in this sense. This requires one to take δαίμονα στυγνὸν to refer to some deity, which is implausible in itself (cf. Barrett ad loc.) and does nothing for the force of ἀνθαιρουμένα: Phaedra *substitutes* good reputation for something (or tries to do so), namely, for the life that she has led and would have to go on leading with her passion. This is her δαίμονα, and καταιδεσθεῖσα means that she is ashamed of it.

45. *Hipp.* 1074 seq.

46. "Shame and Purity in Euripides' *Hippolytus*," *Hermes* 98 (1970), p. 287. Segal follows R. P. Winnington-Ingram, "*Hippolytus:* A Study in Causation," in *Euripide: Entretiens sur l'antiquité classique,* vol. 6, p. 185, in drawing a parallel between Hippolytus's situation and Plato's description of the misunderstood just man (which follows in the text). It is difficult to determine how close the parallel is, because we are not told exactly how Plato's just man is misunderstood (and the reference to Aeschylus does not help; see n. 47). But the echoes of Socrates' case and the general force of the example surely suggest that this man has an unconventional conception of justice: he "appears" unjust because others wrongly construe the character he really has as an unjust one, not because they falsely think that his activities are unjust by standards that both he and they would accept. If this is right, the contrast of appearance and reality in Plato's example does not coincide exactly with any of the contrasts deployed in the *Hippolytus*.

An idea attributed to Democritus (also cited by Segal) certainly comes close to concerns of the *Hippolytus:* frag. 244 DK πολὺ μᾶλλον τῶν ἄλλων σεαυτὸν αἰσχύνεσθαι; frag. 264 DK ἑωυτὸν μάλιστα αἰδεῖσθαι. The latter fragment, at any rate, makes it clear that the main concern is that one should not choose to act badly because other people will not know about it. It is thus not a new thought, though its expression may be original.

Three other fragments of Democritus (62, 68, 89 DK) say that when you are assessing a man's character, what he wants is as significant as what he does. There is a slightly moralistic spin on W. K. C. Guthrie's report of these fragments: "In assessing a man's worth, intention is no less important than action" (*A History of Greek Philosophy,* vol. 2, p. 491). The thought is clearly (and very un-Kantianly) expressed in frag. 89, ἐχθρὸς οὐχ ὁ ἀδικέων, ἀλλὰ ὁ βουλόμενος.

47. *Rep.* 361A–C. The reference to Aeschylus seems to be to *Septem* 592, about Amphiaraus, οὐ γὰρ δοκεῖν ἄριστος, ἀλλ᾽ εἶναι θέλει. Cf. 361B8 οὐ δοκεῖν ἀλλ᾽ εἶναι ἀγαθὸν ἐθέλοντα. It is unclear what contrast precisely Plato intends to mark (see n. 46), but it is certainly different from the point about Amphiaraus, in a way to which the shift from ἄριστος to ἀγαθός contributes. With Amphiaraus, the contrast between εἶναι and δοκεῖν, reality and mere appearance (or repute), is that between delivery and promise, actual deeds as contrasted with mere boasts and display.

48. See my "The Analogy of City and Soul in Plato's *Republic.*"

49. These interlocking assumptions are particularly clear in Adkins, MR.

50. *Il.* 11.762. There are four other places in Homer where the phrase occurs. Editors have discussed the exact force of εἰ; but the general effect is that there was in the past a reality that it is now difficult to bring before one. The present passage is usually read as though τώς went with the second ἔον: "So I was, if ever I was so." But I think it is clear that ἔον should be read absolutely. This is what is meant elsewhere. At *Il.* 3.180, Helen does not mean "Agamemnon was my brother-in-law, if he was my brother-in-law," but ". . . if there was such a person"; at *Il.* 24.426 ἐμὸς πάϊς, εἴ ποτ᾽ ἔην γε means ". . . if I ever had one"; and it is particularly useful to compare with each other and with the present passage *Od.* 15.267–68 πατὴρ δέ μοί

ἐστιν Ὀδυσσεύς, / εἴ ποτ' ἔην and *Od.* 19.315 οἶος Ὀδυσσεὺς ἔσκε μετ' ἀνδράσιν, εἴ ποτ' ἔην γε.

51. *All's Well That Ends Well* 4.3.330–34, 337–38.

NOTES TO CHAPTER V

1. *Il.* 1. 5; cf. chap. 3, n. 5.

2. Homer often refers to elsewhere, above all where the heroes have come from, e.g., *Il.* 18.101–2, 9.393–94; to past time and peace time, as in the activities described in the similes and the description of the shield in book 18; and to future time, as in the account, 12.13–34, of how Poseidon and Apollo after the war swept away all traces of the Greek wall, and in Hector's challenge, 7.67–91, which links the future to his own deeds, when he speaks of a man who in time to come may see from his boat the tomb of a hero who died long before, killed by Hector, τὸ δ' ἐμὸν κλέος οὔ ποτ' ὀλεῖται.

3. Hes. *Theog.* 385 seq. West ad loc. mentions the passage from Pausanias, 2.4.6. προσάγοντες τὰς ἀνάγκας Thuc. 1.99.1.

4. *Il.* 24.750–53. However, the standard practice on capturing a city was rather to kill the men and enslave the women; on this and the present passage, see Redfield, p. 120. This occurred in historical times, e.g., in the Peloponnesian war: for Scione in 421 B.C. see Thuc. 5.32.1; and there is the case of Melos, 416 B.C., famous from the dialogue in Thucydides book 5. A man can be a slave among a foreign people in the *Odyssey*: 14.272, 297.

5. *Il.* 6.450 seq.

6. E.g., AS, p. 67. I am heavily indebted to this and other work by Finley on this subject.

7. Plato assimilated them to slaves in *Leg.* 776B seq.; they were called ἡ δουλεία in a treaty between Sparta and Athens of 421 B.C., reported by Thucydides, 5.23.3. For the terms of the conditions on the Messenians, see Pausanias 4.14. G. E. M. de Ste. Croix claims that they were "state serfs" in "Slavery and Other Forms of Unfree Labour" (in a volume of that title edited by Leonie Archer). The ephors on taking office each year had to make a declaration of war on the helots so that they became official enemies of the state and could be killed as necessary without incurring pollution (Plut. *Lyc.* 28.7). De

Ste. Croix has remarked (p. 24) that this extraordinary practice of a government's formally declaring war on its own work force is probably unparalleled. For their readiness to revolt, cf., among others, Thuc. 4.80.3, Arist. *Pol.* 1269a38–39.

8. Arist. *Pol.* 1253b32, 1254a9.

9. Quem patrem, qui servos est? Plaut. *Capt.* 574, quoted by Finley, AS p. 75. Practice was by no means everywhere the same. The Gortynian code in Crete allowed marriage between a free woman and a man who was not free (but perhaps not the converse); this example is cited by R. F. Willetts in a discussion of the situation in Argos in the early fifth century: "The Servile Interregnum at Argos," *Hermes* 87 (1959).

10. In Rome, cf. Hor. *Serm.* 1.2.116–19; and the remarks of Seneca the Elder (*Controv.* 4 praef. 10) on passive buggery, that it is *impudicitia* in the free, a necessity for a slave, and an *officium* for a freedman.

11. E.g., Ar. *Thesm.* 930–1125; *Lys.* 435–52. Other material in Thomas Wiedemann, *Greek and Roman Slavery*.

12. Cf. Ar. *Plut.* 520 seq. "A species of hunting or war": Arist. *Pol.* 1255b37.

13. Xen. *Mem.* 2.3.3. Finley, AS p. 81; the Erechtheum, p. 101. It seems that master sculptors, master painters, and architects were not slaves: for the last, see James Coulton, *Ancient Greek Architects at Work,* chap. 1. (I owe this point to Mr. Andrew Stewart.)

14. Ar. *Vesp.* 1297–98, 1307.

15. σεσημασμένα τῷ δημοσίῳ σημάντρῳ *Poroi* 4. 21. Xenophon is proposing a new departure in the state ownership of slaves, but he must be referring to a familiar practice. Ar. *Av.* 760 is compatible with the brand being applied just to recaptured runaways.

16. Dem. 22.3; Antiphon *1 Tetral.* 2.7; Arist. *Rhet.* 1376b31 seq.; Lys. 4.10–17.

17. E. Levy, quoted by Finley, AS p. 97.

18. *Digest* 1.5.5 [Marcianus].

19. The first fragment was attributed to the comic writer Philemon, of the fourth century B.C., by Kock (frag. 95), but in this he followed, after Meineke, an error made by Rutgers in 1618 in copying out the name of a Roman collection, the so-called *Comparison of Me-*

nander and Philistion: see R. Kassel and C. Austin, *Poetae comici Graeci,* 7: 317. The author and the date of the verses are unknown.

Alcidamas ap. schol. Arist. *Rhet.* 1. 13.3: ἐλευθέρους ἀφῆκε πάντας θεός, οὐδένα δοῦλον ἡ φύσις πεποίηκεν. The translation attempts to capture two senses of ἀφῆκε, "sent out" and "set free".

20. W. L. Newman, *The Politics of Aristotle,* vol. 1, pp. 139–42.

21. *Pol.* 1253b20–23.

22. For an attempt to show that Aristotle's argument is at least successful on his own premisses, see W. Fortenbaugh, "Aristotle on Slaves and Women," in *Articles on Aristotle,* vol. 2, ed. J. Barnes, M. Schofield, R. Sorabji (London, 1977); well criticised by Nicholas D. Smith, "Aristotle's Theory of Natural Slavery," *Phoenix* 37 (1983). See also Malcolm Schofield, "Ideology and Philosophy in Aristotle's Theory of Slavery," in *Aristoteles' "Politik",* XI Symposium Aristotelicum, ed. G. Patzig.

23. *Pol.* 1255b13; *EN* 1161b5.

24. R. G. Mulgan, *Aristotle's Political Theory,* pp. 43–44.

25. *Pol.* 1254b fin., 1330a25.

26. Note the order of the derivation at 1254a15–17 and the question that immediately follows at the start of chapter 5. Hegel, in this as in many other respects, was following Aristotle when he gave a deeper content to the obvious fact that slavery is a relational concept.

27. At 1259b34 seq. Aristotle has to make a special point that there are no degrees of command and obedience. Inasmuch as this is not just a verbal point, it is the product of assuming that the institution needed must be slavery.

28. Theognis 535; *Pol.* 1254b27 seq.

29. Cf. Aristotle's own argument that barbarians do not observe the differences between slaves and women and treat women like slaves, because everyone among them is like a slave: 1252a34 seq. For the commonplace about slavish barbarians, cf. Eur. *Hel.* 246 (the verse Aristotle quotes is *IA* 1400). For various implications of the word βάρβαρος, and what peoples were counted as barbarian, cf. Helen H. Bacon, *Barbarians in Greek Tragedy.* On some physiognomic materials in the Aristotelian corpus, see G. E. R. Lloyd, *Science, Folklore and Ideology,* pp. 22–25 [SFI]. For the "scientific" investigation in mod-

ern times of physical traits of the kinds in question, see Stephen Jay Gould, *The Mismeasure of Man.*

30.   AS p. 18.

31.   Seneca *Ben.* 3.20. The view that Christianity was responsible for the abolition of ancient slavery—or indeed was notably opposed to it—was attacked by John Millar in 1771, destroyed by Overbeck in 1875; see Finley, AS p. 14.

32.   1260a12–13. "Lacks authority" is a standard translation for ἄκυρον: it has the disadvantage of its not even looking as though the phrase provided a reason. The word can sustain a more neutral sense of inefficacy: at *GA* 772b28 it means "impotent".

33.   The remark in the Funeral Speech is at Thuc. 2.45.2. For differing views of the situation, see A. W. Gomme, "The Position of Women in Athens in the Fifth and Fourth Centuries," *CP* 20 (1925); and John J. Gould, "Law, Custom and Myth: Aspects of the Social Position of Women in Classical Athens," *JHS* 100 (1980). Source materials can be found in M. R. Lefkowitz and M. Fant, *Women's Life in Greece and Rome.* Dover, GPM p. 95 seq., gives a helpful summary with references, and for a useful outline with bibliography see Helene P. Foley, "Attitudes to Women in Greece" in *The Civilization of the Ancient Mediterranean,* ed. M. Grant and R. Kitzinger. Eva C. Keuls, *The Reign of the Phallus,* emphasises Athenian males' fear of women.

34.   See Nicole Loraux, *Les enfants d' Athéna;* John K. Davies, "Athenian Citizenship," *CJ* 73 (1977): cited by Goldhill, p. 58, who stresses the degree of anxiety generated by questions of citizenship.

35.   See S. C. Humphreys, *The Family, Women and Death,* chap. 1. Humphreys also discusses in this connection the representation of women in tragedy, which is of course a very striking feature of the genre (of the surviving plays, only one, the *Philoctetes,* has no female character). On this see also the very suggestive discussion by Nicole Loraux, FT.

36.   GPM p. 95.

37.   *Od.* 5.117 seq.; "resent" renders ἀγάασθαι (119, 122), which is also the word for the attitude that the gods had towards Odysseus and Penelope being together and enjoying their youth, *Od.* 23.211.

38.   Frag. 524 Nauck (the *Tereus*). Helene Foley, *Ritual Irony:*

Poetry and Sacrifice in Euripides, p. 87, comments that this passage brings marriage very near to slavery.

39.   Recent work has brought out the unique character of Medea's final apotheosis, and the conflict of "male" and "female" elements in her character: Bernard Knox, "The *Medea* of Euripides," *YCS* 25 (1977), reprinted in WA; Ann Norris Michelini, *Euripides and the Tragic Tradition,* p. 87 al. [ETT]; Helene P. Foley, "Medea's Divided Self," *CA* 8 (1989). Her famous final speech has been much discussed in connection with questions of ἀκρασία and the Platonic division of the soul: for an interesting discussion of Stoic views, see Christopher Gill, "Did Chrysippus Understand Medea?" *Phronesis* 28 (1983).

For some scholars, the famous final speech does not belong to the play. Their proposals offer a striking example of the pretensions of textual criticism when it is not controlled by a sense of its function. The whole of *Medea* 1056–80 was deleted by Bergk as spurious, and in this he is followed by Diggle in the latest Oxford text, who refers us to an article by M. Reeve, "Euripides *Medea* 1021–1080," *CQ* n.s. 22 (1972). The passage does present some difficulties of dramatic interpretation. One of the more serious is in fact soluble, if 1079 θυμὸς δὲ κρείσσων τῶν ἐμῶν βουλευμάτων is understood to mean not "my anger is stronger than my reasonings"—βουλεύματα up to this point has always referred to Medea's murderous plans—but "my anger is in charge of my plans": see Hans Diller, "ΘΥΜΟΣ ΔΕ ΚΡΕΙΣΣΩΝ ΤΩΝ ΕΜΩΝ ΒΟΥΛΕΥΜΑΤΩΝ," *Hermes* 94 (1966), supported by G. R. Stanton, "The End of Medea's Monologue: Euripides *Medea* 1078–80," *RhM* N.F. 130 (1987), replying in particular to H. Lloyd-Jones, "Euripides *Medea* 1056–80," *WJA* N.F. 6 (1980). The present concern, however, is not with this or any other particular proposal. The point—and it is a fundamental one—is that even if there are unsolved difficulties of interpretation, it is quite inappropriate to mark the fact by parentheses meaning that the entire passage (a passage well known in antiquity and offering few difficulties at a purely linguistic level) is not part of the play. As Fraenkel wisely said, "when a careful examination of the language and the style has produced no evidence of a corruption and yet the sense remains obscure, then there may be a case, not for putting a dagger against the passage, but for admitting the limits of our comprehension" (*Aeschylus Agamemnon,* vol. 1, p. ix).

In this case, moreover, reflection is called for on what constitutes a difficulty, and whether the notions of "coherence" that the critics so freely deploy are those appropriate to Euripides and this text. Reeve, p. 58, remarkably and revealingly says, referring to an editor who condemned the passage, "If Medea is swaying to and fro, Müller has every right to insist that the audience should know at each moment exactly what is in her mind." For a sensitive treatment, comparing the speech (in particular, the sense in which it is a monologue) with Seneca *Medea* 893–977, see Christopher Gill, "Two Monologues of Self-Division," in *Homo Viator: Classical Essays for John Bramble,* ed. M. and M. Whitby and P. Hardie.

40. Ar. *Ran.* 949–50. See now Anton Powell, ed., *Euripides, Women and Sexuality* (London, 1990).

41. Hermippus: Diog. Laert. 1.33. Aesch. *Ag.* 918 seq.

42. Brown, p. 9 seq.; Thomas Laqueur, "Orgasm, Generation, and the Politics of Reproductive Biology," *Representations* 14 (1986); and see now Laqueur's *Making Sex.* For various theories of the female role in reproduction, and other material on the attitude of Greek medicine to women, see Lloyd, SFI pp. 58–111. It has been remarked that Aristotle's theory of the generation of females is rather oddly related to his general teleology: an essential element in the reproductive economy depends on something going wrong roughly 50 percent of the time. It may be relevant to this anomaly that there is an ethical connection at this point: see below, chap. 6, p. 161.

43. I am indebted to Luc Brisson, *Le mythe de Tirèsias.*

44. Frag. Hes. 275, Merkelbach and West, p. 136 seq. Cf. Hyg. *Fab.* 75; Ov. *Met.* 3.316–39. Brisson refers to the idea that in the animal kingdom the Teiresian analogy is the hyena, which was thought to be male one year and female the next (Ael. *NA* 1.25); the story, often repeated, that it had both organs of sex is dismissed by Aristotle, *GA* 757a2–14.

45. τὸν θηλύμορφον ξένον *Bacch.* 353; cf. 453 seq. Teiresias's persona in the play is interestingly discussed by Paul Roth, "Teiresias as *Mantis* and Intellectual in Euripides' *Bacchae*," *TAPA* 114 (1984). For Teiresias's role elsewhere, see Rebecca W. Bushnell, *Prophesying Tragedy: Sign and Voice in Sophocles' Theban Plays,* p. 56.

46. See, for the second century A.D., Brown, *The Body and Soci-*

ety, p. 9, with references on the importance of the threefold division.

47.   The distinction of sex and gender can itself be criticised from a radical point of view as encouraging a too easy distinction between nature and convention, and an assumption that the body simply belongs to the former. See Carole Pateman, "Sex and Power," *Ethics* 100 (1990), particularly pp. 401–2.

48.   There has been a good deal of debate in recent years about the extent and depth of Plato's feminism: for a helpful discussion, see Gregory Vlastos, "Was Plato a Feminist?" *Times Literary Supplement,* 17–23 March 1989. For a negative view, see Julia Annas, "Plato's *Republic* and Feminism," *Philosophy* 51 (1976).

49.   Complacency in this direction is not necessarily suppressed, and may merely be concealed, by relativism. "Unjust for us" still sounds like an improvement.

50.   GI p. 32.

NOTES TO CHAPTER VI

1.   On Greek conceptions of the natural see in particular G. E. R. Lloyd, *The Revolutions of Wisdom,* esp. chap. 1.

2.   An instructive example is offered by Galileo's false inertial theory of the tides. He took it to be a virtue of this theory that it did not demand any action at a distance by the sun and moon, a type of "influence" that he regarded as—in effect—supernatural: see *Dialogue Concerning the Two Chief World Systems,* The Fourth Day. It has been suggested that, rather similarly, Hippocratic doctors may have ignored infection because they thought it was a superstition: Palmer, *Miasma,* p. 220.

3.   *Metaph.* Λ 7.

4.   This question is sensitively discussed by T. M. Luhrman, *Persuasions of the Witch's Craft: Ritual Magic in Contemporary England;* it is important, and central to her treatment, that her subjects, unlike the ancient Greeks, live in a culture in which the practice of magic runs cognitively against prevailing belief systems. For a valuable discussion of magic and ritual in traditional societies and their relations to scientific explanation, see John Skorupski, *Symbol and Theory.*

5. "Decision and Responsibility in the Tragedy of Aeschylus," *JHS* 86 (1966); reprinted in *Oxford Readings in Greek Tragedy,* ed. Erich Segal [OGT].

6. Denniston and Page, *Agamemnon,* p. xxiv n. 4. For Page's authorship, see n. 24 to chap. 1, p. 173 above.

7. Prometheus: ἀνάγκαις ταῖσδ᾽ ἐνέζευγμαι *PV* 108. Hector: κρατερὴ δέ ἑ λύσσα δέδυκεν *Il.* 9.239.

8. Søren Kierkegaard, *Fear and Trembling* (1843), translated by Alastair Hannay, pp. 87–89. It is in a sense true, as Kierkegaard says, "that the eye of the beholder rests confidently upon" the tragic hero, but that is not because of ethical certainty, but because the spectator is given the confidence of a tragic representation (something that is often not given, in fact, by Euripides). Kierkegaard was contrasting the tragic hero with indeed a different figure, Abraham, whose willingness to proceed against the ethical is not mediated by the ethical at all but proceeds "on the strength of the absurd." "Such a relationship to the divine is unknown to paganism": that, for sure, is true.

9. I used the Agamemnon passage as an example in a purely philosophical discussion in "Ethical Consistency," *PAS Suppl.* 39 (1965), reprinted in *Problems of the Self.* This made the points in question here but distinguished less clearly than I would now want to do between deliberative and moral categories and their relations to "*ought* implies *can*": for some further reflections, see *Ethics and the Limits of Philosophy,* esp. chaps. 1 and 10. Lloyd-Jones correctly argued in "The Guilt of Agamemnon," *CQ* n.s. 12 (1962), reprinted in OGT, that Agamemnon was confronted with a necessary choice between two crimes.

10. FG pp. 32–38. She sees that "there is no incompatibility of choice and necessity here," but gives an inadequate account of the necessity itself. Agamemnon "is under necessity in that his alternatives include no very desirable options" (p. 34). But that formula is not enough to make the point. It captures, at most, the necessity expressed in "he has to choose between X and Y." The necessity at which Agamemnon arrives is that of having to choose X. See further n. 11, on putting on the yoke.

11. The point that we are not intended to see Agamemnon's murderous fury as a reprehensible failing on his part will stand even if

we accept Nussbaum's interpretation of the difficult lines 214–17: παυσανέμου γὰρ θυσίας / παρθενίου θ' αἴματος ὀρ/γᾷ περιόργως ἐπιθυ/μεῖν θέμις. εὖ γὰρ εἴη. But in any case there are objections to it:

1.   She takes the last three words to show that Agamemnon has by this stage come to think that the act is not merely the better of two evils but is "pious and right" (p. 35). This is an over-reading of what sounds like simply a desperate utterance: "[It] may sound hopeful, but there is no real hope in it," as Fraenkel says ad loc.

2.   She takes the previous sentence to express a movement by Agamemnon from thinking the act pious and right to thinking it pious and right to desire it furiously. The text of 215–16 is uncertain, and many editors since the sixteenth century have rejected ἐπιθυμεῖν as a gloss (most recently West). Nussbaum defends the MS text, with Fraenkel (it is certainly better than περιόργῳ σφ' ἐπιθυμεῖν Schoemann, preferred by Denniston and Page, which ascribes the desire to the soldiery or, on a very implausible interpretation, to Artemis). But the MS text itself does not require that the desire should be Agamemnon's own: it merely says that it is appropriate for religious reasons (= θέμις) to have this desire—which can mean for people to have it, for someone to have it, and so on. There are two grounds for not taking it as Nussbaum does:

(*a*)   The γὰρ in 214 should introduce a reason for what has gone before. A general statement that θέμις enjoins a desire for the sacrifice *can* be taken to explain, in a compressed way, why refusing it would be a desertion: I prefer this to supposing it to signal that the decision has already been taken, an idea that applies better to the γὰρ of 217 (cf. Hermann, quoted by Fraenkel). But on any showing it is hard to see how γὰρ in 214 can introduce a decision of Agamemnon's.

(*b*)   Nussbaum's reading weakens the sequential, indeed contrastive, relations between these lines and the following strophe: ἐπεὶ δ' . . . τόθεν . . . μετέγνω. The Chorus is telling us how something strange and terrible followed on Agamemnon's putting on the yoke of necessity, but for Nussbaum, putting on the yoke *is* the step, supposedly expressed in 214–17, of adopting the desire to do these terrible things.

This last point involves what is perhaps the most significant issue, that this reading weakens further the powerful image of the yoke. Besides her vague account of what the necessity is (see n. 10), Nussbaum's reading here has the paradoxical result that Agamemnon puts on the yoke precisely when he finds a way of making things easier for himself.

12.   Cf. "Politics and Moral Character," in *Public and Private Morality,* ed. Stuart Hampshire, and other articles there; it is a special case of a more general phenomenon, of the location of a particular deliberation or class of deliberations in a life or practice, on which see my "Moral Luck," *PAS Suppl.* 50 (1976), reprinted in *Moral Luck.*

13.   Cf. A. A. Long in his notice of Nussbaum's *Fragility of Goodness* (*CP* 83 [1988]), with reference to the *Agamemnon* and also the *Septem* and *Antigone:* "What the audience surely feels, as the principal characters face their predicaments, is the inadequacy of any language, moral sententiousness especially, to do justice to their loss and ruin." The Chorus is of course perfectly capable of criticising Agamemnon, as at 799 seq., a passage that Nussbaum mentions as possibly supporting her interpretation of 214–17: she refers particularly to θράσος [θάρσος Tri.] ἑκούσιον 803, a phrase of which some editors have despaired. But, granted the clear reference to *Od.* 11.438, Ἑλένης μὲν ἀπωλόμεθ᾽ εἵνεκα πολλοί (and cf *Ag.* 1455 seq.), there is no reason to associate 799 seq. with the sacrifice of Iphigeneia at all (as Fraenkel makes very clear in criticism of Ahrens). Nussbaum's assumption that the context "all has to do with Aulis" (p. 433 n. 58) is baseless.

14.   ὡς Soph. *El.* 571. She has said that she is speaking τοῦ τεθνηκότος θ᾽ ὕπερ 554; when she continues in the next line τῆς κασιγνήτης θ᾽ ὁμοῦ, ὕπερ moves from "on behalf of" to "about" (it is "slightly zeugmatic," as Kamerbeek says ad loc.). It is characteristic of Sophocles that he should set the note of advocacy and then neutralise it retrospectively. In Electra's account, Agamemnon's reluctance is of course emphasised, and she says that he was βιασθείς by the divine requirements (575).

15.   Compare Paul Mazon's statement that "la vérité est qu'il eut jamais poème moins religieux que l' *Iliade*" (*Introduction à l'Iliade,* p. 294; quoted by Lesky, GM p. 26). Lesky dismisses the judgement on the ground that the *Iliad* is much concerned with the activities of

gods, but Nietzsche had already seen that it is precisely the way in which Homer treats the gods that makes the point: "Homer is so much at home in the humanised world of his gods and, as a poet, takes such delight in it, that he must have been profoundly irreligious" (*We Classicists* [V 196], UO p. 387).

16. Heracl. frag. 119 DK; Vernant, MT p. 30; R. P. Winnington-Ingram, "Tragedy and Greek Archaic Thought," in *Classical Drama and Its Influence: Essays Presented to H. D. F. Kitto,* ed. M. J. Anderson.

17. *Cho.* 435–37.

18. MT p. 30. Eteocles' "decision": *Sept.* 653 seq.

19. As A. A. Long has remarked in "Pro and Contra Fratricide—Aeschylus *Septem* 653–719," in *Studies in Honour of T. B. L. Webster.* Long comments on the extraordinary effect of Eteocles' outburst at the beginning of his speech, as a response to the Messenger's speech and its closing remark that Eteocles knows how to govern the city.

20. γὰρ 695.

21. O. Regenbogen, quoted by R. P. Winnington-Ingram, *Studies in Aeschylus,* p. 16.

22. Herodotus (9.16) tells the story of a Persian who sees that the Persian army is soon going to be annihilated. A Greek asks whether he should not tell those in charge. He replies, ὅ τι δεῖ γενέσθαι ἐκ τοῦ θεοῦ ἀμήχανον ἀποτρέψαι ἀνθρώπῳ. But he does give a reason why he cannot affect the outcome—no one believes you, even when you are telling the truth. Cf. Seth Benardete, *Herodotean Inquiries,* p. 210.

23. Eurymachus: *Od.* 2.181–82. The oracle is a device most typically of Aeschylean and Sophoclean tragedy. Cf. J. C. Kamerbeek "Prophecy and Tragedy," *Mnemosyne* 4 (1965), p. 38: "It is only logical that as *tuche*'s part in the dramatization of human destiny grows, the essential significance of oracles and prophecies is lessened, and as a matter of fact we hardly find in Euripides any scene of prophecy equal to the Cassandra scene of the *Agamemnon* or the Teiresias scene in the *Oedipus Tyrannus* in depth or scope of meaning," quoted by Bushnell, p. 114. Parker, *Miasma,* p. 13 seq., gives a useful caution against assuming that these tragic devices straightforwardly represent popular belief; remarking in particular that there are no grandiose divine causes in Old Comedy and that in high literature

the seer is always right, in comedy always wrong (p. 15; references given in n. 69).

24.   *Cho.* 297–98 τοιοῖσδε χρησμοῖς ἆρα χρὴ πεποιθέναι; / κεἰ μὴ πέποιθα, τοὐργόν ἐστ᾽ ἐργαστέον. It is simplest to refer χρησμοῖς to the conditionally predictive part of the oracle, which tells the hideous things that will happen to him if he does not obey. This leaves ambiguous, and perhaps properly so, θεοῦ τ᾽ ἐφετμαὶ at 300, and whether they do or do not belong with his other motives. 900–901 ποῦ δαὶ [δὴ Auratus] τὸ λοιπὸν [Nauck: τὰ λοιπὰ M] Λοξίου μαντεύματα / τὰ πυθόχρηστα, πιστά τ᾽ εὐορκώματα; There are here and in many other places genuine textual problems, but, as usual, some editors have expressed their own puzzlement or alarm in unnecessary violence to the text. On the whole matter, see Deborah H. Roberts, *Apollo and His Oracle in the Oresteia,* who is sensitive to the relations between oracular credibility and other religious and ethical considerations.

25.   The story is that a man in Baghdad hears that Death is coming for him tomorrow, so he leaves for Samarra. Another meets Death and asks him to stay for dinner, but Death refuses, explaining that he has an appointment in Samarra. It gave the title to a novel by John O'Hara.

26.   The archetypal text is Arist. *Int.,* chap. 9, the "sea battle". For materials on the history of this and related controversies, see Richard Sorabji, *Necessity, Cause and Blame: Perspectives on Aristotle's Theory.* One of the most famous philosophical arguments of antiquity, the "Master Argument" of Diodorus Cronus, was concerned with these questions: see Sorabji, chap. 6, for references.

27.   *Ajax* 753–57; trans. John Moore. 756–57 ἐλᾷ γὰρ αὐτὸν τήνδ᾽ ἔθ᾽ ἡμέραν μόνην / δίας ᾽Αθάνας μῆνις P Oxy. 1615, Pearson, Kamerbeek; τῇδε θἠμέρᾳ μόνῃ A᷄ rec Schol[1]. The text is not certain, but ἔτι is very effective, since it sharpens the truth of what Calchas said when we know what actually happens. The following two lines quoted are *Ajax* 778–79.

28.   Seth Schein, *The Mortal Hero,* p. 127.

29.   See above, chap. 3, n. 42.

30.   *Die dramatische Technik des Sophokles.*

31.   For an interesting discussion of Aristophanes' relations to

Euripides, see Harry C. Avery, "'My Tongue Swore, But My Heart Is Unsworn,'" *TAPA* 99 (1968).

32. The issues of whether Euripides was a religious skeptic and whether his general outlook is more "modern" in tendency are run together in the title and the substance of A. W. Verrall's famous book *Euripides the Rationalist: A Study in the History of Arts and Religion.* To Verrall the two questions were no doubt bound to seem much the same. Michelini remarks, ETT p. 13, that Verrall's position required the gods in Euripides' plays to be "both liars and lies."

33. Euripides continues to be a puzzling writer, even for a time that might be expected to appreciate the more deconstructive aspects of his works. Michelini offers, in ETT chap. 1, a valuable history of Euripidean interpretation, including the observation (pp. 49–51) that the installation at the beginning of the nineteenth century of Sophocles as the finest expression of the fifth century and the downgrading of Euripides, who had for centuries been the most popular of the tragedians, was itself part of the self-definition of the modern as opposed to the classical.

34. See Michelini, ETT p. 86.

35. Arist. *Poet.* 1453a29: a remark that, like others in that unsatisfactory book, looks better if you already have an idea to apply to it. The comment is attached to the question of plays ending in disaster. The suggestion that τραγικώτατος means something like "the most theatrical" I owe to Gregory Vlastos: cf. the use of τραγικός to mean "high-flown", Plato *Meno* 76E; Ar. *Pax* 136; Dem. 18.313 ἐν τούτοις λαμπροφωνότατος, μνημονικώτατος, ὑποκριτὴς ἄριστος, τραγικὸς Θεοκρίνης; and τραγῳδία in Hyperides for an exaggerated speech, *Pro Lyc.* 12, *Pro Eux.* 26. By the third century B.C., Euripides was sometimes called "the tragedian" (cf. LSJ s.v. τραγικός); this was presumably a measure of his enormous and enduring popularity.

36. *Catastrophe Survived: Euripides' Plays of Mixed Reversal,* p. 15.

37. Bernard Knox, "The *Hippolytus* of Euripides," YCS 13 (1952); p. 226 in WA. For the point about the prologue, see p. 216. The general point about the adequacy of the human motivation has been made by many writers, e.g., R. P. Winnington-Ingram, "*Hippolytus:* A Study in Causation," pp. 188–89: "It is by the tragedy that we understand

the gods, not by the gods that we understand the tragedy." This is not to say that the appearances of the gods do nothing: on this, see Charles Segal, "The Tragedy of the *Hippolytus*," *HSCP* 70 (1965), reprinted in his *Interpreting Greek Tragedy: Myth, Poetry, Text*.

38. Plato *Phaedo* 98B–C; cf. Arist. *Metaph.* 985a18.

39. ἐνδέχεται γὰρ τὰς ξυμφορὰς τῶν πραγμάτων οὐχ ἧσσον ἀμαθῶς χωρῆσαι ἢ καὶ τὰς διανοίας τοῦ ἀνθρώπου Thuc. 1.140.1. ἀμαθής has virtually everywhere else this "active" sense; see Edmunds, CI p. 16; Ronald Syme, "Thucydides," *PBA* 48 (1960), p. 56; and see now the Supplement to LSJ s.v., also cited by Edmunds. For the contrast between Pericles and Solon, cf. Edmunds, CI p. 81: "For Pericles, chance is mere randomness. . . . For Solon, the vicissitudes of life are an expression of *Moira* and the god's purposes."

40. Solon 13 West 63–70, cf. Hdt. 1. 32. 4; Theognis 129–30; Archilochus frag. 16 West.

41. σύμβολον δ' οὔ πώ τις ἐπιχθονίων / πιστὸν ἀμφὶ πράξιος ἐσσομένας εὗρεν θεόθεν / τῶν δὲ μελλόντων τετύφλωνται φραδαί. / πολλὰ δ' ἀνθρώποις παρὰ γνώμαν ἔπεσεν Ol. 12. 10–13. It is relevant to recall the derivation of σύμβολον: an object such as a sherd is broken in two, and each party keeps one of the matching parts.

42. The claim is that there is no inconsistency between causal explanation and an everyday psychology of action. This is not the position often called compatibilism, which claims that causal explanation is compatible with our present moral conceptions. This is very doubtful: for some of our moral conceptions, it is not clear that they are consistent with an everyday psychology of action. I have argued this, and that a contracausal (or, again, nondeterministic) notion of choice would be useless, in "How Free Does the Will Need to Be?"

43. *EN* 3, chap. 1.

44. Hdt. 7.172, 174.

45. 58A–B. The general idea that persuasion can be sweet was of course familiar: e.g., *Il.* 14.216–17; *PV* 172–73, καί μ' οὔτι μελιγλώσσοις πειθοῦς / ἐπαοιδαῖσιν θέλξει. For a helpful account, including the point, touched on below, about the various contrasts to πειθώ, see R. G. A. Buxton, *Persuasion in Greek Tragedy*. The idea implicit in Protarchus's remark, that there is collaboration by the per-

suaded, can plausibly be attributed in a quite sophisticated form to Gorgias himself: "The process of persuasion is thus for Gorgias more complex than a simple conquest of reason by the irrational powers of the *logos*. There is rather a psychic complicity in the emotive action of the *logos*" (Charles Segal, "Gorgias and the Psychology of the Logos," *HSCP* 66 [1962]).

46. See chap. 2, pp. 42–44. In the *Republic,* sexual desire is treated in the same way as the desire for food (558D–559C); in the *Phaedo,* however, it is not regarded as a necessary desire for the wise man (64D). The contrast is pointed out by Martha Nussbaum in the course of an interesting discussion of Epicurean attitudes to sex: "Beyond Obsession and Disgust: Lucretius' Genealogy of Love," *Apeiron* 1989.

47. Artemidorus *Oneirocriticon* 1.79. I owe this reference to Brown, *The Body and Society,* p. 84. Plato, above: e.g., *Rep.* 458D.

48. *Rep.* 514E. The combination of the ideas that "the sign is full and the sign is empty," as Stephen Greenblatt has put it, is not peculiar to Plato. "In renaissance English literature the paradox is perhaps most exquisitely realized in Prospero's double fantasy: art as absolute illusion ('the baseless fabric of this vision') and art as absolute power ('graves at my command / Have wak'd their sleepers, op'd and let 'em forth / By my so potent Art')" (Greenblatt, *Marvelous Possessions,* p. 116).

49. See chap. 5, pp. 110, 117. However, it is important that Aristotle emphasised the differences between the ἀρχή of a political leader and that of a master over slaves: see, for example, *Pol.* 1252a17–18; and Schofield, p. 16 seq.

50. The demand for exchange rather than monologue is particularly emphasised in the presence of sophists and rhetoricians: *Grg.* 462A, *Prt.* 334C–336D, *Rep.* 348A7–B9, 350E11–351A2. In the *Phaedrus* Plato's procedures more openly display his own acceptance of the point that in avoiding monologue, one does not necessarily escape the problems of persuasion: "Plato accepts and acts upon rhetoric's insistence that truth is impotent without persuasion" (Ferrari, *Cicadas,* p. 58).

51. *Timaeus* 51E is one passage in which Plato unfavourably contrasts persuasion with reason and knowledge, but in the same dia-

logue, 48E, νοῦς controls ἀνάγκη by persuasion, and in the *Gorgias* itself, 453E–454E, there is a πειθὼ διδασκαλική, which can lead to ἐπιστήμη. At *Leg.* 719E9, 722B6, πειθώ is contrasted with threatening a penalty: this is in line with a standard contrast between πειθώ and βία or, indeed, ἀνάγκη, e.g., Isoc. *Antid.* 293–94, Hdt. 8.111; for this, see Buxton, esp. p. 42 seq.

52.   Such an account must itself allow for the basic point that some beliefs and conclusions are inescapable: that there are constraints of fact and logic. How some beliefs have such a character remains a central question of epistemology, not adequately met by some theories that correctly reject Platonic (and Cartesian) models of rationality. A central consideration is that a correct understanding of how, for instance, true factual beliefs are formed has no tendency to undermine them, while the opposite is typically true of ideological beliefs, for example. This is a truth—admittedly far from clear—at the heart of the Enlightenment enterprise.

53.   See chap. 4, pp. 94–95, 100, and Endnote 1. We should recall once more the difficulty that progressivist thinkers encounter in deciding how far Plato had travelled in the direction of true moral autonomy.

54.   See the works referred to in chap. 1, n. 17. A similar point is pressed in criticism of Rawls by Michael Sandel, *Liberalism and the Limits of Justice:* it is unclear how far he is committed to the strongly Hegelian alternative that his formulations often seem to imply.

55.   *EN* 1103a24.

56.   *Daybreak,* translated by R. J. Hollingdale, p. 168. See also *The Twilight of the Idols,* "What I Owe to the Ancients," sec. 2.

57.   See the full quotation, p. 17 above: the words "unsoftened, unmoralized" point to wider possibilities.

58.   As with Plato's and Kant's conceptions of the characterless moral self, mentioned above, historians of philosophy will rightly insist that Kant was conscious of this criticism of earlier philosophy and indeed effectively invented it; the project of a critical, as opposed to a dogmatic, philosophy was designed to overcome this problem. But in his transcendental psychology and the moral philosophy that depends on it, Kant failed to overcome it. Though practical reason, in Kant's

phrase, makes law for itself and does not draw it from any external source, it is still true that reason's constraints intrinsically yield the moral law. Much post-Kantian philosophy has been concerned with the fact that the critical philosophy, in this as in other respects, destroys itself.

59.   The kind of relation suggested here between Thucydides and Sophocles should not be confused with the association between the historian and tragedy proposed by F. M. Cornford, in *Thucydides Mythistoricus,* who claimed that Thucydides fell unconsciously into tragic styles of narration because he lacked the resources to produce a properly positivist history.

60.   *Réflexions sur la tragédie* [1829], pp. 945, 952–53. In the course of his long discussion of this theme, Constant also says: "L'ordre social, l'action de la société sur l'individu, . . . ce réseau d'institutions et de conventions qui nous enveloppe dès notre naissance et ne se rompt qu'à notre mort, sont des ressorts tragiques qu'il ne faut que savoir manier. Ils sont tout à fait équivalents à la fatalité des anciens; leur poids a tout ce qui était invincible et oppressif dans cette fatalité; les habitudes qui en découlent, l'insolence, la dureté frivole, l'incurie obstinée, ont tout ce que cette fatalité avait de désespérant et de déchirant" (p. 952).

61.   ἦθος ἀνθρώπῳ δαίμων, the Heracleitean phrase quoted earlier in this chapter, can hold true without the daimonic. If the notions of character, self, or individual project are themselves abandoned, then of course a larger gap opens between ourselves and not only tragedy but most other works discussed in this study. I have not discussed the arguments for abandoning those notions: all such arguments known to me rest on supposing that the notions have Platonic, Cartesian, or Kantian implications, which it is precisely one aim of this study to detach from them.

62.   In *The Rhetoric of Reaction;* this is what he calls "the perversity thesis". As he points out (pp. 16–17), the thesis also exists in an explicitly supernatural version, for instance in de Maistre.

63.   Hes. *Op.,* esp. 90 seq., 109 seq.

64.   *Pyth.* 4.263–69. The suggested translation is possible and makes more interesting sense of γνῶθι νῦν τὰν Οἰδιπόδα σοφίαν: for

this (and the association with *Il.* 1.234–38, first suggested by Schroeder) cf. Charles Segal, *Pindar's Mythmaking: The Fourth Pythian Ode*. The conventional view, adopted by, among others, B. K. Braswell, *A Commentary on the Fourth Pythian Ode of Pindar*, takes it merely as a way of drawing attention to a riddle; this follows the scholiast: Προτρέπεται τὸν Ἀρκεσίλαον ὁ Πινδάρος συνορᾶν αὐτοῦ τὸ αἴνιγμα.

Mechanisms of Shame and Guilt

The psychological model for each emotion involves an internalised figure. In the case of shame this is, I have suggested in the text, a watcher or witness. In the case of guilt, the internalised figure is a *victim* or an *enforcer*.

If an account using such models is to be helpful, it must not involve at the most primitive level an appeal to the emotions that it is trying to explain: it is no good saying that there is some internalised figure that elicits in the subject guilt or shame. In the case of guilt, this condition can be met by supposing that, at the most primitive level, the attitude of the internalised figure is anger, while the reaction of the subject is fear. The fear, most primitively, is fear *at* anger, rather than fear *of* anger, which is a more complex development, as is fear of the loss of love.

From this primitive basis, it is possible, by what is sometimes called "bootstrapping", to develop the model to allow for reactions that are progressively more structured by social, ethical, or moral notions. So mere fear at mere anger becomes fear of recrimination, and this can develop into a reaction that is restricted to what the subject regards as justified recrimination. In guilt-centred, autonomous, moralities the point is supposedly reached where there is no distance at all between subject and internalised figure, and guilt is pictured as an emotion experienced in the face of an abstraction, the moral law, which has become part of the subject himself. This idealised picture serves the false conception of total moral autonomy, which is criticised in the text. But in addition to that, by blotting out the primitive basis of guilt, it also conceals one of its virtues, a point I shall come back to at the end of this appendix.

In the case of shame, the story is in one respect more complex. If we start from the elementary situation of actually being seen naked, there is no direct route to internalisation, for the reason mentioned in the text: nakedness before an imagined watcher is no exposure. It may seem mysterious how any process of internalisation can explain shame. The answer lies in the fact that the root of shame lies not so much in observed nakedness itself, but in something of which that is, in most cultures but not all, a powerful expression. (The cultures in which observed nakedness has this force include our own and that of the Greeks, though the conventions governing what counts as nakedness, and what is inappropriate observation, of course differ between us and them, as indeed it varies among us and varied among them.) The root of shame lies in exposure in a more general sense, in being at a disadvantage: in what I shall call, in a very general phrase, a loss of power. The sense of shame is a reaction of the subject to the consciousness of this loss: in Gabriele Taylor's phrase, quoted in the text, it is "the emotion of self-protection."

The case of nakedness is at once very directly experienced and also unusual, because the loss of power is itself constituted by actually being seen. An interesting comment on this is provided by an example originally suggested by Max Scheler and discussed by Taylor (pp. 60–61), of an artist's model who has been posing for a painter for some time and comes to feel shame when she realises that he is no longer looking at her as a model but as a sexual object. Taylor explains this case by introducing a second, imagined, viewer, but I do not think that this is necessary. It is rather that the change in the situation introduces the relevant kind of unprotectedness or loss of power: this is itself constituted by an actual gaze, which is of a special, sexually interested, kind. She had previously been clothed in her role as a model; that has been taken from her, and she is left truly exposed, to a desiring eye.

More generally, the loss of power is not actually constituted by the presence of a watcher, even though it is still a loss of power "in the eyes of another." A process of internalisation is now possible, and "bootstrapping" can proceed in terms of an increasing ethical content given to the occasions of shame.

There are some cases that are very near to needing an actual watcher, without quite doing so. I stumble over my shoelaces in the street, try to recover falling packages, knock off my own hat. I feel a fool and experience some mild variant of shame or embarrassment. The feeling is worse if someone is looking, but does not entirely evaporate if no one is. (A solitary castaway might reasonably cease to have such feelings; but it is illuminating that he might intelligibly want not to lose them, as part of a discipline to keep himself in touch with the possibility of social life.) The farther that "bootstrapping" has proceeded and ethical considerations are involved, the less a watcher needs to be in the actual offing; the idealised other will do. But that other still performs a function, of recalling to the subject a person in the eyes of whom the subject has failed, has lost power, is at a disadvantage.

In contrast to guilt, there is no need with shame that the viewer should be angry or otherwise hostile. All that is necessary is that he should perceive that very situation or characteristic that the subject feels to be an inadequacy, failing, or loss of power. (In the case of literal nakedness, the viewer must, to occasion shame, be taken by the subject to have actually seen that the subject is naked.) However, we should not say that the viewer has to see the loss of power *as* a loss of power. This is clear from the case of the artist's model (the painter may think that she is privileged to have aroused his lust), and from the more general point made in the text, that one can be ashamed of being admired by the wrong people.

This point can apply equally to internalised figures. A subject might be ashamed of certain conduct when he brings to mind how it would have been regarded with approval by his headmaster. But this is clearly a secondary mechanism, involving a process that probably needs to be conscious, or near consciousness. If we are modelling the ethical operations of shame, we naturally do it through the internalisation of a figure who sees the subject's failing just in virtue of seeing it as a failing—that is to say, who shares the standards or expectations in terms of which it is a failing.

We can see in terms of these models why shame might be thought to be in its very nature a more narcissistic emotion than guilt. The viewer's gaze draws the subject's attention not to the viewer, but to the subject himself; the victim's anger, on the other hand, draws attention to the victim. The suspicion of narcissism, I have argued in the text, can be overcome on the side of shame by widening one's view of its possible objects, and by making the kinds of distinction that figure, notably, in the *Hippolytus*. But there is another consideration that should be borne in mind, on the side of guilt. If it is to be an inherent virtue of guilt, as opposed to shame, that it turns our attention to the victims of what we have wrongly done, then the victims and their feelings should remain figured in the construction of guilt, as they are in the primitive version of the model. When the conception of guilt is refined beyond a certain point and forgets its primitive materials of anger and fear, guilt comes to be represented simply as the attitude of respect for an abstract law, and it then no longer has any special connection with victims. The victims may reenter, of course, in an account of what the subject has done in violation of that law, but that gives them, or thoughts of them, no more intimate connection to guilt than they have to shame. This is what I had in mind when I said earlier that the refinement of guilt in this direction can conceal one of its virtues.

It is almost always assumed by those who defend the modern conception of morality that this conception harmoniously and significantly combines four things: the primacy of guilt over shame; the overcoming of narcissism, through the direction of attention to victims rather than to the subject; moral autonomy; and the insistence on the voluntary. I have claimed in the text (p. 93) that the first two, the primacy of guilt and the overcoming of narcissism, do not combine at all easily with the insistence on the voluntary. The present argument suggests that the first two do not combine any more easily with moral autonomy.

Phaedra's Distinction: Euripides *Hippolytus* 380–87

τὰ χρήστ᾽ ἐπιστάμεσθα καὶ γιγνώσκομεν,   380
οὐκ ἐκπονοῦμεν δ᾽, οἳ μὲν ἀργίας ὕπο,
οἳ δ᾽ ἡδονὴν προθέντες ἀντὶ τοῦ καλοῦ
ἄλλην τιν᾽. Εἰσὶ δ᾽ ἡδοναὶ πολλαὶ βίου,
μακραί τε λέσχαι καὶ σχολή, τερπνὸν κακόν,
αἰδώς τε. Δισσαὶ δ᾽ εἰσίν, ἣ μὲν οὐ κακή,   385
ἣ δ᾽ ἄχθος οἴκων· εἰ δ᾽ ὁ καιρὸς ἦν σαφής,
οὐκ ἂν δύ᾽ ἤστην ταῦτ᾽ ἔχοντε γράμματα.

387   ταῦτ᾽ L; ταῦτ᾽ rell.

The passage raises several difficulties, which have attracted the attention of scholars.

1. Does *ἄλλην τιν᾽* at 383 mean "another pleasure" or "something else, namely, a pleasure"? Barrett argues that the latter interpretation is possible (citing Plato *Phaedo* 110E and other passages) and also that it is necessary, on the ground that *ἀργία* is not a pleasure. But it has been disputed that the interpretation is linguistically natural in this context, in particular because *ἄλλην ἀντί* is a recognised alternative to *ἄλλην ἤ*. Willink and Claus have in any case established that it is not necessary. Whether or not one thinks that Euripides or his character would have regarded *ἀργία* as a pleasure, this is not in fact the

contrast in question, which is with τοῦ καλοῦ, the pursuit of which is itself a pleasure: Claus well cites Democritus (frag. 207 DK): ἡδονὴν οὐ πᾶσαν, ἀλλὰ τὴν ἐπὶ τῷ καλῷ αἱρεῖσθαι χρεών.

2. How can αἰδώς be classed as a pleasure? Barrett says, "Taken literally, Phaedra is calling αἰδώς a pleasure, which it is not; so the literal-minded editors have sought to emend. But she must not be taken literally"; and he claims that αἰδώς is introduced as a further thing, not a pleasure, that stops one doing τὸ καλόν. Barrett's conclusion may be right, but the question whether αἰδώς can be a pleasure cannot be answered so briskly; the answer depends on the central matter of what is being said about αἰδώς.

3. Above all, is a distinction being drawn between two kinds of αἰδώς? This is the traditional interpretation, but it has often been thought to give rise to a linguistic difficulty, that there is no parallel for the plural of δισσός being used with a singular noun, let alone with a singular noun that has no plural. It is used in the singular even when it means "two" (δισσὴ μέριμνα Hec. 297): *a fortiori* (it is argued) when it means "of two kinds". The passage has been condemned, by Mahaffy and Bury, for example, on the strength of this argument.

Willink, accepting that this is a problem, has suggested that δισσαὶ δ᾽ εἰσίν applies to pleasures, not to αἰδώς. But it is quite unexplained why a distinction of pleasures should be relevant at this point, and as Kovacs, who adopts the interpretation, admits, it yields by itself an improbably condensed list. (Kovacs himself desperately suggests that a line and a half have fallen out.)

The point about the unusual construction of δισσαί perhaps answers itself. There are two things in question, and they are referred to as such at 387: they are two things called by the same name, "αἰδώς". The fact that the word has no plural itself helps the construction to introduce strikingly the subsequent thought, that αἰδώς is one thing that is two things: that there are, as it might be put, two αἰδώςes.

4. So what are they? Barrett suggests that the bad αἰδώς consists in indecisiveness, saying that the "best commentary" on the passage is to be found in Plut. *De vit. mor.* 448 seq.: παρὰ τὸν λόγον ὄκνοις καὶ μελλήσεσι καιροὺς καὶ πράγματα λυμαινόμενον. But this, in the context, is no help. These hesitations just *are* the failure to follow τὸ καλόν; the supposed explanation offers the effect, not a cause. Barrett rightly draws attention to an archetypal passage on the ambivalence of αἰδώς, Hes. *Op.* 317–19, and cites Sinclair for an explanation of bad effects of αἰδώς there as "a feeling of inferiority that makes [a poor man] hesitate to act on his own initiative." (The related thought at *Od.* 17.347 does not introduce two kinds of αἰδώς—only the disadvantage to a poor man of what certainly is αἰδώς; for a similar view of the Hesiod passage, see West ad loc.) The Hesiod passage does offer a cause and not just an effect—social embarrassment (cf. the passage from Isocrates quoted in the text, p. 79). The question is, What is the most general description of this kind of cause, as contrasted with αἰδώς as a beneficent influence?

The essence of the contrast is well expressed by Méridier ad loc.: "*La mauvaise honte,* c'est-à-dire cette lâche complaisance aux entraînements du dehors qui fait oublier le devoir (et empêche de faire le bien), tandis que *la bonne honte,* la pudeur, retient de commettre le mal" (his emphasis). This is a traditional view of the contrast. As Valckenaer well put it (1768), "pravam [sc. verecundiam] damnabat Phaedra; qua, vel aetatem vel dignitatem vel potentiam aliorum reveriti, mala suadentibus obsecundamus, quemque nobis ipsis primum debemus pudorem violamus." The bad kind of αἰδώς is a form of fear, or other such motive, that overimpresses the agent with external social forces.

It is clear on such an explanation of Phaedra's words how

αἰδώς can be more than a fear of conventional opinion but sometimes fails to be more than that. The explanation also shows how αἰδώς can be a pleasure: as Charles Segal says ("Shame and Purity"), it is a social pleasure—a comfort or reassurance. A similar distinction was understood by Dodds, in an interesting article of 1925, who further related it to the two previous (and only other) references that Phaedra makes to αἰδώς: "At v. 244 αἰδώς saves Phaedra; at v. 335 it destroys her."

Willink claims that Barrett's approach is not sufficiently in touch with fifth-century values. But his own account is marked by progressivist assumptions, and it is a striking illustration of their power that he should conclude that a fifth-century writer would have been incapable of thinking that αἰδώς could be a cause of wrongdoing. But the ambivalence of αἰδώς was directly expressed by Euripides himself, in lines from the *Erechtheus,* which are quoted by several editors (frag. 367 Nauck): αἰδοῦς δὲ καὐτὸς δυσκρίτως ἔχω πέρι· / καὶ δεῖ γὰρ αὐτῆς κἄστιν αὖ κακὸν μέγα. (Cf. also Democritus frags. 244, 264 DK, cited in n. 46 to chap. 4). It is reasonable to suppose that the ambiguity of αἰδώς referred to in this fragment is the same as that represented in the present passage in terms of two kinds of αἰδώς. It is that between an αἰδώς that is timid, reactive, and conventional and one that is steady, active, and (if need be) independent of merely conventional expectations. It is a duality that, on the account given in the text, is inherent in shame itself.

The *Erechtheus* fragment does not simply mean that the speaker finds it hard to make up his mind about the value of αἰδώς; rather, there is something in it obscure or ambiguous or hard to discern. The word δύσκριτος is associated with the idea that it is hard to tell the identity or meaning of something; so in its several occurrences in *PV*: the rising and setting of the stars 458, cries 486, oracles δυσκρίτως εἰρημένους 662; and at Ar. *Ran.* 1433 τὸν σωτῆρα δυσκρίτως γ᾽ ἔχω means "I find it hard to tell which of them is the saviour". This *prima facie* fits well with the reference to καιρός in the present passage. But there is a considerable problem.

5. What is meant by εἰ δ᾽ ὁ καιρὸς ἦν σαφής? Two things at least are clear, both well argued by Barrett. One is that καιρός need not refer to time and can apply to appropriateness more generally: from Euripides he cites *Hec.* 593 (cf. 594), *Or.* 122, frag. 628 Nauck. Second, καιρός *does* imply appropriateness and cannot simply mean, neutrally, "the distinction", as Wilamowitz claimed in explanation of the present passage. καιρός always favours the right end of some contrast.

If we hold on to these points, we have to say what it is in the present context that can be καίριος, "appropriate", or, alternatively, ἄκαιρος, "inappropriate". If we take it to be the two kinds of αἰδώς (or the actions and motivations associated with them), we face the obvious difficulty that one form of αἰδώς, the bad one, is never appropriate. So Phaedra cannot say (as Barrett, for one, makes her say) that if the καιρός for shamelike action were σαφής, there would be two different words for the two different kinds of action: if the occasion for appropriate action—that is to say, for action that would express good αἰδώς—were clear, one of these types of action would not exist.

The solution lies in seeing that this is exactly what the last line says. In the supposed circumstances, in which it would always be clear how we should react, there would not be two things to have this one name, "αἰδώς". The line does not mean, as is generally supposed, that there would be one more name; it means that there would be one less thing. The thought is, "If we could always see clearly the appropriate way to act from these kinds of motivations, there would not be these two things—good and bad αἰδώς, self-respect and mere embarrassment or social conformity—that, as things are, bear this one name."

It might be thought an objection to this account that it makes correct action follow on the καιρὸς being σαφής, and so introduces an intellectualist conception, contrary to what is said at

the beginning of the passage. This would be a misunderstanding. Phaedra says in 381–82 that we know τὰ χρηστά. These
include typical expressions of good αἰδώς and exclude typical
expressions of bad αἰδώς, and, at a general level, we know these
expressions to be χρηστά or not. We do not always act rightly,
however, because in a particular case the καιρός is not σαφής:
we fail to see the appropriate thing to do, fail to see what action
would be the expression of what kind of motive. This very recognisable description would be intellectualist only if the *cause*
of the failure were characterised in intellectualist terms, as stu-
pidity or ignorance or inattention, but it is not. The cause lies
in the motivations of bad αἰδώς, such as the fear, desire for
approval, or misplaced respect listed by Valckenaer; and, in association with such motives, the pleasure (of social reassurance)
that Phaedra mentions.

It is perhaps worth mentioning that while this interpretation
does not exclude the reading ταῦτ’ at 387, it does not demand
it. Perhaps ταῦτ’ is the correct reading, and L's ταῦτ’ is a clever
conjecture by someone who, like most subsequent scholars,
took Phaedra to be discussing a refinement of our language
rather than an improvement in our sentiments.

Bibliography

GENERAL ABBREVIATIONS

AJP:	*American Journal of Philology.*
BICS:	*Bulletin of the Institute of Classical Studies, University of London.*
CA:	*Classical Antiquity.*
CJ:	*Classical Journal.*
CP:	*Classical Philology.*
CQ:	*Classical Quarterly.*
CR:	*Classical Review.*
DK:	*Die Fragmente der Vorsokratiker,* ed. Hermann Diels, rev. Walther Kranz. 6th ed. Zurich, 1951.
HSCP:	*Harvard Studies in Classical Philology.*
JHS:	*Journal of Hellenic Studies.*
LSJ:	Liddell, Scott, and Jones, *A Greek Lexicon.* 9th ed.
PAS Suppl.:	*Proceedings of the Aristotelian Society, Supplementary Volume.*
PBA:	*Proceedings of the British Academy.*
PCPS:	*Proceedings of the Cambridge Philological Association.*
RhM:	*Rheinisches Museum.*
SHAW:	*Sitzungsberichte der Heidelberger Akademie der Wissenschaften.*

TAPA: *Transactions of the American Philological Association.*
WJA: *Würzburger Jahrbuch für die Altertumswissenschaft.*
YCS: *Yale Classical Studies.*

Adkins, A. H. [MR] *Merit and Responsibility: A Study in Greek Values.* Oxford, 1960.

———. [MO] *From the Many to the One: A Study of Personality and Views of Human Nature in the Context of Ancient Greek Society.* London, 1970.

Annas, Julia. "Plato's *Republic* and Feminism." *Philosophy* 51 (1976).

Austin, Norman. *Archery at the Dark of the Moon.* Berkeley and Los Angeles, 1975.

Avery, Harry C. "'My Tongue Swore, But My Heart Is Unsworn.'" *TAPA* 99 (1968).

Bacon, Helen H. *Barbarians in Greek Tragedy.* New Haven, 1961.

Baiter, J. G., and H. Sauppe, eds. *Oratores Attici.* Zurich, 1839–43.

Barrett, W. S., ed. Euripides *Hippolytus.* Oxford, 1964; corrected ed., 1966.

Benardete, Seth. "XPH and ΔEI in Plato and Others." *Glotta* 43 (1965).

———. *Herodotean Inquiries.* The Hague, 1969.

Benjamin, Walter. *Ursprung des deutschen Trauerspiels.* Frankfurt, 1963. Translated by John Osborne as *The Origin of German Tragic Drama.* London, 1977.

Braswell, B. K. *A Commentary on the Fourth Pythian Ode of Pindar.* Berlin and New York, 1988.

Brisson, Luc. *Le mythe de Tirèsias.* Leiden, 1976.

Broadie, Sarah. *Ethics with Aristotle.* Oxford, 1991.

Brown, Peter. *The Body and Society: Men, Women, and Sexual Renunciation in Early Christianity.* New York, 1988.

Burkert, Walter. *Griechische Religion der archaischen und klassischen Epoche.* Stuttgart, 1977. Translated by John Raffan as *Greek Religion.* Cambridge, Mass., 1985.

Burnet, John. *The Ethics of Aristotle.* London, 1900.

Burnett, Anne Pippin. *Catastrophe Survived: Euripides' Plays of Mixed Reversal.* Oxford, 1971.

Bushnell, Rebecca W. *Prophesying Tragedy: Sign and Voice in Sophocles' Theban Plays.* Ithaca, N.Y. and London, 1988.

Butler, E. M. *The Tyranny of Greece over Germany.* Boston, 1958.

Buxton, R. G. A. *Persuasion in Greek Tragedy.* Cambridge, 1982.

Clarke, Howard. *Homer's Readers.* New Brunswick, N.J., 1981.

Claus, David. "Phaedra and the Socratic Paradox." *YCS* 22 (1972).

———. [TS] *Toward the Soul.* New Haven, 1981.

Constant, Benjamin. *Réflexions sur la tragédie* [1829]. In *Oeuvres.* Pléiade ed. Paris, 1957.

Cooper, John. "Plato's Theory of Human Motivation." *Hist. Phil. Quarterly* 1 (1985).

Cornford, F. M. *Thucydides Mythistoricus.* London, 1907.

Coulton, James. *Ancient Greek Architects at Work.* Ithaca, N.Y., 1977.

Crosby, Harry. *Transit of Venus.* Paris, 1931.

Davidson, Donald. *Essays on Actions and Events.* Oxford, 1980.

Davies, John K. "Athenian Citizenship." *CJ* 73 (1977).

Denniston, J. D. *The Greek Particles.* 2d ed. Oxford, 1954.

Denniston, J. D., and Denys Page, eds. Aeschylus *Agamemnon.* Oxford, 1957.

Descartes, René. *Passions de l'âme.* In *Oeuvres de Descartes,* vol. 11, edited by C. Adam and P. Tannery. Paris, 1974.

Diggle, J., ed. Euripides *Fabulae.* Vol. 1. Oxford, 1984.

Dihle, Albrecht. *The Theory of Will in Classical Antiquity.* Berkeley and Los Angeles, 1982.

Diller, Hans. "ΘΥΜΟΣ ΔΕ ΚΡΕΙΣΣΩΝ ΤΩΝ ΕΜΩΝ ΒΟΥΛΕΥΜΑΤΩΝ." *Hermes* 94 (1966).

Dodds, E. R. [GI] *The Greeks and the Irrational.* Berkeley and Los Angeles, 1951.

Dover, K. J. [GPM] *Greek Popular Morality in the Time of Plato and Aristotle.* Oxford, 1974.

Easterling, Pat. "The Tragic Homer." *BICS* 31 (1984).

Edmunds, Lowell. [CI] *Chance and Intelligence in Thucydides.* Cambridge, Mass., 1975.

Ellmann, Richard. "The Uses of Decadence." Reprinted in *a long the riverrun.* New York, 1989.

Engels, F. *Anti-Dühring.* Marx-Engels Werke 20. Berlin, 1962.

Euben, J. Peter. *Greek Tragedy and Political Theory.* Berkeley and Los Angeles, 1986.

———. *The Tragedy of Political Theory: The Road Not Taken.* Princeton, 1990.

Ferrari, G. R. F. *Listening to the Cicadas: A Study of Plato's Phaedrus.* Cambridge, 1987.

Finley, M. I. [AS] *Ancient Slavery and Modern Ideology.* London, 1980.

Foley, Helene P. *Ritual Irony: Poetry and Sacrifice in Euripides.* Ithaca, N.Y., and London, 1985.

———. "Attitudes to Women in Greece." In *The Civilization of the Ancient Mediterranean,* edited by M. Grant and R. Kitzinger. New York, 1988.

———. "Medea's Divided Self." *CA* 8 (1989).

Fortenbaugh, W. "Aristotle on Slaves and Women." In *Articles on Aristotle,* vol. 2, edited by J. Barnes, M. Schofield, and R. Sorabji. London, 1977.

Fraenkel, E., ed. Aeschylus *Agamemnon.* Oxford, 1950.

Fränkel, Hermann. [EGP] *Early Greek Poetry and Philosophy.* Translated by M. Hadas and J. Willis. Oxford, 1975.

Furley, David. "Euripides on the Sanity of Herakles." In *Studies in Honour of T. B. L. Webster,* vol. 1, edited by J. H. Betts, J. T. Hooker, and J. R. Green. Bristol, 1986.

Galilei, Galileo. *Dialogue Concerning the Two Chief World Systems.* Translated by Stillman Drake. Berkeley and Los Angeles, 1962.

Gaskin, Richard. "Do Homeric Heroes Make Real Decisions?" *CQ* n.s. 40 (1990).

Gauthier, R. A., and J. Y. Jolif. Aristote: *L'Ethique à Nicomaque.* Vol. 2. Louvain, 1970.

Gibbard, Alan. *Wise Choices, Apt Feelings.* Cambridge, Mass., 1990.

Gill, Christopher. "Did Chrysippus Understand Medea?" *Phronesis* 28 (1983).

———. "Two Monologues of Self-Division." In *Homo Viator: Classical Essays for John Bramble,* edited by M. and M. Whitby and P. Hardie. Bristol, 1987.

Goldhill, Simon. *Reading Greek Tragedy.* Cambridge, 1986.

Gomme, A. W. "The Position of Women in Athens in the Fifth and Fourth Centuries." *CP* 20 (1925).

———. *A Historical Commentary on Thucydides.* Vol. 1. Oxford, 1959.

Gould, John J. "Law, Custom and Myth: Aspects of the Social Position of Women in Classical Athens." *JHS* 100 (1980).

Gould, Stephen Jay. *The Mismeasure of Man.* New York, 1982.

Greenblatt, Stephen. *Marvelous Possessions.* Oxford, 1991.

Griffith, Mark. *The Authenticity of "Prometheus Bound."* Cambridge, 1977.

Guthrie, W. K. C. *A History of Greek Philosophy.* Vol. 2. Cambridge, 1965.

Hampshire, Stuart, ed. *Public and Private Morality.* Cambridge, 1978.

Harrison, Jane. *Prolegomena to the Study of Greek Religion.* Cambridge, 1903.

Hart, H. L. A. *Punishment and Responsibility.* Oxford, 1968.

Hart, H. L. A., and A. M. Honoré. *Causation in the Law.* Oxford, 1959.

Hirschman, Albert. *The Rhetoric of Reaction.* Cambridge, Mass., 1991.

Homer. *Iliad.* Translated by Richmond Lattimore. Chicago, 1951.

———. *Odyssey.* Translated by Richmond Lattimore. New York, 1965.

Hooker, J. T. "Homeric Society: A Shame-culture?" *Greece and Rome* 34 (1987).

Hornsby, Jennifer. "Bodily Movements, Actions, and Mental Epistemology." *Midwest Studies in Philosophy* 10 (1986).

Housman, A. E. M. Manilii *Astronomicon* Liber I. Cambridge, 1937.

Hume, David. *An Enquiry Concerning the Principles of Morals,* edited by L. A. Selby-Bigge. Oxford, 1894.

Humphreys, S. C. *The Family, Women and Death.* London, 1983.

Irwin, T. H. *Plato's Moral Theory: The Early and Middle Dialogues.* Oxford, 1977.

Jahn, Thomas. *Zum Wortfeld 'Seele-Geist' in der Sprache Homers.* Munich, 1987.

Jaynes, Julian. *The Origin of Consciousness in the Breakdown of the Bicameral Mind.* Boston, 1976.

Jenkyns, Richard. *The Victorians and Ancient Greece.* Oxford, 1980.

Kamerbeek, J. C. "Prophecy and Tragedy." *Mnemosyne* 4 (1965).

Kassel R., and C. Austin. *Poetae comici Graeci.* Vol. 7. Berlin and New York, 1989.

Keuls, Eva C. *The Reign of the Phallus*. New York, 1985.

Kierkegaard, Søren. *Fear and Trembling*. 1843. Translated by Alastair Hannay. Harmondsworth, 1985.

Kirk, G. *The Iliad Books I–IV*. Cambridge, 1985.

Knox, Bernard. "The *Hippolytus* of Euripides." *YCS* 13 (1952).

———. "Why Is Oedipus Called Tyrannos?" *CJ* 50 (1954).

———. *The Heroic Temper*. Berkeley and Los Angeles, 1964.

———. "Second Thoughts in Greek Tragedy." *Greek, Roman and Byzantine Studies* 7 (1966).

———. "The *Medea* of Euripides." *YCS* 25 (1977).

———. [WA] *Word and Action*. Baltimore and London, 1979.

Kock, T. *Comicorum Atticorum fragmenta*. Leipzig, 1880.

Kovacs, D. "Shame, Pleasure and Honor in Phaedra's Great Speech." *AJP* 101 (1980).

Laqueur, Thomas. "Orgasm, Generation, and the Politics of Reproductive Biology." *Representations* 14 (1986).

———. *Making Sex*. Cambridge, Mass., 1990.

Lefkowitz, M. R., and M. Fant. *Women's Life in Greece and Rome*. London and Baltimore, 1982.

Lesky, Albin. [GM] "Göttliche und menschliche Motivation in Homerischen Epos." *SHAW* 1961.

———. "Decision and Responsibility in the Tragedy of Aeschylus." *JHS* 86 (1966). Reprinted in Erich Segal, ed., OGT.

Lloyd, G. E. R. *Magic, Reason and Experience*. Cambridge, 1979.

———. [SFI] *Science, Folklore and Ideology*. Cambridge, 1983.

———. *The Revolutions of Wisdom*. Berkeley and Los Angeles, 1987.

Lloyd-Jones, Hugh. "The Guilt of Agamemnon." *CQ* n.s. 12 (1962).

———. [JZ] *The Justice of Zeus*. Berkeley and Los Angeles, 1971; 2d edn., 1983.

———. "Euripides *Medea* 1056–80." *WJA* N.F. 6 (1980).

———. *Blood for the Ghosts*. London, 1982.

Long, A. A. [MV] "Morals and Values in Homer." *JHS* 90 (1970).

———. "Pro and Contra Fratricide—Aeschylus *Septem* 653–719." In *Studies in Honour of T. B. L. Webster*, vol. 1, edited by J. H. Betts, J. T. Hooker, and J. R. Green. Bristol, 1986.

———. Review of Nussbaum, FG. *CP* 83 (1988).

———. Review of Jahn. *CR* n.s. 42 (1992).

Loraux, Nicole. "Socrate, contrepoison de l'oraison funèbre." *L'antiquité classique* 43 (1974).

———. *Les enfants d' Athéna.* Paris, 1981.

———. "Corps des dieux." *Le temps de la réflexion* 7 (1986).

———. [FT] *Façons tragiques de tuer une femme.* Paris, 1985. Translated by Anthony Forster as *Tragic Ways of Killing a Woman.* Cambridge, Mass., 1987.

———. *Les expériences de Tirèsias.* Paris, 1989.

Luhrman, T. M. *Persuasions of the Witch's Craft: Ritual Magic in Contemporary England.* Cambridge, Mass., 1989.

MacCary, W. Thomas. *Childlike Achilles: Ontogeny and Phylogeny in the Iliad.* New York, 1982.

MacIntyre, Alasdair. *After Virtue.* London, 1981.

———. *Whose Justice? Which Rationality?* London, 1988.

Mazon, Paul. *Introduction à l'Iliade.* Paris, 1948.

Méridier, L., ed. Euripide. Vol. 2. Budé ed. 2d ed. Paris, 1956.

Merkelbach, R., and M. L. West, eds. *Fragmenta Hesiodea.* Oxford, 1967.

Michelini, Ann Norris. [ETT] *Euripides and the Tragic Tradition.* Madison, 1987.

Morris, Herbert. "Guilt and Shame." In *On Guilt and Innocence.* Berkeley and Los Angeles, 1976.

Mulgan, R. G. *Aristotle's Political Theory.* Oxford, 1977.

Murnaghan, Sheila. *Disguise and Recognition in the Odyssey.* Princeton, 1987.

Nauck, A. *Tragicorum Graecorum fragmenta.* 2d ed. Leipzig, 1889.

Newman, W. L. *The Politics of Aristotle.* Oxford, 1887.

Nietzsche, F. *The Birth of Tragedy.* 1872. Translated by Walter Kaufmann. New York, 1974.

———. [UO] *Unmodern Observations.* 1873. Edited by William Arrowsmith. New Haven and London, 1990.

———. *Human, All Too Human.* 1878. Translated by R. J. Hollingdale. Cambridge, 1986.

———. *Daybreak.* 1881. Translated by R. J. Hollingdale. Cambridge, 1982.

———. *The Gay Science.* 1882. Translated by Walter Kaufmann. New York, 1974.

————. *The Genealogy of Morals.* 1887. Translated by Walter Kaufmann and R. J. Hollingdale. New York, 1967.

————. *The Twilight of the Idols.* 1888. Translated by R. J. Hollingdale. Harmondsworth, 1968.

————. *The Anti-Christ.* 1888. Translated by R. J. Hollingdale. Harmondsworth, 1968.

————. *Nietzsche contra Wagner.* 1888. Translated by Walter Kaufmann. New York, 1954.

Nussbaum, Martha C. "Consequences and Character in Sophocles' *Philoctetes.*" *Philosophy and Literature* 1 (1976–77).

————. [FG] *The Fragility of Goodness.* Cambridge, 1986.

————. "Beyond Obsession and Disgust: Lucretius' Genealogy of Love." *Apeiron* 1989.

O'Brien, Michael J. *The Socratic Paradoxes and the Greek Mind.* Chapel Hill, 1967.

Page, D. L. *Homeric Odyssey.* Oxford, 1955.

Parker, Robert. *Miasma: Pollution and Purification in Early Greek Religion.* Oxford, 1983.

Pateman, Carole. "Sex and Power." Review of *Feminism Unmodified,* by Catherine Mackinnon. *Ethics* 100 (1990).

Powell, Anton, ed. *Euripides, Women and Sexuality.* London, 1990.

Rahn, H. "Tier und Mensch in der Homerischen Auffassung der Wirklichkeit." *Paideuma* 5 (1953–54).

Rawls, John. *A Theory of Justice.* Cambridge, Mass., 1971.

Redard, G. *Recherches sur χρ`η, χρῆσθαι.* Paris, 1953.

Redfield, James M. *Nature and Culture in the Iliad.* Chicago and London, 1975.

Reeve, M. "Euripides *Medea* 1021–1080." *CQ* n.s. 22 (1972).

Regenbogen, O. "Bemerkungen zu den *Sieben* des Aischylos." *Hermes* 68 (1933).

Restatement of the Law of Torts. Promulgated by the American Law Institute. St. Paul, 1965.

Ricks, Christopher. *T. S. Eliot and Prejudice.* London, 1988; Berkeley and Los Angeles, 1989.

Roberts, Deborah H. *Apollo and His Oracle in the Oresteia.* Göttingen, 1984.

Romilly, Jacqueline de. "Le refus du suicide dans l'*Heraclès* d'Euripide." *Archaiognosia* 1 (1980).

Rorty, Amélie Oksenberg. *Mind in Action*. Boston, 1988.

Roth, Paul. "Teiresias as *Mantis* and Intellectual in Euripides' *Bacchae*." *TAPA* 114 (1984).

Sandel, Michael. *Liberalism and the Limits of Justice*. Cambridge, 1982.

Schein, Seth. *The Mortal Hero*. Berkeley and Los Angeles, 1984.

Schofield, Malcolm. "Ideology and Philosophy in Aristotle's Theory of Slavery." In *Aristoteles' "Politik"*, XI Symposium Aristotelicum, edited by G. Patzig. Göttingen, 1990.

Segal, Charles. "Gorgias and the Psychology of the Logos." *HSCP* 66 (1962).

———. "The Tragedy of the *Hippolytus*." *HSCP* 70 (1965). Reprinted in *Interpreting Greek Tragedy*.

———. "Shame and Purity in Euripides' *Hippolytus*." *Hermes* 98 (1970).

———. *Tragedy and Civilization*. Cambridge, Mass., 1981.

———. *Interpreting Greek Tragedy: Myth, Poetry, Text*. Ithaca, N.Y., 1986.

———. *Pindar's Mythmaking: The Fourth Pythian Ode*. Princeton, 1986.

Segal, Erich, ed. [OGT] *Oxford Readings in Greek Tragedy*. Oxford, 1983.

Sharples, R. W. "But Why Has My Spirit Spoken with Me Thus?" *Greece and Rome* 30 (1983).

Shipp, G. P. *Studies in the Language of Homer*. 2d ed. Cambridge, 1972.

Sicherl, M. "The Tragic Issue in Sophocles' *Ajax*." *YCS* 25 (1977).

Silk, M. S., and J. P. Stern. *Nietzsche on Tragedy*. Cambridge, 1981.

Sinclair, T. A. "On αἰδώς in Hesiod." *CR* 39 (1925).

Skorupski, John. *Symbol and Theory*. Cambridge, 1976.

Smith, Nicholas D. "Aristotle's Theory of Natural Slavery." *Phoenix* 37 (1983).

Snell, Bruno. *Die Entdeckung des Geistes*. Hamburg, 1948. Translated by T. G. Rosenmeyer, with the addition of an extra chapter, as *The Discovery of the Mind in Greek Philosophy and Literature*. New York, 1953.

Sophocles. *Oedipus at Colonus*. Translated by Robert Fitzgerald. New York, 1941; Chicago, 1954.

———. *Ajax*. Translated by John Moore. Chicago, 1957.

Sorabji, Richard. *Necessity, Cause and Blame: Perspectives on Aristotle's Theory*. London, 1980.

Ste. Croix, G. E. M. de. *The Origins of the Peloponnesian War*. London, 1972.

———. "Slavery and Other Forms of Unfree Labour." In a volume of that title, edited by Leonie Archer. London, 1988.

Stanton, G. R. "The End of Medea's Monologue: Euripides *Medea* 1078–80." *RhM* N.F. 130 (1987).

Steiner, George. *Antigones*. Oxford, 1984.

Stich, Stephen. *From Folk Psychology to Cognitive Science: The Case against Belief*. Cambridge, Mass., 1983.

Strong, Tracy B. *Nietzsche and the Politics of Transfiguration*. Berkeley and Los Angeles, 1975.

Syme, Ronald. "Thucydides." *PBA* 48 (1960).

Taylor, Charles. *Sources of the Self*. Cambridge, Mass., 1989.

Taylor, Gabriele. *Pride, Shame and Guilt*. Oxford, 1985.

van Fraasen, Bas. "Peculiar Effects of Love and Desire." In *Perspectives on Self-Deception*, edited by Brian McLaughlin and Amélie Rorty. Berkeley and Los Angeles, 1988.

Verdenius, W. J. "*Aidos* bei Homer." *Mnemosyne*, 3d ser., 12 (1945).

Vernant, Jean-Pierre. [IMA] *L'individu, la mort, l'amour*. Paris, 1989.

Vernant, Jean-Pierre, and Pierre Vidal-Naquet. [MT] *Mythe et tragédie en Grèce ancienne*. Vol. 1. Paris, 1972. Translated by Janet Lloyd as *Tragedy and Myth in Ancient Greece*. Brighton, 1981. Vol. 2. Paris, 1986.

Verrall, A. W. *Euripides the Rationalist: A Study in the History of Arts and Religion*. Cambridge, 1913.

Vlastos, Gregory. "Happiness and Virtue in Socrates' Moral Theory." *PCPS* 1984.

———. "Was Plato a Feminist?" *Times Literary Supplement*, 17–23 March 1989.

———. *Socrates*. Cambridge, 1991.

von Staden, Heinrich. "Nietzsche and Marx on Greek Art and Literature: Case Studies in Reception." *Daedalus*. Winter 1976.

Warren, Mark. *Nietzsche and Political Thought*. Cambridge, Mass., 1988.

West, M. L., ed. Hesiod *Theogony*. Oxford, 1966.

———, ed. *Iambi et Elegi Graeci*. Oxford, 1971–72, 2nd ed. 1989.

———, ed. Aeschylus *Tragoediae*. Stuttgart, 1990.

Whitlock-Blundell, Mary. *Helping Friends and Harming Enemies: A Study in Sophocles and Greek Ethics*. Cambridge, 1989.

Wiedemann, Thomas. *Greek and Roman Slavery*. London, 1981.

Wilamowitz, Tycho von. *Die dramatische Technik des Sophokles*. Zurich, 1969.

Wilamowitz-Möllendorff, U. von. "Excurse zu Euripides *Medeia*." *Hermes* 15 (1880).

Wilde, Oscar. *The Critic as Artist*. In *Intentions*. London, 1913.

Willetts, R. F. "The Servile Interregnum at Argos." *Hermes* 87 (1959).

Williams, Bernard. "Ethical Consistency." *PAS Suppl.* 39 (1965). Reprinted in *Problems of the Self*.

———. "The Analogy of City and Soul in Plato's *Republic*." In *Exegesis and Argument: Essays Presented to Gregory Vlastos,* edited by E. N. Lee, A. P. Mourelatos, and R. M. Rorty. Assen, 1973.

———. *Problems of the Self*. Cambridge, 1973.

———. "Moral Luck." *PAS Suppl.* 50 (1976). Reprinted in *Moral Luck*.

———. *Moral Luck*. Cambridge, 1981.

———. *Ethics and the Limits of Philosophy*. London and Cambridge, Mass., 1985.

———. "How Free Does the Will Need to Be?" Lindley Lecture 1985. Lawrence, Kans., 1986.

———. Review of *Whose Justice? Which Rationality?* by Alasdair MacIntyre. *London Review of Books,* January 1989.

Willink, C. W. "Some Problems of Text and Interpretation in *Hippolytus*." *CQ* n.s. 18 (1968).

Winnington-Ingram, R. P. "*Hippolytus:* A Study in Causation." In *Euripide: Entretiens sur l'antiquité classique*. Vol. 6. Geneva, 1960.

————. "Tragedy and Greek Archaic Thought." In *Classical Drama and Its Influence: Essays Presented to H. D. F. Kitto,* edited by M. J. Anderson. London, 1965.

————. *Sophocles: An Interpretation.* Cambridge, 1980.

————. *Studies in Aeschylus.* Cambridge, 1983.

Wollheim, Richard. *The Thread of Life.* Cambridge, Mass., 1984.

Woods, Michael. "Plato's Division of the Soul." *PBA* 73 (1987).

General Index

Achilles: character, 81; and divine intervention, 30; extremity, 192n41; and Hector's corpse, 24; honour and shame, 80, 101; inner life, 47–48; obstinate, 75, 76; supposedly childish, 77

Adkins, A. H., 171n8, 171n9, 181n43, 189n28, 191n39, 193n4; on competitive values, 81, 187n9, 195n17, 200n49

Aeschylus, 98, 174n34; as thinker, 15; *Ag.*, 119, 132–36; *Cho.*, 136, 140; *Sept.*, 136–39

Agamemnon: (in *Iliad*) apology, 52–55; (in *Agamemnon*) decision, 132–35

Aitios, aitia, 52–54, 58, 64

Ajax (in Sophocles): decision, 73–74; madness, 55, 72; and shame, 84–85, 101; and Tekmessa, 104–5

Akrasia, 44–46

Anaxagoras, 149

Annas, Julia, 207n48

Anthropologists, cultural, 1–3, 6

Antigone (in Sophocles), 77, 85–87

Antiphon, 60; *Tetralogies*, 60–63, 68

Aristarchus, 23

Aristophanes, 119, 148

Aristotle: and agency, 5; on *akrasia*, 44; on commands of reason, 182n43; on constraint, 113–14, 117, 153; cosmology, 126, 131; on Euripides, 148–49; on generation, 120; on modality, 143; moralised psychology, 44,

160–62; on needs, 155; on the *polis*, 113; on slavery, 106, 110–16, 122–25, 156; on the soul, 177n15; on women, 117–18, 156, 161

Ate, 52–55

Austin, J. L., 175n6

Austin, Norman, 177n17, 184n58

Autonomy. See Heteronomy

Avery, Harry C., 213n31

Bacon, Helen H., 203n29

Barrett, W. S., 184n57, 194n9, 199n44, 225–30

Benardete, Seth, 184n57, 211n22

Benjamin, Walter, 15, 16, 19, 46, 74

Bentley, Richard, 169

Body: in Homer, 23–25; and soul, 26, 176n15

Bootstrapping, 219, 221

Braswell, B. K., 218n64

Brisson, Luc, 206n43, 206n44

Broadie, Sarah, 183n50

Brown, Peter, 12, 120, 207n46, 215n47

Buñuel, Luis, 148

Burkert, Walter, 187n13, 189n23

Burnett, Anna Pippin, 149

Bushnell, Rebecca W., 206n45, 211n23

Butler, E. M., 170n4

Buxton, R. G. A., 214n45, 216n51

Calderón de la Barca, Pedro, 101

Cardozo, B., 190n34

Index Locorum